Economics
A Student's Workbook

John Beardshaw and Andy Ross

Pitman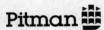

PITMAN PUBLISHING
128 Long Acre, London, WC2E 9AN

A Division of Longman Group UK Limited

First published in Great Britain 1989

British Library Cataloguing in Publication Data
Beardshaw, John
  Economics: a student's workbook
  1. Economics
  I. Title II. Ross, Andy
  330

ISBN 0 273 03014 0

Printed and bound in Great Britain

Acknowledgements

Every effort has been made to trace all the copyright holders but if any
have been inadvertently overlooked the publishers will be pleased to
make the necessary arrangement at the first opportunity.

Contents

Contents

1

Learning and studying economics

1
What's in the book

The aim this book is simple; it is *to help you to pass an exam in economics*.

This introduction gives some guidance on how to *study*, *revise for* and *take exams*. The book is intended to prepare candidates for an 'A' level examination in economics, but because it is intended to demonstrate excellent rather than mediocre answers it will be useful for students on other courses up to and including first year degree level. Most of the questions are 'typical' of the types of question set by the various examination boards, but we have also designed questions in order to *develop* your understanding of important areas.

It is essential that you have studied the relevant sections of at least one major textbook before attempting the problems in this book. This workbook is based on the textbook *Economics: A Student's Guide* by John Beardshaw. If you compare the two you will see that the eight parts of the study section of this book follow the form of the other. Naturally we hope that you will have the textbook but it is not necessary in order to use this workbook; there are no exercises of the sort which say 'see page 245 of the textbook'.

In each section of the workbook you will find:

(a) *Essay questions*. To many of these we have given suggested answers, which are roughly of the length that is required in most exams. They would gain a very high grade in the exam, so do not be put off if your attempts fall short of their standard. But note their *concise* and *precise* style and the *logical* structure; you will have to work with great speed in exams and the student who can pack in most relevant material is likely to score highest! Moreover, examiners invariably favour such essays as against long, meandering, and usually repetitive, essays. The suggested answers not only will show you how to organise an essay but also contain many useful phrases and additional information that will be helpful to you in your exam.

(b) *Data response questions*. Again we have provided suggested answers to many of these and the same comments apply to these as to the essay answers above. The length of answers expected, however, varies between examination boards and from paper to paper or even question to question. To allow for this we have set a variety of questions of differing expected length of response.

(c) *Multiple-choice tests*. In all there are eight of these, each with 20 questions. Answers are provided for all of these.

2
Studying economics

Economics is often described as a 'feel' subject, i.e. it is one for which you either have an inherent grasp or not. This is an exaggeration but it is certainly a subject which is not readily learned from textbooks. The first few chapters of most economics texts are often enough to put many people off. We hope that the following few points may help you to develop your study of the subject.

Economics and current affairs

Few other subjects give students such easy access to their subject. You are unlikely to hear on the news an item on quantum physics, but each day the raw material of economics is pumped out by the media. You must make it part of your everyday life to be familiar with this.

Remember, however, that economics is *not* just current affairs. It is necessary to think about and *process* the information you are receiving and turn it into economics. Let us illustrate this by an example: suppose that in today's news we were to be told that, 'The EC has today imposed a community-wide system of quotas on dairy farmers'. By itself this is simply an item of current affairs. However, as an economics student, you should have thought something like, 'The butter mountain is an example of excess supply. The EC is now trying to deal with this by imposing a quota system. This should work by artificially moving the supply curve to the left', and so on.

Economists and textbook writers

You will need to refer to economists when writing your answer. You will say things such as: 'As so-and so argues . . .', or, 'Research by Professor Blank indicates that . . .', and so on. In other words you are referring to *original* work on the subject.

Textbook writers, on the other hand, are typically *teachers* of economics; they are practised in putting economics across to students in a simplified way. It is therefore usually of little use to quote a textbook to support your argument.

Occasionally the two combine. The most influential textbook on economics written since the 1939–45 war is Paul A. Samuelson's *Economics*. Samuelson is also one of the greatest economists of this period and a Nobel Prize winner in the subject.

Opinions

One of your authors once ventured to say in a university seminar, 'In my opinion . . .' and was somewhat unkindly rebuked by the tutor who said, 'Your opinion! Who wants to know your opinion?'.

Alas, this seems generally true. Despite what some may say, it does appear that examiners do not want to know your opinions at length. They are far more interested in seeing you demonstrate that you understand the work of established economists. And, without disrespect, students at this level seldom astound their tutors with some original and profound insight (nor would all tutors recognise it as such!), but we have all unfortunately seen essays which consist solely of misinformed or superficial opinion. Nevertheless, you *will* have to think for yourself, as will be seen when you read the section on assessment criteria in this book.

Formal English

There are many types of English, both written and spoken. In the exam *you are required* to write in formal English. We do not presume in five or six paragraphs to teach you what this is, let alone how to write it, but you must be aware of it and practise writing it.

If you look very carefully at how writers on economics express themselves you will realise that no one speaks like this (not even on Radio 4). However, they will be writing good, formal English and you should try to emulate them. Economics is a subject of words and argument (and, at a higher level, mathematics). It follows that a sophisticated command of the language will help you express yourself more accurately. For example, economists tend to 'hedge' their statements around with all kinds of conditions. Consider the following statement by way of example: 'Inflation is caused by wage rises'. As it stands the statement might be useful as political rhetoric, but it is far too strong a statement for the economist. The economist would say something like: 'Under certain circumstances wage rises can give rise to inflation'. It is probably better for you to say 'Some economists believe that inflation is often caused by wage increases'.

An eloquent use of language is always impressive, but examiners do not appreciate flowery English. They do appreciate a *sophistication of tone*, *a wide vocabulary* and *varied sentence construction*. Many writers on exam technique will tell you to use simple direct sentences. We wish to qualify this advice: obviously you should try to be concise when time is pressing, but you should not waste time attempting to achieve greater simplicity and conciseness, as this is not the object of the exercise. Remember Winston Churchill's remark about one of his pieces; 'I would have made it shorter but I did not have the time'. It is our experience that students who write good English often achieve better grades than equally informed colleagues who do not.

The use of diagrams

Diagrams and graphs are often useful and their effective use can greatly enhance an answer. Some textbooks illustrate their contents by the use of photographs and pictures; such pictorial illustrations will not earn you marks. Diagrams and graphs should be used as analytical devices or where they aid exposition. They should also be used, where appropriate, to structure the exposition in the text and should not repeat in a different form points already made. It follows that they should also not be disembodied from the text; they should be *integrated* with the text and not just 'thrown in for luck'.

Remember that if it is worth drawing a diagram, then time should be taken to ensure that it is *fully labelled*, *clear*, and *accurate*. These objectives are easiest to achieve by drawing diagrams fairly large. Do not squeeze them into little boxes crammed in by text. If several points need to be made, it may be neater and clearer to draw an additional diagram rather than superimposing more and more lines or resorting to complex notations which will confuse and frustrate the examiner. If you cannot remember a diagram correctly leave it out; nothing reveals lack of understanding more clearly than a wrongly drawn diagram. Be careful to avoid violating the many mathematical relationships that hold in economics, e.g. MC cutting the minimum of AC, MR lying half way between the vertical axis and a straight line demand curve. If you draw a '45 degree' line, make sure it is at 45 degrees. Such inaccuracies are very easy to spot and give a bad impression.

5

Avoid the habit of unthinkingly trotting out diagrams every time a particular technical term is mentioned; it may be that the points highlighted by the standard diagrams are not the ones focused upon in the question. For example, if you were asked to compare the free market with a planned economy, you should not spend most of your time drawing supply and demand diagrams. Indeed, you will notice in the text that an essay on the price mechanism contains no such diagrams (see page 36). Instead time is taken to *explain* the nature and basis of such a system so that it can be contrasted and compared with an alternative system, rather than 'filling up space' by engaging in an abstract shifting of lines. This is not to say that a good answer could not include such a diagram, but you should not think that reproducing a diagram automatically earns you a mark.

Equilibrium and the 'Rule of Three'

In your economics exam and coursework you will no doubt have to explain the concept of equilibrium, e.g. market equilibrium, consumer equilibrium, national income equilibrium etc. You must avoid regarding equilibria as simply being points where two lines cross or touch! When you think of equilibrium think of the following 'Rule of Three':

(a) First, you must explain *why* the point indicated is an equilibrium; for example, in market equilibrium it is because all economic agents are doing what they want to do, given the constraints they face. That is to say, at the prevailing market prices consumers can buy the amounts they wish to purchase and suppliers can sell the amounts they wish to sell, hence supply equals demand and there is no upward or downward pressure on price and therefore no reason to change behaviour.

(b) Second, explain what would happen 'below' the point of equilibrium. For example, in the case of normal supply and demand, a below equilibrium price would cause excess demand (i.e. consumers wish to buy more than producers wish to sell). This would lead to a rise in price and a consequent contraction of demand, accompanied by an extension of supply until demand again equals supply and equilibrium is restored. If time permits or if the question seems to require it you could explain how price actually changes, for example, by suppliers responding to stock depletion or demanders competing against each other as at auction. If you are familiar with the concept of a 'Walrasian Auctioneer' you may use this to demonstrate your awareness of the model's essentially abstract nature.

(c) Third, explain what would happen 'above' equilibrium. For example, in the case of Keynesian national income determination, if income exceeds planned/desired expenditure then the volume of output exceeds that which is being purchased. Firms will thus respond by cutting back production, but as they do this the derived demand for the factors of production also decreases. The consequent fall in factor incomes will lead to a fall in planned/desired expenditure, thus output will fall still further. However, as MPC is less than one, planned/desired expenditure will fall at a slower rate than output/income. Hence, when the multiplier process has finally worked through, equilibrium will be restored when planned/desired expenditure again equals income/output.

In short, the Rule of Three' should remind you to explain why an equilibrium *is* an equilibrium and what forces are set up below and above it which act to restore equilibrium (assuming, of course, a stable equilibrium).

3
Study techniques

The study environment

The environment at your college/school is probably largely beyond your control. Make sure, however, that you make the most of it. Become familiar with your *library* and with *public libraries*. Remember that inter-library loans can usually be arranged. The main public library for your local authority is likely to have a designated quiet study/reference area. It is often worth the extra travel to avoid the often noisy environment of many branch libraries. Many colleges allow students from other institutions to use libraries, but it is unlikely that they would permit you borrowing privileges.

At home you should create a study environment. This means a quiet place where you can work (preferably alone) which is well lit, comfortable and where you can keep your books, notes, etc. in good order. It is all too easy to deceive yourself that you can study effectively in front of the television. In general, this just cannot be done. Admittedly, at times you may well find studying rather tedious or just plain dull. The way to respond is to try to get more out of your studies rather than looking for some distraction to take the pain away! (See the advice on passive learning below.)

If you have a home environment in which it is impossible to get away from distractions you are at a disadvantage. Nevertheless, there are steps you can take. Make clear to your family the im-

portance of what you are doing; if necessary ask your tutor for a letter explaining your need for uninterrupted study. If you are living away from home at college, nag the accommodation office for better conditions. Make sure your teacher/tutor is informed about your difficulties. Find out about and use libraries for studying. You may find earplugs are useful: these can be purchased from chemists and the wax type are particularly effective sound barriers. Above all, keep going!

Passive learning – or how to succeed without really trying!

Passive learning is the technical term for the process by which we learn from the environment around us rather than in the more formal way from textbooks, lectures, etc. Not only can you learn things without conscious effort; it can dramatically increase your enjoyment of your studies. In economics we are lucky in that our everyday lives are surrounded by material which is useful for our studies. You should develop an active interest in using what you have learned to explain the world around you. For example: Why are two shops able to charge different prices for the same good? Why are people paid different amounts? Why is there a heavy tax on some goods but not on others?

By supplementing your studies with 'quality'

newspapers and magazines, together with certain radio and TV programmes, you will find that, as your knowledge of economics improves, many previously unintelligible and therefore boring sources of information come to life. You will be aware of seeing the world around you in new ways. Thus those lonely hours of study will seem more worthwhile and not nearly so dry. Hopefully you will actually *enjoy* your study of economics; it really is a fascinating subject once you get into it. What's more, there will be a pay-off in the exam!

By passive learning, therefore, we actually mean *active listening and looking*. Once you begin to get more out of the world about you, rather than relying solely on textbooks, you will find the subject much easier. You will be aware of knowing more than you have consciously learned. Many things that are current in economics you will simply know about in the same way that you know what the best-selling records of the moment are. This does not mean that you will not have to slog through a difficult piece of 'textbook' economic analysis any more, but when you do you will find that your motivation has been greatly increased.

Notes

Notes are the very stuff of which many of your exam answers will be made. It is through the framework of your notes and marked coursework that your knowledge will tend to be organised and learned.

Your notes are your business and doubtless you will find the way of organising them which seems best to you. However, here are a few points you may find useful:

(a) Always use loose-leaf paper. This is most convenient for adding to your notes at a later date or rearranging them. Always try to ensure that you do not have two topics on one sheet of paper; this will allow you to re-order and arrange your notes under different headings for revision purposes.

(b) Try to make a pattern in your notes: use as much space as you can afford with sub-headings, sub-sub-headings and so on. You will find that a strong visual pattern to your notes helps you to remember them.

(c) Use abbreviations but be consistent, otherwise you will forget what they stand for. Economics abounds in conventionally accepted symbols: DD for demand, Y for income, MC for marginal cost, etc. Try to use these as a matter of course.

(d) It is no use copying chunks out of books. You must think about the information and *process* it so that it makes sense to you in your own words. There is a place for formal definitions and these can be reproduced word for word, but the emphasis must be on deciding how *you* are going to explain things. Much time and anguish can be saved in the exam if you practise explaining things in your own words *throughout* your period of study. Remember that it is impossible to hide your lack of understanding by memorising chunks of textbooks; moreover, you will not be able to memorise much that does not make sense to you. You will get more marks for a clear explanation of what you *have* understood than for a garbled recollection of reams of material you have read but not understood.

(e) Take notes on all that seems useful in lectures and classes, not just when the teacher appears to be 'giving notes'. Do not, however, get into the habit of taking notes of things you do not understand in place of asking the teacher for an explanation or elaboration.

(f) Look after your notes. Consider their opportunity cost! Suppose you are studying on a two-year 'A' level course: it costs the local authority around £3000 per year to educate you in three 'A' level subjects. Thus we have an explicit cost of your economics notes (to taxpayers etc.) of around £2000. Then consider that in order to do 'A' levels you are not earning wages for two years. Further, suppose that as a result of losing your notes you fail to obtain your desired grade and do not go on to higher education and because of this your salary for the rest of your life is 20 per cent less than it might have been.

Hang onto your notes – it looks like you've got something in excess of £50 000 tucked under your arm!

Reading

It is essential that you read widely and are critical of what you read. We still use the expression 'reading for a degree'. This is a telling phrase. One of the best ways to achieve a good grade is to demonstrate the breadth of your reading (and of course your understanding of what you have read!). You will find material in our suggested answers which is not contained within any single textbook. You, too, should seek information beyond a single text.

(a) *Textbooks*. We recommend that as you come to each topic you read carefully the relevant chapters in your textbooks and make notes as you go. Ensure you only make notes: avoid copying as it is time-consuming.

(b) *The reading list*. You might be given a reading list by your tutor; if not you will find suggestions for further reading in most textbooks (including this one). Do not be put off by the sheer quantity of sources that are recommended. It is better just to 'dip into' a book or article than not to try it at all. Again make notes of what you find useful and *note the source* so that you can refer to it in your answers.

(c) *Newspapers and magazines*. A glance at the sources of material for data response questions should convince you how important newspapers are. Try to cultivate the habit of reading at least one 'quality' daily newspaper (e.g. *The Financial Times, The Times, The Guardian, The Independent* etc), making a note of any information that could be used to make your notes more topical. Avoid, however, believing everything you read and do not reproduce a reporter's opinion as 'fact'. Remember our previous warning that economic analysis is not simply current affairs. Some magazines are also useful, e.g. *The Economist*. Ploughing through the 100 plus pages of *The Economist* every week may seem a daunting task on top of everything else you have to do but you can be selective and single out those features and articles of most relevance. *The Economist* has published a series of 'Schools Briefs' and 'Economist Briefs'; try to get hold of these if you can as they are a masterpiece of concise writing.

(d) *Journals*. Today's students of economics are most fortunate in that there is a considerable number of journals written specifically for them. These journals are topical and avoid the difficult, 'arcane' and mathematical analysis of the more advanced journals. Notable are *The Economic Review* and *Developments in Economics*. Ask your tutor or librarian about these. It would be very foolish not to make use of them because others will! Your tutor is also probably a member of the 'Economics Association' and can refer you to many useful articles published in *Economics: The Journal of the Economics Association*. There are also a number of reviews published quarterly by banks which are free and usually not too technical.

(e) *Statistics*. You should make yourself familiar with some or all of the following:

The Annual Abstract of Statistics (CSO)
Economic Trends (CSO)
National Accounts: Blue Book (CSO)
UK Balance of Payments (CSO)
Social Trends (CSO)
Employment Gazette (Department of Employment)
OECD Economic Outlook
World Bank – World Development Report (Oxford)

They are all, with the exception of the last named, fiendishly expensive and therefore best consulted in libraries.

Make the most of your teacher

If you have a teacher or lecturer, remember that they are your most valuable resource. Make sure that you get the maximum value out of each class. Make notes of what seems useful, ask questions **9** and discuss points with your teacher and class-mates.

One of the most effective methods of learning is to note which topics are to be covered next and prepare in advance. Go through the relevant chapters in the textbooks ahead of the lesson.

Afterwards go through your notes, making sure you understand what has taken place, and take your problems along to your next class/tutorial. Virtually all teachers respond well to interested students.

4
Exams

Syllabuses

As there are a number of examination boards, and as syllabuses are subject to change, this book does not contain a list of the specific syllabuses set by the various boards. No doubt your teacher will have a copy of your examination board's syllabus. Alternatively you can obtain one directly from the examination board (the addresses are listed in the Appendix). You might be disappointed however; it is our experience that the lists of topics contained in these syllabuses are usually far more meaningful to teachers than to the students themselves!

Nevertheless, it is essential that you familiarise yourself with the assessment pattern of your examination board. These differ in terms of the types of paper set, the weightings to be given to each paper, the degree of choice allowed, and the nature of the questions actually set. Again your teacher will have the relevant details or these can be obtained from the examination board, together with past papers.

There has been a welcome move towards the standardisation of topics across the various boards. This has resulted in a booklet published by the GCE Boards – entitled 'Common Cores at Advanced Level'. The result has been that the examination boards differ more in terms of their assessment pattern than in their coverage of topics. This is fortunate in that no textbook is written with just one examination board in mind, but rather a modern text should cover all these core topics.

Textbooks are usually written as an integrated whole, with extensive cross-referencing and reliance on concepts and information developed in earlier chapters. As 'A' level textbooks should now cover the common core topics fairly closely, it would not seem useful for the student to spend a great deal of time 'editing' in order to tailor such a text to a specific board. Nevertheless, you should check that no topics in the syllabus you are following are omitted by your textbooks. Even if your main textbook contains material not strictly included in your syllabus, it is likely that the author has integrated the topic with the material in the rest of the book and hence it is useful as additional reading.

Your teacher will have compiled a list of reading which reflects the particular emphasis given by your examination board. But as a general rule your main reading should consist of a textbook *specifically* designed for 'A' level students. It is *essential* that the text you choose is up to date; economics should be about the real world and real economies are constantly changing. Moreover, the types of question that are set and the answers expected change in the light of economic events, developments within economics itself, and the policies adopted by governments. The date of publication is to be found in the first few pages of any book: do not use an edition which was published more than a few years ago.

Practice

One of the most important things you can do in preparing for an exam is to practise. During Wimbledon fortnight you can become a great expert on tennis but it still doesn't mean that you could take a single point off Boris Becker or Steffi Graf. It is the same with the economics exam. You must learn to perform under match conditions. This means *doing* essays, data response and multiple-choice questions under as near examination conditions as you can. The sheer speed with which you must think and write is something you can only acquire with constant practice.

Assessment criteria

Examiners require more than a simple recall of knowledge; you will also have to demonstrate that you *understand* and can *apply* such knowledge. In particular, the following abilities are looked for by examiners:

- Knowledge
- Comprehension
- Application
- Analysis and synthesis
- Evaluation
- Expression

Data response is often the form of assessment that students are most in fear of. But it should be noted that it was introduced *specifically* to allow examiners to assess performance over the full range of criteria as listed above. Although the criteria should be borne in mind in all papers (excluding expression in multiple choice!), it is most helpful to illustrate them in relation to data response questions: *knowledge*, i.e. of the terminology used, specific facts about the economic environment relating to the data, methods of data presentation and of relevant economic concepts, principles and theories; *comprehension*, i.e. the ability to understand data and make generalisations; *application*, i.e. the ability to apply known economic principles to the data; *analysis and synthesis*, i.e. the ability to recognise assumptions, test hypotheses using the data and to draw inferences and conclusions; *evaluation*, i.e. the ability to assess the quality of the data in terms of its reliability, logical consistency and conclusiveness; *expression*, i.e. the ability to present your response in a clear, logical and appropriate form.

The incline of difficulty

If you read the literature put out by examining boards you will become aware that they place great emphasis on 'higher order skills'. *Lower order skills* are things such as simple *factual recall* of terminology, data, institutions and so on. '*Higher order skills*' are the ability to *analyse*, *evaluate* and *apply* the information you have. Some boards publish a, supposedly, precise weighting of marks allocation attached to a breakdown of the abilities to be tested. However, these weights are unlikely to be of much use to the student when engaged in actual question-answering. We think it will be more useful for you to think of an 'incline of difficulty'. Looked at from your point of view, you will only get high marks if you can demonstrate the higher order skills.

We have devised a diagram to illustrate the incline of difficulty (*see* Fig. 4.1). On the left hand side you will see the order of skills plotted against factual recall on the horizontal axis. The mark achieved is then read off the right hand axis according to the level of skills reached.

Experience suggests the shape of the line with the grades F to A on it. The diagram is illustrative rather than precise; nevertheless consider carefully the implication: You can have excellent factual recall, but if you do not demonstrate the higher order skills you will achieve only a low grade.

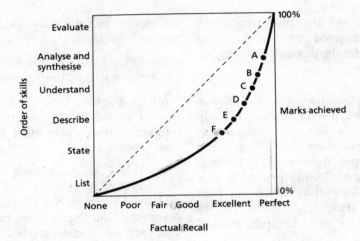

Fig. 4.1 The incline of difficulty

Data response questions

Most 'A' level examining boards now have a data response section. Many other examination bodies have also been influenced by this approach. In such questions you are required to respond to the *stimulus material* provided. This tends to fall into two main categories:

(a) Articles from the press and journals, etc, to which you are required to respond.

(b) Numerical material which may either be *real-world data* or *simulated data*. With this material you may be required to undertake various calculations and also to comment upon it. Real world data are statistics drawn from any source such as government statistics, car sales, housing starts, etc. Simulated data are completely fictitious and are used to test your knowledge of various parts of economic theory, such as demand and supply, theory of the firm, comparative advantage, etc.

You must read the stimulus material very carefully. This is vital both to understand the question and also because it should contain at least part of the answer you require. There is a danger that when you are presented with a long piece of prose as the stimulus you will only skim it

and then try to answer the questions from your own knowledge while the information you so badly need remains unnoticed in the material.

You may find that, where there are several parts to the question, they follow the incline of difficulty approach described above. This being the case, the early questions may be very straightforward and consist of your having to do little more than comment on the data, e.g. 'the figures show that over the period real income rose by 8 per cent' or, perhaps, 'the figures show that 25 per cent of all manufactured goods were exported'. It sometimes really is as simple as this, so do not always go looking for 'deep dark meanings'.

However the later parts may be much more difficult. You may have to demonstrate the higher order skills to gain marks. The sort of things to consider are:

- What conclusions might be *inferred* from the data.
- What *assumptions* are implicit in the material.
- What *economic theories* do the data support or refute.
- Above all ask yourself *'what data are relevant to answering the question and what other data do I need to reach any of the above conclusions?'*. By answering this question you will answer **13**

many others. You will also prevent yourself from being 'mesmerised' by the data and meandering pointlessly through it using up your valuable time.

The data response questions you will find in this book are of all the types mentioned. In addition there are some which are designed as 'exercises' to expand your knowledge and understanding of a topic. When working through the question you may well find the need to look at outside sources. As well as increasing your understanding this should also help you to answer our 'What else do I need to know?' question.

Essay questions and essay techniques

Essay papers (sometimes known as 'free response papers') present the greatest opportunities and difficulties for examinees. The opportunities lie in the fact that you have a choice of topics and can select those in which you are stronger. Also, since there is no 'model' answer, you can adopt the response which suits you best (*warning*: see the note on relevance below). You may also be able to disguise your weaknesses in a way which is not possible with data response and multiple-choice questions. Indeed, it was for this very reason that the latter two types of paper were introduced.

The difficulties with essay papers and essays may be all too obvious to you. If this is the case you may like to consider the following points which will help you:

(a) *English*. There is a premium on the use of good English. Perhaps there should not be but there is. This does not mean marks will be deducted for every spelling mistake and grammatical transgression, but the candidates with a better command of the language will express themselves with greater precision. The examiner can thus award marks with greater confidence; examiners guard against 'giving the benefit of the doubt' to candidates who do not express themselves clearly.

(b) *Practice*. As we have noted, you *must* practise writing essays under exam conditions.

(c) *Conciseness*. Your answer must be concise. Do not waffle! There is not time in the exam for longwindedness; you must try to make every word count!

(d) *Take 5*. Spend at least five minutes at the beginning of an exam to *read the paper carefully* and decide your plan of attack. This is absolutely essential. Nothing is more guaranteed to sink you than misreading a question or making the wrong selection, which is so easily done if you panic.

(e) *Essay Plans*. Your two authors have a confession to make: neither of us have ever written essay plans in examinations. We note, however, that many students find them useful, but be careful you do not spend too long on them. As examiners we have both been confronted with scripts where the essay plans have been longer than the essays! The benefit of an essay plan is that it makes you think about the question before wading in. We have found that we can do this without constructing a 'formal' essay plan, perhaps just jotting down a few key words. In either case the moral is the same; *think* about the question. In particular: what material from the syllabus is *most* relevant and must be explained in detail; what should be explained only briefly; and how are you going to structure your answer? Do this *before* starting to write. While you are writing ideas are likely to occur to you which are relevant to other paragraphs of your answer. Jot these ideas down quickly in the margin or in your plan.

(f) *Space*. Leave lots of space when you are writing. This will allow you to go back and amend your answers if you have time and/or new thoughts occur to you. Leave several lines at the end of each paragraph. *Never* start a new question on the same side of paper as you finished the last one. Leave lots of space at the end of each essay even if this means leaving a whole page blank.

(g) *Relevance*. Probably the commonest mistake made by students is writing material that is irrelevant to the question actually set. No matter how brilliant your essay is, if it is not relevant to the question set you will receive no marks. You must answer the question set and not the one you would have liked to have seen set! Admittedly, if you have done a lot of practice essays during your studies you are likely to find that you can remember parts that can in fact be 'plugged' straight into your answer, e.g. a paragraph defining the price mechanism. This can save a great deal of time which can then be used to compose the original material you will need for the rest of the essay. The danger is that your previous essay 'takes over' the present, so after each paragraph check that what you are writing is relevant to the question. Do not try to 'bend' the question round to one you can answer or have prepared previously.

(h) *Plan your time*. It is essential to allocate your time correctly. If there are five questions, you *must* answer five. Consider the *law of diminishing returns* – once you have written enough to gain 60–70 per cent of the marks available for an essay, every additional five minutes spent on an answer buys you less and less additional marks. This being the case, it pays you to get onto the next question. Prop your watch in front of you. If you are over-running the time on the early questions, stop and go onto the next question. If you are short of time at the end write down the remaining part of your answer in note form.

(i) *Quotes*. To use or not to use quotes in an essay is a topic of some controversy. Those that dislike them say that they waste time, they are often irrelevant, they add nothing to your essay, examiners dislike them and you spend fruitless hours trying to memorise them. On the other hand, reference to learned authorities is part of academic debate, although this does not necessarily mean quoting verbatim. The best advice is to use quotes only when they add significantly to your answer, when they are relevant and when you can remember them with total accuracy.

(j) *Correcting fluid*. Do not use correcting fluid. First, it is forbidden by most examining boards and second, it wastes time. If you make a mistake simply cross it out.

(k) *Essay structure*. Try to give your essay a logical structure. A good essay usually begins by defining the relevant terms and concepts that are mentioned or implied in the question. It should then progressively develop a theme in such a way that the points made in the essay link together, i.e. it should be clear where the essay is 'going' and how one point is related to another through its relevance to the question. If you are successful in this you will find that the points you make prepare the ground for subsequent points; this jogs your memory and makes it easier to remember to include all the points of relevance.

In contrast a poor essay often wanders about in a confused fashion like a ship without a rudder. It is clear that the student does not know at any point where he or she has got to in the essay or where to go next. The student often resorts to merely listing points in a haphazard way. Repetition and irrelevance is common. The student is constantly searching for another point to make and cannot draw the material together into a conclusion which rests upon the material of the essay and which answers the question set.

Everyone knows that good essays need an introduction and conclusion. However, beware of the old formula 'say what you are going to say/say it/say what you have said'. This may be good teaching practice but it is no good as the basis of an essay plan. You do not have the time to say things twice, let alone three times.

Your introduction should be a lead into the topic. If you are not sure how to do this then one way is to look very carefully at the question and construct your introduction around this. Your conclusion should be a conclusion and not

15

simply a summary of what you have said. Often the best way to look at it is to say to yourself that you are making the statement, 'On the basis of the arguments and evidence presented we can conclude that . . .'. If the essay title is a direct question you must answer it in your concluding paragraph. If the essay is not actually a question, e.g. 'Compare and contrast . . .', your conclusion should still round off what has been said rather than restate it. It is most important that your conclusion is not 'drawn out of thin air'; it must be supported by what you have written in the essay.

You may well feel these points on structure are rather abstract; essay writing is a subtle skill which is best learned through example and practice. For examples we refer you to the suggested essay answers in this book; it is not just their content which you should absorb – most of that can be found in books and journals; what is even more important is the style and construction of the essays. It is for this reason that the essays are written out in full instead of a mere plan of relevant topics.

Multiple-choice questions (MCQs)

The types of question used by different boards vary but in all there are three sorts of question you may come across:

(a) *Single completion (or stem) questions*. In these the *stem* is the question itself followed by four or five possible answers. The correct answer is known as the *key* and the incorrect answers as *distractors*. It is often the practice that two of the distractors will seem temptingly correct while the others are nonsense. Remember that you are required to select the *most* appropriate answer. All the multiple-choice tests in this book start with single completion items and conclude with a number of the other types.

(b) *Multiple completion questions*. In these you are given a number (usually three) of statements of which all may be correct, none may be correct,

only the first statement is correct and so on. You select the correct combination from the possibilities offered (*see* page 31).

(c) *Assertion/reason questions*. Students often find these the most difficult form of question. In these you are presented with two statements. From these you must first decide whether the two statements are correct when considered as separate statements. If both are correct then you must decide if the second statement provides an explanation of the first (*see* page 79).

You will find that some questions may be answered quickly while others take a comparatively long time. Here is a suggested plan of attack for an MCQ paper:

(a) Go through the paper once, answering the questions which may be answered quickly. Leave out those which you cannot do or which seem to involve lengthy calculation.

(b) Return to the questions which involve calculation and do these.

(c) Leave yourself time to consider the questions which you could not answer. *Never* leave any question unanswered; as the end of the exam approaches, make your best guess at any questions you still cannot do. Sometimes it is possible to eliminate answers which you can see are wrong. If so, cross them out and guess from those remaining. Remember that even if you have no idea at all which is the correct answer you still have a 20 or 25 per cent chance of guessing correctly.

Multiple-choice questions only work properly when undertaken under rigorous conditions. In the MCQ tests in this book you will find sets of 20 questions. Allow yourself precisely 30 minutes for each test. Write down the answer so that there is no possibility of your cheating yourself. When you have finished the test and checked it against the answers provided, make sure you know why the correct answer is the most appropriate of the answers listed. It is vitally important to do this.

Revision

Obviously you cannot revise what you do not know. By this we mean that you should work hard consistently throughout your period of study and learn each topic as you go along. If you do not do this, then your programme of revision is not revision at all but study, and you will be at a serious disadvantage.

Start your revision several weeks before the exam. Set out a timetable of topics which you are going to revise.

If you are doing an exam with multiple-choice questions and/or data response then you must revise the whole syllabus.

Revise in sessions of two to three hours. With longer sessions the law of diminishing returns sets in quite viciously. Set yourself little targets within the session, allowing yourself, say, a hot drink every 45 minutes. If you want to check your recall of a particular essay you have prepared during the year, or read in this book, it often makes a change to use a tape recorder. You must practise, however, writing under time-constrained conditions; only then will you know how much *you* are capable of fitting in the time allotted. You should tailor your answers in the exam according to this ability.

Arrange your notes in topic order. The loose-leaf format of notes allows you to rearrange and to cross topic boundaries. Increasingly, examination questions cross topic boundaries so that you may need to understand and to revise things in a different order from that in which you learnt them. Try to be aware of these interrelationships throughout your study. For example, it is essential to understand elasticity of demand if you are going to understand international trade and exchange rates.

You will find this book a valuable aid to revision. You should have worked your way through all the questions by the end of your revision.

Do not revise late into the night the day before your exam. Also, try to avoid revising on the day of the exam. By the morning of the exam you should be fully ready. Try to clear your mind and relax.

Nerves

It is no use pretending that exams are not important. Your exam results can determine much of the rest of your life, even the way you regard yourself. If at present you are beginning to be frustrated by studying and want to 'get out there and do something' instead, remember that you will change with time and different things will become important to you. You are likely to find that without adequate exam results many opportunities in later life will be closed to you. Most students instinctively know these things and that is perhaps why a debilitating dread of failure sometimes develops.

The best way to tackle nerves is to accept them as entirely normal. In fact you can learn how to use them to your advantage!

Psychological studies suggest that for most people a certain amount of anxiety or 'arousal' is necessary to achieve optimum performance; most teachers have seen students who fail to reach their potential because of 'over-confidence'. The thought of the impending examination may enable you to put aside distractions and get down to work. 'Nerves', then, are not all bad.

The danger comes from too much anxiety; not only can this be extremely unpleasant but it can also lower your performance level. Accept a certain amount of anxiety and trepidation as the sign of a healthy attitude, but do not allow yourself to enter a vicious circle where your fears pile up upon each other.

Get plenty of sleep and allow yourself time for relaxation. Some people find it is useful to work out a timetable which lays down definite times for work and pleasure; there may be a member of staff at your school or college who helps students do this. If things are all becoming too much, *seek help* from a teacher, parent, welfare officer, student counsellor etc. Never take drugs of any sort to reduce your nerves before an exam, unless of course these are part of a medical treatment prescribed by your doctor.

It's up to you!

No one can learn for you and no one can take the exam for you. You must realise that it is not your teacher's fault if you do not know something, nor is it the fault of the textbook. These days there is such a wealth of guidance available that there is no excuse. Do not become 'teacher dependent'; shake yourself free from this and make the leap to realising that it's up to you to do the work that will bring exam success.

2
Study section

5

Economics and the economy: an overview

Questions

Essay paper   Attempt all questions. Compare your answers with those provided.

1   (Answer provided.) Why do economists disagree?

2   Examine the advantages and disadvantages of large-scale production.

3   'If the government paid producers to produce more at a lower price consumers could purchase more of everything.' Evaluate this statement.

4   (Answer provided.) How might changes in population affect the standard of living in a country?

5   (Answer provided.) 'If the price mechanism did not exist it would be necessary to invent it.' Discuss.

6   Evaluate the arguments for and against planned and free market economies.

7   What is meant by 'the conditions of supply' and how would a supply curve be affected by changes in these conditions?

8   Trace the development of the mixed economy in the UK. To what extent are the guiding principles of this development still relevant today?

9   (Answer provided.) To what extent does Gross National Product provide a reliable measure of a nation's standard of living?

10   Is economic growth a desirable policy objective?

Data response paper   Attempt all questions. Compare your answer with those provided.

Question 1 (Answer provided.)
Assume an economy can produce two goods which we will call X and Y. We are told that if all resources are fully utilised and allocated with maximum efficiency, the economy is capable of producing (per week):

	Output of Y		Output of X
Combination 1	50 units	and	0 units
Combination 2	40 units	and	300 units
Combination 3	20 units	and	500 units
Combination 4	0 units	and	550 units

(a) Draw the production possibility boundary (assume a smooth curve).

(b) Can an output of 40 units of Y and 400 units of X per week be attained? If not, why not? (Only a short answer is required, but avoid a tautological answer.)

(c) State the two types of reason why the economy may in practice be producing, say, 10 units of Y and 400 units of X per week.

(d) What is the opportunity cost of increasing the production of X from 300 units to 500 units per week?

(e) How would technical innovation in the X industry alone affect the production possibility boundary? Illustrate your answer with a diagram (assume the existing flow of resources to be unaltered).

(f) Does the above prove that a combination of 50 units of Y and 550 units of X per week will always be beyond the potential of the above economy?

(g) Offer an explanation as to why the production possibility boundary is curved (i.e. concave to the origin).

Question 2

Read the following passage which is adapted from an article in *The Economist*, and study Fig. 5.1 which accompanies the article.

Governments in most industrial countries are trying to trim the size of their public spending. And finding it damnably difficult for three reasons:

i) *Slow economic growth*: since 1979 the depression started by the oil price rises has resulted in rising unemployment and the need to give financial support to industry.

ii) *Demography*: the number of pension-age dependants has risen everywhere, both absolutely and as a proportion of the population.

iii) *Indexation*: many transfer payments – pensions, unemployment pay etc. – are indexed to inflation, so if an economy is actually contracting (e.g. Britain 1979–83), their share of GDP is bound to rise. Higher transfers accounted for more than half the growth in spending between 1961 and 1986 in the countries shown in Fig. 5.1. In America public consumption (defence, education etc.) actually fell as a proportion of GDP, while transfers increased their share from 8.8% to 12.7% of GDP over the same period.

Spending and deficits are not always related: Japan has frequently had large deficits (4–5% of GDP) whilst having one of the smallest public sectors. But the desire to cut fiscal deficits is one reason why governments are keen to cut public spending. The alternative is to raise taxes – politically unpopular at the best of times, but especially so when real incomes are being squeezed by slow growth.

So how do governments go about making cuts? Answer: the easy way. Transfers are hard to reduce because they are tied to political and moral ideas about equity: why hit the old and the unemployed when they are already disadvantaged? Cutting public expenditure is always a difficult option, especially when it involves destroying civil servants' empires.

So the government axemen often go first for public investment programmes involving only the cancellation of a few contracts with private companies. By the time the sewers start leaking and the roads have potholes, some other government will have to take the blame.

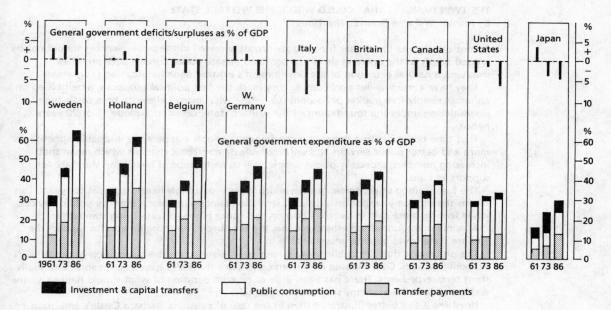

Fig. 5.1 The growth of the public sector

Having studied Fig. 5.1 and read the article, answer the following questions:

(a) For each of the years shown in Fig. 5.1 state the country which had the largest public sector.

(b) For each year state which three countries had the largest percentage of GDP devoted to transfer payments.

(c) Which three countries had the largest budget deficits in 1986?

(d) Which countries had a larger public sector than Britain in 1986?

(e) Explain what is meant by the indexing of transfer payments.

(f) Why might Holland find indexation more burdensome than other countries in the example?

(g) What does the article suggest is the alternative to cutting public expenditure and why is the alternative difficult?

(h) Explain as fully as you can why the cuts described in the final paragraph are potentially the most dangerous to the economy.

(i) What additional information would be useful in assessing the information in Fig. 5.1 and why?

(j) The article and Fig. 5.1 were compiled in 1986. Explain what significant changes (if any) there have been to the situation in Britain since that date.

23

Question 3 (Answer provided.)
Read the following newspaper article:

THE TWIN DANGERS THAT COULD WRECK THE WELFARE STATE
by Frances Williams (Source: *The Times*)

Recent calls by the Chancellor for a bigger private element in the public services should not be judged simply as the opening shots in a confined debate about Conservative priorities involving a natural extension of the Government's existing denationalization programme.

They have a much wider significance. They mark the first political proposals, albeit based on an unashamedly free market philosophy, to defuse what many believe to be a costly time bomb ticking under the foundations of the welfare state, timed to explode 15 or 20 years hence.

That time bomb has two dangerous components: people's apparently insatiable appetite for more and better public services and unfavourable demographic changes which mean that increasing numbers, especially of old people, will come to depend heavily on the state for support and aid.

The fuse is sluggish economic growth which looks increasingly likely to persist for years. This means the economy cannot provide sufficiently to maintain, let alone improve public services, while leaving more cash in people's pockets to finance higher private living standards.

At some point, unless something is done, the tax burden on those in work to support the welfare state could became unsustainable.

The problem is that the public services have been planned on the assumption of rapid economic growth. Cuts imposed by governments since the 1970s have been seen as essentially short term expedients. There has been little or no consideration of what should happen to the welfare state if the economy stagnates indefinitely.

Nowhere is this better illustrated than in the case of pensions. Barbara Castle's ambitious plan enacted in 1975 provides for earnings-related, inflation-proofed (or nearly) pensions for all. The White Paper introducing the scheme stated optimistically:-

"The (new) scheme will lead to a gradual increase in transfer of income and therefore of claims on resources from the economically active sector of the community to those who have retired ... (It) will mean that take-home pay of employees will be restricted and prices increased compared with what would otherwise have been the case ... But the full costs ... will be far outweighed by the improvement in living standards generally resulting from economic growth."

Independent estimates of the cost of the Castle scheme plus some very modest moves towards lower retirement ages and so on suggest that by the first decade of the next century the cost of state pension provision could double in real terms, implying a rise in the average tax burden on those in work from 25 per cent in 1980–81 to 40 per cent.

Even where no significant improvements are planned, the cost of public services seems set to rocket. A confidential paper recently submitted to the Cabinet by an inter-departmental group of officials suggested that health spending could rise in real terms by 25 to 35 per cent during the 1980s, mainly because of population changes, while social security spending could increase by 20 to 25 per cent, in large part the consequence of continuing high unemployment.

With a growth rate of around 2½ per cent a year, close to 'the best we can expect', public spending would absorb roughly the same proportion – 37 per cent instead of 38 per cent – of national output in 1990 as it did in 1979–80. With slow growth – 0.5–0.8 per cent a year – the proportion could rise to 44 per cent.

But the higher growth scenario makes virtually no concession to public demand for better services as national wealth increases. There is plenty of evidence from abroad to show that richer societies choose to spend a higher proportion of their incomes on health care, education and social services. The pressure will always be there for spending on public services to outstrip the growth in economic output, while the gains of prosperity are not willingly relinquished when times are harder.

The Chancellor wants to tackle this problem by diverting demand for improved services away from the state and towards the private sector. Addressing the Institute for Fiscal Studies, a Government spokesman argued in favour of maintaining an absolute basic level of public services rather than a relative level as a proportion of national output.

People had inflated expectations of what the state could provide in straitened economic circumstances. 'The real question,' he suggested, 'is how much the state can afford to provide, free, and still leave the individual citizen with the incentive and ability on top of that ... to provide for his own old age, his own health and his own children's education, directly.'

It is an interesting paradox that people are often prepared to spend more out of their pockets than they grudge the state in taxes to pay for the services they want. But even granted this paradox, the Conservative solution has three critical flaws.

First, simply shifting the financial burden of health, pensions and education from taxes to take-home pay does not leave people better off on balance. In practice it is likely to leave them worse off because private provision tends to be dearer.

Second, such a shift implies that services will be allocated, not on the basis of need – the very *raison d'etre* of the welfare state – but on the basis of ability to pay. In other words, poor people will get a second class service – or none at all. Arguing that the shift would apply only to services above a basic minimum merely begs the question of what the minimum is.

If it is set low the full force of the criticism applies. If it is high the savings on public spending will be trivial.

Third, the very existence of the private sector may detract from the state service, tempting away skilled people with higher salaries and better working conditions and, with schools, removing bright, well motivated children with parents who can afford to pay, to the detriment of those remaining behind.

If two-tier public services is not a solution, however, another must be found. There is a limit to how much in taxes working people are prepared to pay. The danger is that if public services are not carefully planned and expectations deflated to allow for the likelihood that economic growth will not provide, the cost time bomb will explode and the welfare state will collapse.

(a) What reasons are given by the author for the large increase in the cost of the 'welfare state' that is predicted to occur around the turn of the century?

(b) Explain carefully why gradually reducing state aid for the elderly will not necessarily make those in work better off.

(c) How does the privatisation of welfare provision conflict with the 'very *raison d'être*' (i.e. reason for being; purpose that accounts for, justifies or originally caused a thing's existence) of the welfare state?

(d) What assumptions are being made in the conclusion of the article?

Question 4
Study the figures contained in the table.

Now answer the following questions:

(a) Identify the country which

(i) has the greatest density of population.

(ii) has the least density of population.

(iii) experienced the greatest percentage growth rate of population.

(iv) experienced the lowest percentage growth rate of population.

(v) experienced the greatest percentage growth rate in GDP per capita (i.e. per head).

Country	Population (millions) 1985	Area (thousands of square kilometres)	GDP per capita		Average annual growth of population % 1980–85
			Dollars 1985	Average annual growth % 1965–85	
Ethiopia	42.3	1,222	110	0.2	2.9
India	765.1	3,288	270	1.7	2.2
Ghana	12.7	239	380	−2.2	3.3
Brazil	135.6	8,512	1,640	4.3	2.3
Mexico	78.8	1,973	2,080	2.7	2.6
Singapore	2.6	1	7,420	7.6	1.2
Ireland	3.6	70	4,850	2.2	0.9
United Kingdom	56.5	245	8,460	1.6	0.1
France	55.2	547	9,540	2.8	0.7
Japan	120.8	372	11,300	4.7	0.7
United States	239.3	9,363	16,690	1.7	1.0
United Arab Emirates	1.4	84	19,270	–	6.2

Source: World Development Report 1987.

(vi) experienced the lowest percentage growth rate in GDP per capita.

(b) On the basis of these figures and your other reading, comment on the relationship between the density of population and the level of prosperity.

(c) Using these figures as an illustration, comment on the concept of optimum population.

Question 5 (Answer provided.)

(a) The following is a set of instructions and headings which can be used to show how the national income accounts are compiled. The instructions are jumbled up and your task is to rearrange them into a logical and correct order and classification. This will produce a set of instructions showing how to calculate the various national income accounting concepts that are mentioned in capital letters:

Deduct capital consumption.

Add corporate profits (both public and private sectors).

Deduct stock appreciation.

Equals GDP at factor cost.

Add subsidies.

OUTPUT METHOD

Add all incomes from employment and self employment.

Add value of physical increase in stocks and work in progress.

Add residual error.

Add gross domestic fixed capital formation.

Equals GDP at market prices.

INCOME METHOD

Deduct taxes on expenditure.

Equals GDP at factor cost.

Add residual error.

Add rent and interest.

Equals GDP at factor cost.

Add values of all domestically produced goods and services at factor cost (including investment goods).

Equals NNP (National Income).

EXPENDITURE METHOD

Add exports.

Equals GNP

Add net property income from abroad.

Add all expenditures on goods and services made by consumers and by public authorities.

Deduct imports

(b) Study the data and then answer the questions that follow:

	GDP at current prices (£ billion)	GDP deflator
1964	29.9	20.3
1969	40.6	25.2
1974	75.4	39.3
1979	171.7	83.4
1980	199.3	100
1981	217.2	111.9
1982	236.7	120.2
1983	258.0	126.3
1984	277.3	131.8
1985	304.4	139.1

(*Source*: National Accounts)

 (i) Use the above data to compile index numbers of output using 1980 as the base year. Show how your calculations have been made.
 (ii) Which set of figures is most relevant to measuring changes in living standards? Explain your answer.
(iii) Explain why the GDP deflator is not the most relevant measure of inflation for the typical consumer.
(iv) 'The Thatcher government has claimed some success, with a growth rate of 2.6 per cent for the five years 1982–86, third only to Japan and Denmark, and a whisker ahead of the United States. However, the choice of the base year 1981 is misleading.' (C. Johnson; Lloyds Bank Economic Bulletin, April 1987). Use the data you have compiled to explain the point being made here.

Multiple-choice test

Answer all questions. Time allowed: 30 minutes.

1 In Adam Smith's *Wealth of Nations* he sees a competitive market system as:

    A self regulatory.
    B producing what society wants.
    C distributing output among consumers.
    D automatic.
    E all of the above.

2 When economists say that economic goods are scarce goods they mean the word scarce in the sense that

    A there are very few of these goods.
    B there are not enough resources to fill everyone's wants to the point of satiety. **27**

C the goods are limited in supply.

D there are insufficient goods to meet our physical needs.

E the goods are sold at market prices.

Questions 3–4 are based on the following:

Production possibility schedule

Possibility	Wine in mill. litres	Food '000 tonnes
A	0	40
B	20	16
C	36	12
D	48	8
E	56	4
F	60	0

3 If an economy is at present at possibility C, then the opportunity cost of producing 12 million more litres of wine would be:

A 16 000 tonnes of food

B 12 000 tonnes of food

C 40 000 tonnes of food

D 8000 tonnes of food

E 4000 tonnes of food

4 A graph to illustrate these figures would be:

A concave to the origin.

B convex to the origin.

C a straight line.

D a rectangular hyperbola.

E slope upwards at an ever increasing rate.

5 Which of the following best describes the law of increasing costs? The law of increasing costs:

A requires that some inputs remains constant while others are increased.

B is founded on the idea that not all units of any input are equally productive in the output of different goods.

C is another name for the law of diminishing returns.

D results from the fact that buyers will have to pay a higher price as the quantity supplied goes down.

E comes about from the constantly increasing cost of opportunities foregone.

6 It is the case that, *ceteris paribus*, if one or more inputs are held constant while one or more other inputs are increased then the level of total production will:

A after some point increase at a decreasing rate.

B diminish after a certain point.

C increase at a constant rate.

D increase from zero to the point where it begins to lessen.

E never decline absolutely.

7   Of the following the best description of opportunity cost is that it is:

   A   a special sale at below normal price.
   B   a cost that increases at a diminishing rate.
   C   a cost that increases at an increasing rate.
   D   goods that are not produced in order to produce more of another good.
   E   a rightward shift of the production possibility line.

Questions 8–11 are based on the following diagram which illustrates the variations in the total output of goods and services in an economy *ceteris paribus*:

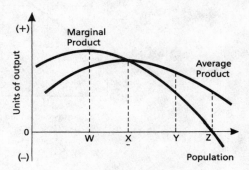

Fig. 5.2

Which of the following:

   A   OW
   B   OX
   C   OY
   D   OZ
   E   cannot be determined from the information given

best describes a situation
where:

8   there are increasing returns to scale.

9   population is at its optimum size.

10   total output of goods and services is at a maximum.

11   there are increasing returns to labour.

12   In a given time period, as an individual increases his or her consumption of a good, then, *ceteris paribus*, the extra amount of utility he or she derives from the consumption of each successive unit will:

   A   increase for a time but then diminish.
   B   decrease.
   C   constantly increase.
   D   increase but at a decreasing rate.
   E   remain constant until utility is maximised.

13 Consider the following diagram:

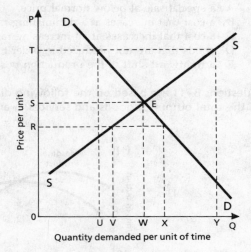

Fig. 5.3

Which of the following dimensions represents excess demand. Is it:

A   OR
B   OT
C   VX
D   UY
E   RT

14 When the price of a good is held above the equilibrium price for any reason the normal result of this will be:

A   an excess demand.
B   an increase in demand.
C   a shortage of this good.
D   a surplus of this good.
E   an increase in supply.

15 From the following information calculate the Gross Domestic Product (GDP) at factor cost.

	£ million
Consumers' expenditure	20 000
General government final consumption	7 000
Gross domestic fixed capital formation	5 000
Exports of goods and services	4 000
Imports of goods and services	4 500
Taxes on expenditure	15 000
Subsidies	2 500
Capital consumption	3 000

Is GDP: (£ million)

A   £58 000
B   £44 500
C   £31 500
D   £19 000
E   £16 000

Questions 16–20

Directions: For each of the questions below, **one** or **more** of the responses given is (are) correct. Then choose

A   if 1, 2 and 3 are correct
B   if 1 and 2 only are correct
C   if 2 and 3 only are correct
D   if 1 only is correct
E   if 3 only is correct

Directions summarised				
A	B	C	D	E
1, 2, 3 correct	1, 2 only	2, 3 only	1 only	3 only

16   *Ceteris paribus* the demand for a product is:

1   inversely related to its price.
2   partly determined by the availability of a product.
3   related to consumers' income.

17   Which of the following are included in the calculation of the national product by the income method?

1   income from employment.
2   gross trading profits of companies.
3   imports.

18   A mixed enterprise is one in which:

1   a company undertakes many different types of activity.
2   a public limited company owns subsidiaries which are private limited companies.
3   both the government and public have shareholdings.

19   The butter mountain resulting from the EC's common agricultural policy (CAP) is an example of:

1   the effect of government intervention in market prices.
2   excess supply.
3   the application of a price 'floor'.

31

20 If a company were to increase the physical input of all resources it uses by 100 per cent and, as a result of this, output were to increase by 100 per cent but, nonetheless, the unit cost of production were to fall, then this would be an example of

1 economies of scale but not of returns to scale.
2 constant returns to scale.
3 economies of scale and of returns to scale.

Answers

1 Why do economists disagree?

It is possible to overstate the extent of disagreement. Mark Blaug estimates that there is a broad consensus among 75 per cent of economists. Nevertheless, there are schools of thought which differ not only in their perception of how the economy works, but also concerning what the subject matter of economics is and the appropriate methods of enquiry.

Problems arise not faced by, say, physicists. For example, the behaviour of people is influenced by perception; they are, for instance, likely to respond to tax increases in different ways according to whether they perceive them as helping the deserving poor or supporting 'spongers'. Hence, some economists feel that the record of past incomes policies shows they are ineffective; others feel it demonstrates the need for incomes policies based on a wider consensus. Moreover, in the laboratory, controlled experiments are often possible, isolating the effect of influences we are interested in. The economist does not have such *ceteris paribus* conditions, and economists can therefore disagree over which particular changes cause which particular events. For example, do wage claims cause or merely reflect other inflationary forces.

Economists such as Adam Smith were social philosophers; their 'Political Economy' was designed to influence political opinion. But from the late nineteenth century onwards economists began to emulate 'scientific' classical physics. This led to emphasis on the 'normative vs positive' distinction, abstract mathematical models, and the separation of analysis from a socio-political context. The subject matter of this 'neoclassical' economics came to be the 'objective' study of the logical consequences arising from competitive market transactions by individuals seeking to maximise individualistic 'innate' human desires.

Most 'mainstream' economists came to see the purpose of economics as being to make predictions rather than to influence political opinion. Following Friedman's 1953 essay 'The Methodology of Positive Economics', it was widely accepted that a theory should be assessed solely on its predictive power and that this does not involve normative considerations, i.e. value judgements. Such, more or less, was the message of Lipsey's influential textbook of the time *Positive Economics*.

There has been growing criticism of the methodology of positive economics, partly because of apparent problems in testing theories by their predictions. Because of the lack of *ceteris paribus* conditions economists resort to highly mathematical and complex statistical techniques. But this 'econometrics' is based on probability theory, not the definite laws of classical physics. Thus not only can economists disagree as to the significance to attach to particular econometric results, but the statistical measures of probability vary with different specifications of the same theory; for example, in testing the relationship between inflation and the money supply, the robustness of the results varies enormously according to which measure of the money supply is **33** used and the postulated mathematical relationship. Causation can also be disputed: Friedman argues that expansion of the money supply increases aggregate demand, but Kaldor argues that increases in aggregate demand cause the money supply to expand.

Lipsey now accepts that evidence is too 'inconclusive', and theories too full of 'tolerated anomalies' for 'dramatic falsification' of a theory to occur. He now argues that theories are only abandoned under the weight of numerous theoretical and empirical conflicts, and that such abandonments are always 'judgemental'. This is closer to Kuhn's view that scientific schools of thought are a 'consensus of experts' involving normative judgements as well as 'objective' criteria.

Some economists argue that 'facts' depend on one's political perspective. Hence 'radical' economists such as Ben Fine claim that the empirical part of any theory *is* part of the theory. Most economists regard this as an extreme view, yet many concede that, for example, the 'correct' measure of unemployment depends on one's perspective. Such considerations blur the positive/normative distinction.

Ironically, by the time that positive economics had achieved its dominance, classical physics had lost its; Eddington had rejected the notion of precise prediction and the work of the physicist Heisenberg suggested that all investigation is ultimately normative in character.

In conclusion, disagreement among economists is not only over 'technicalities' but also over philosophical and ideological positions.

4 How might changes in population affect the standard of living in a country?

The term 'standard of living' usually refers to measures of material consumption. Welfare is a wider concept including the notion of 'quality of life'. Nevertheless, *ceteris paribus*, a higher real disposable income per capita would seem desirable. This is the criterion of a commonly used notion of the 'optimum population', i.e. the level of population at which real income per head is maximised. It is simply an application of the 'law' of diminishing returns: 'If one factor of production is fixed in supply and successive units of a variable factor are added to it, then the extra output derived from the employment of each successive unit of the variable factor must, after a time, decline.

Edwin Cannon (1888) argued that at low levels of population an increase in population allows a more efficient utilisation of resources, for example, through division of labour and the benefits of large-scale production. Hence output per head will at first rise with population. He then used the law of diminishing returns to point out that after a certain level of population is reached, labour will begin to 'run out' of the other existing resources and therefore output per head will begin to fall with increases in population (*see* Fig. 5.4).

The optimum population of a country would be difficult to quantify; it is a short run concept and depends on the level of other resources, technology,

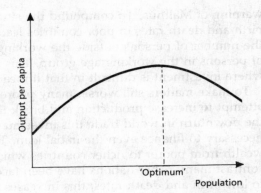

Fig. 5.4

and the composition of the population. Moreover, higher output today could even mean lower output in the future as non-renewable resources are used up. The consideration that population increase might itself affect other variables, such as congestion and pollution, also complicates the notion of an optimum. There could well be moral objections to the term optimum in this context.

The growth of real income per capita depends on the relative growth rates of the volume of national income and population. The growth of population is determined by birth and death rates and migration. The Reverend Thomas Malthus believed ('Essay on Population', 1798) that economic growth could temporarily raise real per capita income, but that this increase in living standards would both increase the birth rate and decrease the death rate. He held that this increase in population would take the form of a geometrical progression (1, 2, 4, 8, 16 etc.), whereas the growth of the means of subsistence proceeds according to an arithmetical progression (1, 2, 3, 4, 5 etc.). Thus he concluded that the natural increase in population would eventually bring per capita income and hence living standards, at least for the 'masses', down to bare subsistence levels.

In the industrially developed countries Malthusian predictions have been thwarted by economic growth which outstripped population growth. Indeed, the decline in birth rates in such countries during this century probably reflects economic growth and its effects on welfare provision, increased job opportunities for women, and the increased opportunity cost of children. In contrast, the poorest countries have both low economic growth and high population growth. Moreover, increased population has occurred largely in the absence of economic growth, due often to advances in medical science. Over half the population of the earth lives in absolute poverty; this is perpetuated by the fact that such poverty leads to large families as insurance against illness and old age.

In many instances a growing population has been advantageous; it may enable a better utilisation of other resources, stimulate demand and investment in the economy, and the constant supply of young persons will increase labour mobility, both geographical and occupational. But on a world scale the unprecedented population growth gives renewed relevance to the

35

warning of Malthus. To compound the situation, the combination of high birth and death rates in poor countries leads to a high dependency ratio, i.e. the number of persons outside the working age group divided by the number of persons in the working age group. This creates a kind of poverty trap where investment is difficult in that it means more hardship in the present.

To make matters still worse, many poorer countries used loans in an attempt to increase production and break the poverty trap. Partly because of the downturn in world trade this investment has not produced the revenues necessary to finance even the initial loan. This has resulted in net transfers of wealth from poorer to richer countries which swamp overseas aid. In contrast many richer nations have been faced with an ageing population due to low birth and death rates; this increases the proportion of resources needed to provide for the elderly.

An important conclusion of the 'Brandt Report' is that the growth of the world's population will lead to yet further tragedy and increased world tension. More controversially, it suggested that disaster could only be avoided through a substantial redistribution of wealth from the rich to the poor countries. It was also claimed this was ultimately necessary for the continued progress of the rich nations themselves, in that increasing productivity would require expanding world markets.

5 'If the price mechanism did not exist it would be necessary to invent it.' Discuss.

The term 'price mechanism' refers to an interaction both within and between markets of supply and demand. In a smoothly functioning free market system this interaction establishes the relative prices (the price of one thing in terms of another) which decide the three basic economic (i.e. arising from scarcity and choice) questions of 'What?, how? and for whom?' Price acts as a signalling device, collecting information and providing incentives for economic agents to act upon. Resource allocation, and the distribution of product, is thus determined by impersonal market forces. Such a system evolved from the need to trade, associated with increasing specialisation, but came nearest in the UK to the competitive *laissez-faire* ideal of Adam Smith under nineteenth-century capitalist industrialisation.

The ubiquity of the economic problem makes necessary an allocating mechanism: if the wants of the human race exceed its means, then choice is forced upon it. This problem of scarcity and choice is encapsulated in the concept of 'opportunity cost', i.e. that, because our resources are not sufficient to meet all our wants, to have one thing is to incur a cost in terms of forgone alternatives. It is this problem of choice that is settled by the workings of the price mechanism.

'What?' is decided by the money votes of consumers. Changes in the desires of consumers will be reflected in changes in the way their money is spent. This will lead to a change in relative prices. The relative profit earned across industries will be altered. This will lead to a change in the activities of businesspersons and hence a new allocation of resources. Finally, this reallocation of resources will produce a change in output which reflects the change in consumer desires.

'How?' refers to the method of production. In a competitive market cheaper methods will drive out more expensive methods and this will lead to efficient production and economising on scarce resources. 'For whom? is decided by the interaction of factor supply and demand and the pattern of resource ownership. It should be noted that in practice the questions are interrelated and therefore determined simultaneously, i.e. in general equilibrium.

Although some method of settling the inevitable economic questions is needed, allocation does not have to be by a price mechanism. The major alternative today is the planned economy in which economic decisions are taken by committees and implemented through direction of resources either centrally or at local level. Under this system planning committees provide the answers to the three economic questions. They settle the 'What?' problem by deciding, for example, on whether more buses or more tractors should be produced. They solve the 'How?' problem by directing labour and other resources into certain areas of production. They solve the 'For whom?' question by allotting goods and services on the grounds of social and political priorities. We can see that under this system the question of 'For whom' can be separated from the other two questions.

Both systems face practical problems. For price mechanisms these include inequality, market failure and instability. Market failure arises when the workings of the price mechanism fail to satisfy consumer wants efficiently; this might be the result of monopoly, externalities, ignorance or lack of co-ordination. Planned economies face the problems of information concerning consumer desires, production techniques and resources supply; inequality caused by political patronage and corruption; excessive bureaucracy and lack of incentive.

In conclusion, alternatives to a price mechanism do exist but, because of the practical problems with each system, in practice all economies are mixed. The actual mix is determined by the severity of the problems faced and ideology. Many observers now prefer the concept of the 'social market' in which market transactions are seen as *socially* valuable, reflecting the mutual benefit of voluntary transactions. Hence the marketplace is accepted as an essential social tool, even by many on the 'left', albeit within the context of a regulated distribution of income and wealth. There has been a movement towards greater use of market solutions not only in this country but also in such countries as Hungary, Russia and even China.

9   To what extent does Gross National Product provide a reliable measure of a nation's standard of living?

GNP is the most common measure of a nation's standard of living. GNP of a nation is GDP plus net income received by domestic residents from investments abroad. GDP measures the total flow of goods and services produced by aggregating through market prices. NNP ('National Income') is the more accurate measure of economic performance as the nominal value of   **37** consumer goods usually includes an element for capital amortisation (i.e. capital consumption). This figure is roughly equal to 'replacement capital' which is also included in gross investment. Hence by adding to the total expenditure on consumer goods gross, instead of net, investment we are counting replacement capital roughly twice.

Although 'the standard of living' is a vague term, an increase in GNP is seen by virtually all governments as a prerequisite to 'better' living standards. If it is taken to refer only to the ability to purchase goods and services this is reasonable. But the overall welfare of a nation's population also depends on many non-marketed things, e.g. the equality of the environment, the level of stress and anxiety, the quality of human relationships, the standard of education, etc. The link between GNP and these variables is far less direct.

GDP measured at current prices can increase due to increases in both prices and output. Only the latter has a direct relevance for the standard of living and hence nominal National Income figures are deflated by using an index of prices in order to indicate changes in 'Real National Income'. Per capita (i.e. per head) income is more relevant than total income. It is obviously vital to adjust for population size when comparing the UK with, say, the USA. It is not meaningful to speak of a 'nation's' standard; clearly there are vast differences in the equality of income distribution between say, South Africa and Sweden.

In making international comparisons it is necessary to convert national income figures to a common currency, but this can be misleading if international exchange rates do not accurately reflect domestic purchasing power. To allow for this a 'Purchasing Parity Index' must be constructed; a recent study by the European Commission reported that on such a basis the standard of living in the UK in 1986 was only 3 per cent below that in France compared to a 30 per cent gap when compared via exchange rates.

There are differences in the range and quality of goods available both through time and internationally. The amount of time available for leisure can also vary. Similarly one would want to adjust national income figures to allow for differences in the proportions of recorded and non-recorded economic activity, for example, home-grown vegetables or goods traded via barter. The proportion of such activity differs particularly between industrialised and non-industrialised nations. Tax evasion also leads to unrecorded transactions, i.e. the 'informal' economy. The problem with attempting to adjust for such items is precisely the fact that they are unrecorded!

What is regarded as final product varies between countries; final product consists of goods and services that are purchased for their own sake in contrast to intermediate products which are required only to produce other products. For example, in many countries public transport is excluded from national product in that it is mainly used for transporting human factors of production and therefore is intermediate production.

Related to the distinction between final and intermediate products is the concept of 'regrettable necessities'. Following Ruggles, both Nordhaus and Tobin have attempted to adjust GDP for regrettables such as defence and negative externalities such as pollution, in an attempt to obtain a measure of income more closely related to welfare. Their measure of economic welfare (MEW) suggested that welfare advances less rapidly than GDP. But the problem arises in deciding whether something is wanted for its own sake or not: medical care can be considered as regrettable but necessary; some of our food simply fuels our work effort.

The problem with MEW is that it is possible to argue that all productive activity might do no better than satisfy the wants it creates! This consideration is taken seriously by Mishan. He believes that much effort is used up in producing goods and services which cater for human needs that were better met in some pre-industrial civilisations. He concludes that it is far from certain that economic growth as measured by GNP should be accepted even as a rough measure of the growth in 'living standards'.

Clearly GNP is not synonymous with welfare. The vital question is whether the benefits of GNP outweigh the costs (although a constant level of output also incurs costs, for example, the depletion of non-renewable resources and added pollution). A topical consideration is that, unless output expands, productivity increases can cause unemployment.

Suggested data response answers

Question 1

(a)

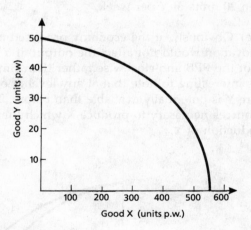

Fig. 5.5

(b) This combination of goods cannot be attained as it is outside the production possibility boundary (PPB). This in itself is a tautology as the PPB is defined as the limit of what is attainable. The reason is that at any given time there is only the existing supply of resources and technology. It is because of this scarcity of resources that there is an upper limit to what is possible.

(c) There are many individual reasons why the economy might in practice be operating at less than its full productive potential, i.e. producing combinations of goods *within* the PPB. But all of these reasons can be classified under two headings. First, *unemployment* might exist; this occurs when resources which are currently available for productive use are not being utilised. Second, there might be *production inefficiency* in the economy; this occurs when resources are being used, but in a way which does not maximise production. Inefficiency in economics is normally taken to mean that by reallocating resources it would be possible to increase the amount of at least one thing which is desirable without having to reduce the amount of other desirable things. If such an improvement is possible, then the present situation represents a *misallocation* of resources.

(d) If the economy is operating within the production possibility boundary it would be possible to increase the output of X without reducing the output of Y, e.g. given the right economic policies, the economy could move from 10 units of Y and 300 units of X per week to 10 units of Y and 500 units of X per week. Nevertheless, if more resources are used in the production of X, the *potential* output of Y is reduced. Once the PPB is reached *any* increase in the output of X must involve a sacrifice in the actual output of Y. Therefore, if the economy is already on the PPB, an increase in the output of X from 300 to 500 must involve a sacrifice in the weekly output of Y of at least 20 units. Thus the opportunity cost of the 200 unit per week increase in X would have been 20 units of Y per week.

(e) Obviously, if the economy produced nothing but good Y, the technical innovation would not affect the output of Y. Therefore the effect will be to pivot the PPB anti-clockwise rather than simply shift it outwards (*see* Fig. 5.6). It is interesting to note that at any level of output of X (other than zero), more Y is potentially available than before. This is due to the reduction in resources necessary to produce X which thereby frees resources for the production of Y.

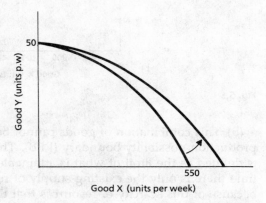

Fig. 5.6

(f) No. The PPB simply shows the limits to possible production that exist at any one time. An increased supply of resources or an improvement in technology would allow economic growth, i.e. an outward shift of the PPB. Hence, although 50 units of Y and 550 units of X per week is at present outside the PPB, future economic growth could one day make this combination attainable.

(g) The concave to the origin curve of the PPB indicates increasing costs of production as the output of a particular good is increased. If the costs of production of all goods remained constant as the output combination is altered the PPB would be a straight line. We would expect increasing costs, however, in that it is unlikely that factors of production are equally suited to all industries or that all industries require, say, capital and labour, in the same proportions. Thus, if the output of an industry expands to the extent that begins to exhaust available supplies of the factors most suited to that industry, it will be forced to change to more costly methods of production.

Question 3
(a) The author includes the following reasons:

(i) The increase in the numbers of retired persons, beginning in about 20 years' time, who will be dependent upon the state. These persons will require pensions and welfare services in general (especially medical).

(ii) Public pressure to maintain or increase the present levels of welfare provision, even though lack of economic growth may mean that financing this provision threatens to restrain or even lower living standards of the working population.

(iii) Any economic growth which does occur might lead to political pressure to increase public spending; the author suggests that this might lead public expenditure to 'outstrip' economic growth and thereby increase it as a proportion of GDP.

(iv) Social security spending could increase, particularly as many economists see continuing high levels of unemployment into the next century.

(b) Assume that private schemes do successfully maintain the living standards of the retired at the levels that would otherwise be provided by the state and that thus the amount of national income received by the retired population would be the same under both schemes. It is now essential to realise that current wants can only be met from current production. If then the total output is unaffected by the method of providing for retirement, the amount of national income left to be consumed by the working population would be unaltered. Moreover, the author suggests that private schemes are less efficient. If this is so then such schemes may actually absorb more resources than a comparable state scheme to the detriment of the then working population.

The move toward private sector retirement schemes might, however, increase economic growth, i.e. to provide for their retirement those in work may forgo a greater amount of present consumption to invest in schemes to provide for their future needs. If these funds are invested in productive

41

investment projects, this will tend to increase economic growth to a level above that which would have occurred under a state scheme involving a transfer payment from those currently in work to those currently retired. Even with this 'extra' economic growth, however, those on low incomes would be unlikely to feel that they can afford a private scheme that would offer the same retirement income as a state scheme which has income redistribution built into it. There is also the additional problem that during the transitional period the beneficiaries of the past state schemes would have to be supported by the transfer payments of taxpayers who are also having to forgo consumption to make investment for their own retirement.

(c) The welfare state was introduced to protect the economically weak from the miseries of poverty. One can argue about how well it performs this function, but it is clear that leaving welfare provision to the free market conflicts with the idea of providing for those with limited or no income; private schemes will pay most to those who can make the largest contributions and least to those who can only afford small contributions. The author also points out that a large private sector in these services might cause a deterioration in the state-run services as the most able and qualified labour is bid away from the state sector. The validity of this prediction, however, depends upon the overall effect on the supply of such labour.

(d) The author is arguing that the standard of the public services that is expected currently, and that will be expected in the future, will be increasingly difficult to finance. It is suggested that this could bring about the demise of the welfare state itself.

The decline in public services could be forced through political pressure as taxpayers, faced with higher tax rates, express their dissatisfaction through the ballot box. To ensure election, governments might then reduce the level of provision to pensioners, the unemployed etc. This assumes that employed workers act out of immediate self interest. In contrast it might be argued that many workers not on high incomes might perceive a reduction in state provision, e.g. in medical care, unemployment provision, education and pensions, to be against their long term interests, or that many taxpayers may take a more altruistic attitude to the reduction of state provision to the less well off.

Alternatively, this decline could be forced if it becomes impossible to raise the necessary finance because of the economic effects of increases in tax rates. The author might be assuming that substantial increases in tax rates have disincentive effects on the working population. This might so lower the tax base as to make it impossible to raise the necessary tax revenue. But it is by no means certain that higher tax rates do have net disincentive effects. It might even be the case that any disincentive effect is itself variable according to the perceived need for taxation.

It should also be noted that variables such as economic growth, unemployment and the dependency ratio are notoriously difficult to predict long term.

Question 5

(a)

Output method	Income method	Expenditure method
Add values of all domestically produced goods and services at factor cost (including investment goods) Add residual error Equals GDP at factor cost	Add all incomes from employment and self employment Add corporate profits (both public and private sectors) Add rent and interest Deduct stock appreciation Add residual error Equals GDP at factor cost	Add all expenditures on goods and services made by consumers and by public authorities Add gross domestic fixed capital formation Add value of physical increase in stocks and work in progress Add exports Deduct imports Equals GDP at market prices Deduct taxes on expenditure Add subsidies Equals GDP at factor cost

Add net property income from abroad
Equals GNP
Deduct capital consumption
Equals NNP (National Income)

(b)
(i) We first need to deflate the figures given for nominal GDP to take out the effect of inflation. This will produce figures for real GDP. To express the GDP in constant price terms we divide by the GDP deflator and multiply by 100. Thus we obtain:

1964 $\dfrac{£29.9}{20.3} \times \dfrac{100}{1} = £147.3$

From the figures for the GDP deflator we can see that the base year used is 1980. Thus GDP at 1980 prices in 1964 was £147.3 bn. We can repeat this procedure to obtain GDP at 1980 prices for all the other years. From these figures for GDP at 1980 prices we can then construct index numbers of output. This is done by dividing the current year GDP at 1980 prices by 1980 GDP and then multiplying by 100. For example:

1964 $\dfrac{£147.3}{£199.3} \times \dfrac{100}{1} = 73.9$

The results of all these calculations are tabulated below:

	GDP at 1980 prices (£ billion)	GDP at constant prices (1980 = 100)/ Index of output
1964	147.3	73.9
1969	161.1	80.8
1974	191.9	96.3
1979	205.9	103.3
1980	199.3	100
1981	194.1	97.4
1982	196.9	98.8
1983	204.3	102.5
1984	210.4	105.6
1985	218.8	109.8

(ii) The figures for GDP at current prices are misleading in that they include the effects of nominal price changes, i.e. inflation. Movements in GDP at constant prices are caused by changes in output and are thus preferable as a guide to changes in living standards. It is easier to see what has been happening to output if one looks at the index of output. But it is important to realise that even these figures do not directly translate into a measure of living standards. There are many adjustments which one might want to make to obtain a more meaningful index of living standards, for example, adjustments for population changes, composition of output, distribution of income, etc.

(iii) The most relevant deflator for any consumer is a composite index of prices for those things which that particular consumer purchases weighted according to the percentage of that consumer's expenditure on each item. The 'Retail Price Index' (RPI) attempts to construct an index of inflation for the 'typical' consumer by using weights obtained by aggregating across all consumer expenditure. There is bound to be some discrepancy between the weights used in the RPI and those of any actual consumer. The GDP deflator is also a composite index but, in addition to consumer expenditure, it also includes expenditure on investment and by the government. Hence, the discrepancy between the weights used for the GDP deflator and the weights relevant for a typical consumer is likely to be large.

(iv) It can be seen from the output index that 1981 was the bottom of a trough for UK output. Therefore, to take the five years from 1981 to 1986 is likely to involve measuring growth from a trough to a peak. Thus the figure obtained would not be representative of UK growth either for the future or of a slightly longer past. Indeed, if we take 1979 as our starting point, we see that output has risen by 6.3 per cent for the whole of a six-year period; this seems far less impressive than the 12.7 per cent in four years we get by taking 1981 as our starting point!

Answers to	**1**	E		**11**	A
multiple-choice	**2**	B		**12**	B
questions	**3**	E		**13**	C
	4	B		**14**	D
	5	E		**15**	D
	6	A		**16**	D
	7	D		**17**	B
	8	B		**18**	E
	9	B		**19**	A
	10	D		**20**	B

6
Markets and prices

Questions

Attempt all questions. Compare your answers with those provided.

1 (Answer provided.) Describe and explain the equilibrium condition of a consumer when faced with a given income and relative prices. Starting from this equilibrium, how would the consumer respond to:
   (a) a rise in the price of one good?
   (b) a rise in the level of prices while the consumer's money income remained constant?

2 'Government intervention in the form of price ceilings and floors is well intended but invariably leads to undesirable side effects.' Explain and discuss.

3 (Answer provided.) Contrast the incidence of a commodity tax imposed in the market for peaches with that of a similar tax in the market for potatoes.

4 'The economic case for regional industrial policy is not self evident.' Discuss.

5 (Answer provided.) 'The advantages of large-scale production will lead to the elimination of all small firms.' Discuss.

6 What are the reasons for the various types of merger between firms?

7 Explain the circumstances under which a firm would continue to produce at a loss.

8 Compare and contrast the market models of perfect competition, oligopoly and monopoly.

9 (Answer provided.) Discuss the view, with reference to official policy, that company mergers are against the public interest.

10 'The government guidelines for nationalised industries that have been laid down since 1948 have been vague, contradictory and often overridden.' Evaluate this statement.

Data response paper

Question 1 (Answer provided.)
Read the following extract from *The Times* newspaper:

EEC SPENDS £16m DISPOSING OF SURPLUS FRUIT AND VEGETABLES TO HOLD PRICES
Under the EEC arrangements designed to prevent market prices falling below an agreed level, Community intervention agencies bought up the surplus product. Some of it was distributed free of charge to charities or used in animal feed. But a considerable amount was simply destroyed.

Expenditure on the fruit and vegetable sector is, in fact, only a tiny part of total spending on the common agricultural policy, which accounts for more than two-thirds of the entire EEC budget.

These surpluses either have to be expensively stored, which is not possible with highly perishable goods like fruit, or exported outside the Community with the aid of subsidies, much to the annoyance of the EEC's trade competitors.

The cost of the common agricultural policy became increasingly controversial because of the British complaints that farm spending, from which Britain derives little benefit, distorts the overall impact of the budget.

Now answer the following questions:

(a) Using supply and demand analysis, offer an explanation for the surpluses mentioned in the above newspaper extract.

(b) Suggest an alternative scheme which would, at least in principle, be a better guarantee of farmers' income and which could possibly be self-financing.

(c) Describe the difficulties such agricultural support schemes face.

(d) Why are the surpluses disposed of in the ways outlined in the extract rather than being resold at cheap prices within the EEC?

(e) Why does the export of surplus foodstuffs annoy the EEC's trade competitors?

(f) Why does Britain derive little direct benefit from the CAP?

Question 2 (Answer provided.)
Study the following data and quotation and then answer the questions that follow:

	Stock of dwellings by tenure UK (millions)		
	1951–60	1977	1981
Owner occupied	6.97 (42%)	11.16 (53.5%)	12.21 (56.25%)
Rented from local authorities or public corporations	4.4 (26.5%)	6.7 (32%)	6.76 (31.25%)
Rented from private owners	5.24 (31.5%)	3.01 (14.5%)	2.72 (12.5%)

(*Source*: Social Trends)

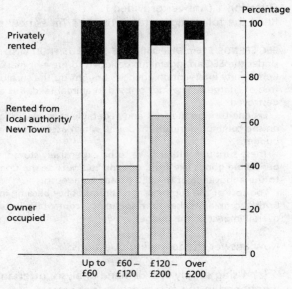

Source: Social Trends

Fig. 6.1 Tenure by weekly income of household

First-time buyers

Year	Number of Loans	Average Dwelling Price	Average Advance (£)	Average Income (£)	Average Percentage Advance	Advance/ Income Ratio	House Price/ Income Ratio
1969	290 000	4 097	3240	1617	79.1	2.00	2.53
1970	329 000	4 330	3464	1766	80.0	1.96	2.45
1971	394 000	4 838	3914	1996	80.9	1.96	2.42
1972	394 000	6 085	4954	2281	81.4	2.17	2.67
1973	283 000	7 908	6115	2734	77.3	2.24	2.89
1974	220 000	9 037	6568	3231	72.7	2.03	2.79
1975	306 000	9 549	7292	3753	76.4	1.94	2.54
1976	352 000	10 181	8073	4285	79.3	1.88	2.37
1977	355 000	10 857	8515	4800	78.4	1.77	2.26
1978	379 000	12 023	9602	5283	79.9	1.82	2.27

(*Source*: The Building Societies Association: 'A Compendium of Building Society Statistics')

Quotation:
The continuing decline in the supply of private rented accommodation (from about 90 per cent of dwellings in 1914 to approximately 12 per cent in 1980) has been a critical factor in the demand for owner occupier housing. The decline can be attributed to several fundamental factors: security of tenure to the unfurnished tenant (and furnished under the 1974 Rent Act); the almost continuous interference by successive governments in landlord-tenant relations; rent control and the low levels of fair rents registered by Rent Officers under the provisions of the 1965 Rent Act; and the tax position of private landlords.

(Balchin and Kieve, (1982) *Urban Land Economics*, 2nd Edition, Macmillan.

(a) Explain, using demand and supply analysis, the arguments in the quotation from Balchin and Kieve.

House prices, inflation and earnings.

Year	Average price of a house (£)	(% increase)	Retail price index (% increase)	Real increase in house prices (% change)	House price earnings ratio
1960	2 480	5.0	1.1	3.9	3.00
1970	5 190	7.0	6.4	0.6	3.40
1971	6 130	18.1	9.4	8.7	3.61
1972	8 420	37.4	7.1	30.3	4.39
1973	11 120	32.1	9.2	22.9	5.11
1974	11 300	1.6	16.1	−14.5	4.41
1975	12 119	7.2	24.2	−17.0	3.74
1976	12 999	7.3	16.5	−9.2	3.47
1977	13 922	7.1	15.8	−8.7	3.38
1978	16 297	17.1	8.2	8.9	3.45
1979	19 885	28.7	13.4	15.7	3.9
1980	21 732	20.6	15.3	5.3	3.6

Source: Department of the Environment, Housing and Construction Statistics; Building Societies Association.

Nominal and real mortgage interest rates %

Year	Average mortgage rate	Net nominal mortgage rate after adjustment for tax concessions	Increase in retail price index %	Net real rate of interest
1970	8.59	5.84	6.4	−0.2
1971	8.59	6.01	9.4	−2.1
1972	8.26	5.78	7.1	−1.1
1973	9.59	6.71	9.2	−3.5
1974	11.05	7.40	16.1	−9.8
1975	11.08	7.20	24.2	−14.2
1976	11.06	7.19	16.5	−6.9
1977	11.05	7.29	15.8	−4.3
1978	9.55	6.40	8.2	−1.8
1979	11.95	8.37	13.4	−7.4
1980	15.00	10.50	15.3	−5.0

Source: A Compendium of Building Society Statistics

(b) The above authors present many additional explanations for the changes apparent from Fig. 6.1 and the Tables. Use the data provided to suggest such possible explanations, indicating, where appropriate, what additional data might be useful.

Question 3 (Answer provided.)

A firm has overheads of £100 per week which are unavoidable in the immediate future. The price of its product has fallen in recent weeks and the directors are convinced that this reflects a permanent change. Before this price decrease the firm was operating at a level of output at which all economies of scale had just been exhausted. This was also the output at which diseconomies of scale would begin.

The firm's product would now fetch £11 per unit on the market, no matter how much the firm sells. £11 is also the addition to cost from producing the fiftieth unit of output per week. To produce this amount the firm must employ 20 people at a wage of £20 per week; in addition it would require £100 of raw materials per week.

49

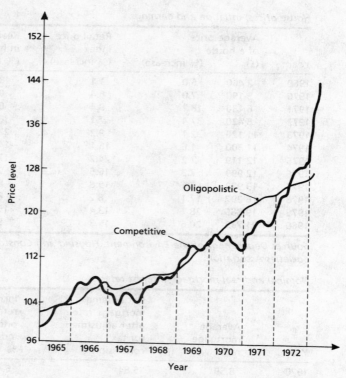

Source: Eichner, 'Determination of the Mark-up under Oligopoly',
The Economic Journal, Dec 1973

Fig. 6.2 Wholesale prices in oligopolistic and competitive industries

Prepare a report for the directors advising them as to whether it would be profitable to close the factory or not. Also, for your future reference, illustrate the firm's situation using the cost concepts employed by economists. (Do as complete a diagram as possible.)

Question 4
Study the graph in Fig. 6.2 above.

(a) Summarise the information that is presented in the graph.

(b) Account for the differences in the time paths shown in the graph.

Question 5
Read the following extracts from an article taken from *The Independent* newspaper:

Industry's burning grievance with privatised British Gas
Richard Hickmet on a threat to the popularity of capitalism

Tomorrow's British Gas AGM, the first since the company was sold to the public last December, offers a timely reminder of the pitfalls which threaten the privatisation of a public utility.
British Gas's bloody-minded attitude, particularly towards industrial customers, was notorious when the company was a public body. A long-running price battle between British Gas and its industrial customers continues, underlining the fact that an over-powerful private monopoly is

not only unacceptable in principle, but is also a grievous threat to the country's economic performance.

Industrial customers account for about 30 per cent of British Gas's income and a healthy £200m of its profits. In return, companies are rewarded with an *ad hoc* pricing policy which can vary by as much as 300 per cent between customers and which can be a staggering 50 per cent higher than those paid by competitors in Belgium, France, Italy, the Netherlands and Germany.

Where gas is a major cost, this sort of pricing nonsense makes fair competition impossible. Major British companies have lost significant orders to European competitors across the whole range of manufacturing industry, where gas costs have been an important element. The consequent effect on jobs is obvious.

Nobody knows how much ICI, BSC or Sheffield Forgemasters pay, yet too often industrial users are frightened to exchange information openly or to join forces publicly, because of British Gas's power and willingness to punish dissenters by increasing prices. There is now no Government control of British Gas, and the regulatory body OFGAS has no powers in this industrial field.

British Gas claims to 'negotiate' with each of its industrial users on the basis of market circumstances. In reality, gas prices can vary from month to month, so no company tendering for a long-term manufacturing contract can confidently estimate its gas costs. Meanwhile British Gas makes no admission of, and thus no explanation for, the fact that there are huge differences in the prices charged to individual customers.

Of course the weaknesses and dangers of a private monopoly are not only exemplified by British Gas. The high-handedness and poor performance of British Telecom have been well publicised, while the toothlessness of the so-called regulatory body OFTEL remains a source of frustration. Meanwhile the failure of the Mercury network to provide major competition is a disappointment.

Popular capitalism in the form of wider share ownership was dramatically extended by the privatisation of British Gas and British Telecom. But the absence of real competition and effective regulatory authorities may lose capitalism some of its popularity.

These unsatisfactory examples provide vital lessons for the Government as it turns its attention to the electricity industry, where the same mistakes must not be made again. Crucially, the CEGB must be split into smaller units rather than sold in its entirety.

Second, the involvement of the Department of Trade and Industry at the planning stage would help ensure that industrial interests were given full consideration when the new system was introduced. Any regulatory authority must also be given proper powers and an adequate budget, to make it more effective than either OFTEL or OFGAS.

What is more, the Government must address the existing problems of Gas and Telecom. They should be split and OFTEL and OFGAS should, in the meantime, be granted greater powers.

There will be a temptation to avoid these issues, as any reorganisation will give the opponents of privatisation a chance to claim they have been proved right. This of course will be nonsense.

Now answer the following questions:

(a) What is meant by the term 'privatisation'?

(b) Explain how higher gas prices in the UK than in major European competitors could lead to job losses in UK manufacturing industry.

(c) Explain how the assumption of profit maximisation could be used to explain, as it is claimed, 'the fact that that there are huge differences in the prices charged to individual customers.'

(d) Evaluate the author's arguments that, despite his claims that monopoly power is being abused, the example of British Gas does not prove privatisation to be a misguided policy.

Multiple-choice test

Answer all questions. Time allowed: 30 minutes.

1 Which of the following is the most accurate statement about the total utility derived from the consumption of a normal good? The total utility:

    A increases with each additional unit consumed.
    B decreases with each additional unit consumed.
    C is less from each additional unit consumed than from the previous one.
    D increases at a constant rate.
    E increases at first but then begins to diminish.

2 Which of the following statements is most likely to be correct?

    A the demand for tobacco is usually inelastic
    B the demand for strawberries is highly inelastic
    C the supply of rubber is elastic
    D the demand for potatoes is elastic
    E the demand for salt is extremely elastic.

3 If in Fig. 6.3 OX is the original price of potatoes, what would be the new equilibrium if consumers' incomes rose and there was an outbreak of potato blight? Would it be:

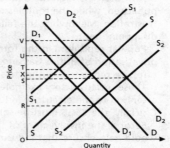

    A OR
    B OS
    C OT
    D OU
    E OV

Fig. 6.3

4 Study the following carefully:

	Price change	Substitution effect		Income effect	Quantity demanded	Slope of demand curve
Good 1: Normal	↓	↑		↑	↑	Downwards
Good 2: Inferior	↓	↑	>	↓	↑	Downwards
Good 3:						

If Good 3 is a Giffen Good the third line in the above should read:

	Price change	Substitution effect		Income effect	Quantity demanded	Slope of demand curve
A	Inferior	↓	↓		↓	↓	Upwards
B	Normal	↓	↑	<	↓	↓	Upwards
C	Inferior	↓	↑	>	↓	↑	Downwards
D	Inferior	↓	↑	<	↓	↓	Upwards
E	Inferior	↓	↑	<	↓	↓	Horizontal

5 Figure 6.4 illustrates the demand and supply curves for JB Rare Brandy in which $S^T S^T$ shows the effect of excise duty. Under these circumstances the revenue which the government receives from the tax is represented by the area:

A ABFG
B ACEG
C BCEF
D BCEJ
E OCEH

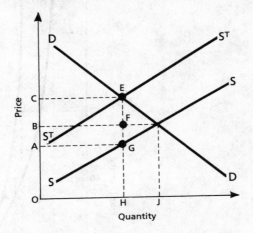

Fig. 6.4

6 In Fig. 6.5 on page 54 the lines DD and SS represent the demand and supply curves for an agricultural product. The government intervenes in this market through a *buffer stock facility* with the intention of stabilising farmers' income. The line $E_d = 1$ represents the theoretical demand curve necessary to stabilise farmers' income at £2.4 million. Suppose that, this year, actual output is 80 000 tonnes. What quantity of the product is required that the government release from/add to buffer stocks in order to maintain farmers' income at £2.4 million?

A 13 000 tonnes
B 20 000 tonnes
C 30 000 tonnes
D 35 000 tonnes
E 40 000 tonnes

7 Suppose that the price of bread were to fall by 10 per cent and that, as a result of this, total expenditure on bread were to fall by 10 per cent. Which of the following best describes the elasticity of demand for bread? The demand for bread is:

A perfectly elastic.
B elastic.
C unitary.
D inelastic.
E perfectly inelastic.

8 The marginal cost curve (MC) of a firm above the average variable cost curve (AVC) for a firm under perfect competition:

A is the supply curve for that firm in the short-run.
B is the same as the curve showing additions to total costs.
C can be used to demonstrate either profit maximisation or loss minimisation.
D is unaffected by fixed costs.
E all of these.

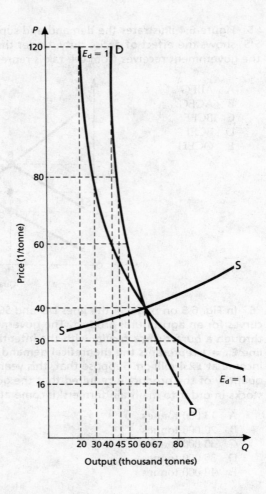

Fig. 6.5

9 Which of following is the most accurate definition of marginal cost. Marginal cost is the:

    A   cost of producing one more unit of a commodity.
    B   change to total cost divided by the change in output.
    C   first derivative of cost with respect to output.
    D   total cost divided by output.
    E   change to average variable cost.

10 Fig. 6.6 on page 55 represents the market for Sperrier Mineral Water. The owner of the Sperrier spring has sold the rights to bottle the water to an international soft drinks company. In return for this he is paid a fixed percentage of the bottler's total sales revenue. At what price per litre (A to E) will Monsieur Sperrier maximise his income from the operation?

11 In the short-run, to stay in business, the total revenue of a business must cover:

    A   total costs.
    B   fixed costs.

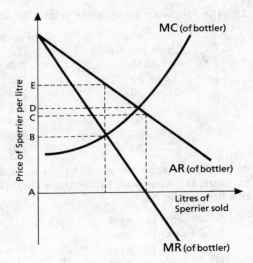

Fig. 6.6

    C variable costs.
    D normal profit.
    E capital costs.

12 Question 12 is based on Fig. 6.7. This shows the cost and revenue curves of a firm. With reference to the diagram, which one of the following statements is **incorrect?**

    A The long-run equilibrium price is OP.
    B At any price above OP the firm would make windfall profits.
    C AR = MR
    D At any output less than OQ, AR is greater than MR.
    E At the output of OQ, MR = MC.

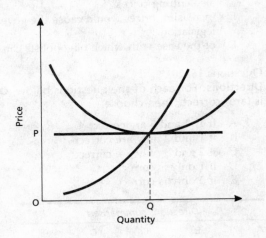

Fig. 6.7

13 The following information relates to an individual firm:

Sales (Units per week)	Total revenue (£s)
10	100
20	180
30	240
40	280
50	300
60	300
70	280

Assume that fixed costs are £100 per week and that average variable cost is constant at £3 per unit. Under these conditions the profit maximisation output for this firm would be:

A   20 units per week
B   30 units per week
C   40 units per week
D   50 units per week
E   60 units per week

14 In many of the large industries in the UK the existence of oligopoly can be best explained by:

A   collusion amongst producers.
B   the small size of the UK market.
C   the impact of technology on the structure of markets.
D   price discrimination.
E   low fixed costs.

15 The 'kink' in an oligopolist's demand curve occurs because:

A   of the peculiar nature of demand in oligopoly markets.
B   there is one price above which consumers would switch to substitutes.
C   any reduction in price would be felt by competitors who would respond by also cutting prices.
D   increasing prices would cause the government to invoke anti-monopoly legislation.
E   of the ease with which oligopolists can fix prices.

Questions 16–20
Directions: For each of the questions below, **One** or **more** of the responses given is (are) correct. Then choose:

A   if 1, 2 and 3 are correct
B   if 1 and 2 only are correct
C   if 2 and 3 only are correct
D   if 1 only is correct
E   if 3 only is correct

Directions summarised				
A	B	C	D	E
1, 2, 3 correct	1, 2 only	2, 3 only	1 only	3 only

16 A firm operating a policy of price discrimination:

    1 attempts to drive its rivals out of business.
    2 relies heavily upon advertising.
    3 achieves an average revenue above its demand curve.

17 If the demand for a product is inelastic then:

    1 if the price is lowered total revenue will increase.
    2 the value of the coefficient of elasticity of demand will be greater than unity.
    3 marginal revenue will be negative.

18 The imposition of a 'price floor' by the government is likely to lead to:

    1 a system of rationing being imposed.
    2 illegal attempts being made to increase prices.
    3 unsold stocks of goods.

19 In the long-run the firm operating under conditions of monopolistic competition will:

    1 produce the output at which AC = AR.
    2 produce an output below that at which unit cost is minimised.
    3 not be able to make more than normal profit.

20 A publicly owned industry may find it difficult to adopt a policy of marginal cost pricing because:

    1 the government may insist on it making profits.
    2 many people will not be able to afford the product.
    3 it is very difficult to calculate marginal cost.

Answers

Suggested answers to essays

1 Describe and explain the equilibrium condition of a consumer when faced with a given income and relative prices. Starting from this equilibrium, how would the consumer respond to:
    (a) a rise in the price of one good?
    (b) a rise in the level of prices while the consumer's money income remained constant?

We shall assume that the purpose of consumption is to maximise individual utility. Thus the consumer is in equilibrium when she is purchasing the bundle of goods and services that yields maximum satisfaction subject to the constraints of a given set of prices and a limited income. In deciding between goods the consumer should consider the rate at which one good must be forgone in order to obtain another. This ratio, and hence opportunity cost, is set by the relative prices of goods, for example, if an egg costs 10p and a loaf 40p, then the relative price of a loaf can be said to be four eggs.

For maximisation the relevant measure of a good's utility is its marginal utility, i.e. the amount added to the consumer's total utility by the consumption of an extra unit of that good. In terms of *indifference analysis*, marginal utility is used only as a mathematical description of consumer's

57

ordinal preference and does not require cardinal measurement. The *Law of Diminishing Marginal Utility* (LDMU) implies cardinal utility in that it states that the the marginal utility of a good declines as consumption of it increases.

The condition for utility maxisation is:

$$\frac{MU_A}{P_A} = \frac{MU_B}{P_B} = \frac{MU_C}{P_C} = \text{etc.}$$

i.e. the ratio of marginal utility to price must be the same for all goods.

Cardinal utility allows an intuitive explanation of this equilibrium condition: the utility derived from the last penny spent on any good must be equal to the utility from last penny spent on any other. If this were not so, utility could be increased by reallocating one's income towards those goods which, on the margin, are yielding a higher utility per penny. In terms of indifference analysis, equilibrium occurs when the rate at which goods can be substituted for one another in the market place is equal to the rate at which the consumer is just prepared to sacrifice one good for another. This latter, subjective, rate is known as the *Marginal Rate of Substitution*. At such a point there is a tangency between the budget line and an indifference curve. If this were not so, the consumer would be able to increase his satisfaction by moving along his budget line so as to reach 'higher' indifference curves. A rise in the price of one good changes its price relative to other goods. In terms of indifference analysis the slope of the budget line will have altered; at the original consumption bundle the slope of the budget line will no longer be equal to the slope of the original indifference curve; there will thus be a substitution effect away from the good which has risen in price as the consumer moves towards a new tangency between the new budget constraint and a lower indifference curve.

Cardinal utility allows an intuitive explanation of the substitution effect: a rise in the price of good A will now mean that less utility is derived from the last penny spent on A than on any other good. The consumer will thus decrease his consumption of good A; but, according to the LDMU, this will cause MU_A to rise; the consumer will cease substituting away from good A when the utility from the last penny spent on A has risen until it is again equal to that derived from the last penny spent on any other good.

By allowing for income effects indifference analysis can explain the 'Giffen Good' situation whereby a fall in price causes a decrease in the consumption of that good.

The real income of a consumer can be represented by the ratio of money income to the price level. If all prices were to, say, double, the relative price of all goods would be unaltered but the real income of the consumer would be halved. Because relative prices would be unaltered there would be no substitution effect. The fall in real income, however, will cause less of a normal good to be consumed but more of an inferior good.

A *ceteris paribus* fall in a good's price will alter relative prices *and* change real income. Real income is increased in that the set of attainable consumption bundles is enlarged. The substitution effect is always negative but if the good is inferior, the income effect will be positive. In principle such an income effect could outweigh the substitution effect, causing a 'Giffen Good' effect.

Indifference analysis is now usually preferred to that of the LDMU in that the assumption of ordinal preference seems less stringent than cardinal utility. In fact, even with cardinal utility, the LDMU is neither necessary nor sufficient for a diminishing marginal rate of substitution. Revealed preference makes even less assumptions than indifference analysis. Radical economists ridicule all such analysis as 'trivial', stressing that it is more important to understand how preferences and tastes are inculcated in the first place.

3 Contrast the incidence of a commodity tax imposed in the market for peaches with that of a similar tax in the market for potatoes.

Commodity taxes, which are an example of an indirect tax, may be *specific*, i.e. so much per unit irregardless of price, or *ad valorem*, i.e. a percentage of price, as with VAT. Incidence refers to on whom the tax burden finally rests. For example, if the demand for the product is perfectly inelastic the price of the product to the consumer will increase by the amount of the tax per unit; thus, although formally the tax is paid by producers, the entire burden of the tax has in fact been shifted to consumers. In general the incidence of a commodity tax will be shared between consumers and producers according to the following relationship:

$$\frac{\text{increase in price to the consumer}}{\text{decrease in price to producer}} = \frac{\text{elasticity of supply}}{\text{elasticity of demand}}$$

Elasticity is a measure of the responsiveness of one variable to changes in another. Thus the price elasticity of demand is defined as the percentage change in quantity demanded divided by the percentage change in price which brought it about.

The relative incidence between producers and consumers will thus depend upon the relative elasticities of the supply and demand for peaches and potatoes. Fig. 6.8 on page 60 demonstrates that, *ceteris paribus*, the greater the elasticity of demand, the greater the proportion of the tax paid by the producers and therefore the smaller the proportion of the tax paid by consumers.

We should expect the demand for peaches to be more price elastic than the demand for potatoes. This is because peaches have more substitutes; they do not form part of a staple diet and can easily be replaced by other fruits. In contrast, potatoes are used to provide bulk in diet and are often purchased out of habit. Although substitutes such as pasta and rice do exist, UK consumers as a whole are more used to potatoes and use them as complements in many 'traditional' dishes. Thus they will not switch as readily from potatoes to pasta as from peaches to pears. From our mathematical relationship and Fig. 6.8, the expected higher price elasticity of demand for peaches suggests that a larger percentage of the tax will be borne by consumers in the case of potatoes. The intuitive explanation of this is that the less sensitive the demand to price the greater the percentage of the

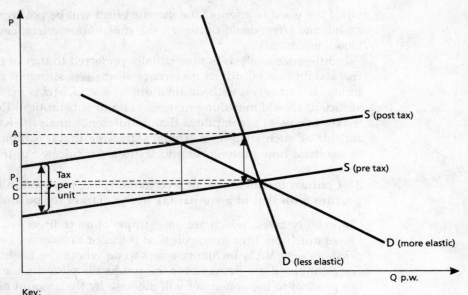

Key:
A-P_1: Increase in price to consumer less elastic demand
B-P_1: Increase in price to consumer more elastic demand
P_1-C: Decrease in price to supplier less elastic demand
P_1-D: Decrease in price to consumer more elastic demand

Fig. 6.8

burden of the tax that producers can pass onto consumers by way of a price increase.

The tax revenue from a commodity tax will, *ceteris paribus*, tend to be higher the lower the price elasticity of demand and the higher the original quantity bought and sold. This suggests that the tax revenue from a specific per unit tax will be greater in the case of potatoes than in the case of peaches. The comparative revenue from an *ad valorem* tax, however, is less certain, as a given percentage tax will mean a higher per unit tax in the case of peaches due to their higher price.

It is probably the case that it is more difficult to increase peach production than potato production. This is because peach orchards take more time to establish than it takes from seeding to harvesting potatoes. Fresh peaches are also more perishable than potatoes. Equally a peach orchard is unlikely to be ploughed over if in one year peach prices fall. All this suggests that the elasticity of suppply will be lower in the case of peaches. If so, then from our previous mathematical relationship, this again suggests that a larger percentage of the tax will be borne by producers in the case of peaches when compared with that of grapes.

Interestingly, the advent of a multi-cultural society has broadened consumers' culinary knowledge. The greater awareness of substitutes is likely to have increased the price elasticity of demand for potatoes. Indeed, demand for potatoes did not return to its previous level following the price increase in the 1976 'drought'. Conversely, disposable incomes have been rising and this tends to reduce the price elasticity of basic food stuffs. Conversely, rising inequality of income distribution in the eighties could increase the percentage of income spent on potatoes among poorer families. In short, the relationship between variables in economics is subject to change.

5 'The advantages of large-scale production will lead to the elimination of all small firms.' Discuss.

The advantages of large-scale production consist of market power and economies of scale. Economies of scale refer to a fall in unit cost caused by an increase in the scale of production. This fall in average cost might be due to *increasing returns to scale*, i.e. an equi-proportional increase in all the factors of production produces a more than proportionate increase in output, or, alternatively, *pecuniary economies*, e.g. market dominance used as bargaining strength to obtain lower input prices.

Market power could also be used for 'predatory' pricing, i.e. large firms using their financial reserves or profits from diversified activity to sustain a period of unprofitable prices designed to drive smaller competitors from the market. For example, many observers feel this has occurred on occasion in the transatlantic airline business.

By exploiting economies of scale, a large firm can profitably set a price below the average cost which can be attained by a smaller firm (*see* Fig. 6.9).

From Fig. 6.9 on page 62 we can see that the small firm will be driven from the market as it will find it impossible to sell at a price which covers its costs. Hence any firm which operates below the *Minimum Economic Scale* (MES) for its industry is at a cost disadvantage to larger firms. MES refers to the output at which a firm's long-run average cost stops falling. One theory of market structure holds that the larger the MES relative to market size the fewer will be the number of firms in an industry and hence the greater the *market concentration ratio*. Scherer has produced evidence which broadly supports this theory.

An increasing importance of economies of scale could thus explain the long-term increase in industrial concentration which has been particularly salient in manufacturing and retailing (particularly grocery retailing). In retailing the economies of scale have also been on the consumer side, reflecting factors such as increase in car and deep freeze ownership; the increased labour market participation of married women, and the growth of 'one-stop' weekly shopping habits. Some observers, Utton, for example, have detected a halt in the increase in industrial concentration, but this is hotly disputed by others, such as Cowling. The issue is contentious as it relates to the efficiency of the free market and Marx's prediction of a 'concentration of capital'.

Although output is concentrated in a comparatively small number of large firms, the great majority of firms *are* small. For example, in 1982 over 90 per cent of manufacturing plants employed less than one hundred workers. In fact, since the late sixties, the number of such small establishments has

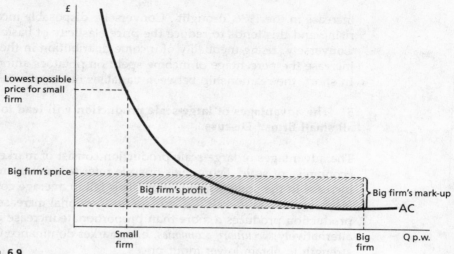

Fig. 6.9

actually increased. The reasons for the continued numerical predominance of small firms can be split into demand side and supply side.

On the demand side there may be no 'room' for economies of scale. For example, small independent retailers might cater for a limited local demand; there might be physical difficulties of transport; the product might be highly specialised or differentiated. Nevertheless, a firm can own many such outlets, hence the managerial economies of centralised control have not been sufficient to compete out such small businesses.

Supply side reasons include the advantages of vertical disintegration and the tax advantages to small firms. Diseconomies of scale might occur at fairly low levels of production, e.g. where attention to detail and/or flexibility is of paramount importance, or a mark-up to large customers mights be the practice among input suppliers. Difficulties in raising finance and managerial attitudes are often cited, but it must be explained why such handicapped firms are not competed away by large firms. In some industries small businesses can survive by accepting lower profit rates than larger firms.

In some industries there are no significant economies of scale, for instance where personal contact is essential, as in the personnel services, or because there is little scope for mass production, as with 'small' building work. Small independents might be able to reap many of the benefits of economies of scale through franchises or common warehousing. Government industrial policy can also play a part. Although structural competition policy is usually directed only at large firms, for example through references to the Monopoly and Mergers Commission, Conservative governments in particular have encouraged small enterprises. Recently such measures have included preferential corporation tax, the income-tax relief of the Business Expansion Scheme and the Loan Guarantee Scheme whereby bank borrowing is underwritten by the government.

Clearly, whatever the trend in industrial concentration, small firms will continue to exist into the foreseeable future.

9 Discuss the view, with reference to official policy, that company mergers are against the public interest.

'Merger' refers to a mutually agreed combining, 'take-over' to a combination which may be against the wishes of the acquired company. When firms in the same market combine, *horizontal combination* is said to have occurred as, for example, with the Nationwide and Anglia building societies. *Vertical integration* occurs when firms that are suppliers or customers of one another combine, for example, Lipton the grocer buying up tea plantations. *Conglomerate combination* creates a diversified firm. BAT, for instance, has diversified into hotels, frozen foods and many other lines.

Conglomerate mergers reduce the risk of relying on a particular activity. Diversity also reduces the variance of a firm's cash flow; this aids planning and investment. Such combination may reflect *administrative economies of scale*; or the replacing of management by a superior one. But it may also allow cross-subsidisation whereby the profits of one activity are used to support *predatory pricing* against rivals in another. Such mergers may reflect managerial desires, not efficiency; hence fears are raised concerning the formation of large economic power blocs which could distort the 'normal' political as well as economic processes. The ability of large firms, however, to overcome the barriers which would debar small firms from many industries has also been cited as a cause of increased competition to previously unassailable monopolies.

Vertical integration can increase efficiency when the links in production are more effectively co-ordinated through administrative procedures than by market transaction. But again it can also lead to increased market power if a firm gains control of a rival's supplier or retail outlets.

Horizontal mergers, by increasing market concentration, pose the most obvious threat to competition because, as concentration increases, firms become increasingly aware of their interdependence and therefore the possibility of collusion to limit competition, either formal or tacit, also increases. But it can be argued that such mergers allow economies of scale or 'rationalise' production in saturated markets. Indeed Labour's Industrial Reorganisation Corporation of the Sixties actively encouraged such mergers on these grounds, for example GEC–AIE and Leyland–BMC.

As the reasons for, and benefits of, mergers clearly vary, the implications for the public interest also differ. The MMC is empowered to investigate mergers which would increase market concentration above the 25 per cent market share monopoly criterion, on increase the ability of firms to engage in anti-competitive tactics, or where the value of assets involved exceeds £30m. As with monopolies, the MMC adopts a cost-benefit, case study approach.

Not only can mergers be for 'good' as well as anti-competitive reasons, even resulting monopolies are not necessarily 'bad'. For example, economies of scale could result in a reduction in price and increased output *vis à vis* more competitive conditions. Failing this, reduced costs nevertheless reflect a saving of resources which might outweigh the loss of consumer surplus from setting price above MC. Mergers might also eliminate wasteful duplication and allow useful product standardisation. Possible disadvantages include: redistribution of national income towards profit: contrived scarcity and allocative inefficiency; price discrimination; cost inefficiency (e.g. Leibenstein's 'X-inefficiency') and complacency towards R&D; excessive oligopolistic non-price competition (e.g. advertising); diseconomies of scale; and lack of consumer choice. The dangers considered most likely depend on one's theoretical perspective. For example, if we assume profit maximisation, then cost inefficiency loses its relevance.

An active takeover market might keep management 'on its toes'; a firm which does not maximise profits will risk takeover from a 'raider' which purchases the shares of its 'victim' and throws out the victim's present management. Increasing profits would then increase the value of the shares which the raider now owns. This is seen as a deterrent against cost inefficiency and the 'wasteful' pursuit of managerial objectives other than profits.

The 'keep on toes' argument has been challenged by evidence (e.g. by Meeks) which suggests that mergers do not typically lead to increased efficiency. This is reflected in a move away from the presumption that mergers are in the public interest towards a more neutral attitude. Developments in economic theory and official attitudes were also reflected in the 1980 Competition Act which stressed that the MMC should consider the competitive environment in general rather than market concentration alone. This may explain the MMC decisions of 1981 when it allowed a merger creating a 100 per cent monopoly of cross-channel hovercraft services, yet decided that European Ferries' bid for Sealink was against the public interest. It was accepted that there were close substitutes for hovercraft travel but less so for the shipping services concerned.

Ferguson (*NW Bank Review* 1985) argues MMC decisions have often taken an ecletic view which pre-empted developments in economics. For example, Demsetz's assertion that monopoly profit reflects efficiency is reflected in the MMC's praise in 1977 for Pedigree Petfoods. The revival of Schumpeter's 'Austrian School' is reflected in the 1976 decision that Rank-Xerox's profits were a largely justified reward for the risk of developing the plain paper copier. Its observation that increased competition would continue to erode Rank-Xerox's profits suggests the 'new' theory of contestable markets which holds that the ease of entry and exit to an industry can be more important than concentration.

Contestability theory has played a large part in the deregulation in the U.S.. But many observers feel that the privatisation of UK state monopolies has been based on assumptions about the relationship between competition and the public interest different from those which have applied in the past.

Suggested data reponse answers

Question 1

(a) Demand and supply refer respectively to the amounts of a product that consumers and producers wish to buy and sell, at any given price, within a certain period of time, all other influences remaining constant. The equilibrium price is the price at which the wishes of buyers and sellers

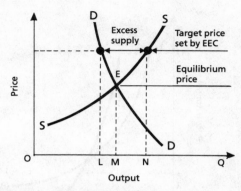

Fig. 6.10 Excess supply created by guaranteed high prices

coincide. In equilibrium, therefore, there will be neither excess demand nor excess supply. In a free and perfectly competitive market, price will adjust until equilibrium is reached.

In contrast to harmonised demand and supply plans, we note from the extract that surpluses (i.e. excess supply) in EC agriculture are chronic. It is clear that the CAP itself is responsible for the surpluses mentioned. This is made explicit by the sentence 'Under the EC arrangements designed to prevent market prices falling below an agreed level, Community intervention agencies bought up the surplus product.' The effect of such a scheme can be illustrated as above:

From the diagram we can see that, on average, Community intervention agencies will have to purchase ON–OL of product to prevent excess supply pushing price below the agreed level.

(b) With a guaranteed price scheme farmers' incomes vary directly with output, making them high in bumper crop years and low in times of poor harvest. The alternative could be a guaranteed revenue scheme, i.e. a scheme aimed at the stabilisation of incomes rather than price. The working of such a scheme can be illustrated as shown in Fig. 6.11 on page 66.

Market demand DD is such, that at an output of 6m tonnes, price would be £4 per tonne. Total revenue would then automatically equal the total revenue guaranteed to farmers. But if there was a bumper crop of, say, 8m tonnes, then market price would fall to £1m per tonne, producing a revenue of only £8m. To prevent this, the intervention agencies will purchase 1.5m tonnes at £3 tonne. This leaves 6.5m tonnes to be sold on the market. As 6.5m tonnes will sell on the market at £3 per tonne the farmers will, overall, have sold 8m tonnes at £3 per tonne. This will therefore give them the guaranteed revenue of £24m.

Similarly, a bad harvest of, say 4m tonnes, would cause market price to rise to £12 per tonne. To prevent this the authorities sell 1.5 tonnes to bring market price down to £6 per tonne. The farmers will then have sold their 4m tonnes at £6 per tonne giving them a total revenue of £24m.

Note that the intervention agencies purchased 1.5m tonnes at £3 per tonne **65**

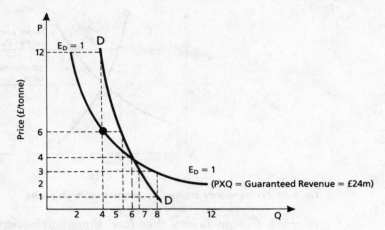

Fig. 6.11 Income stabilisation

and resold it at £6 per tonne. This produced for these agencies an overall trading surplus of £4.5m. This then might be sufficient to finance the storage and administration costs of the scheme.

(c) The stabilisation of the market around equilibrium price entails the storage and reselling of buffer stocks. There is thus the problem of the perishability of agricultural crops. Indeed, if there is a series of bad crops, buffer stocks may become exhausted and the scheme breaks down. If, on the other hand, guaranteed prices or revenue are too generous, surpluses will tend to accumulate each year. This will lead to the embarrassing and costly 'butter mountains' and 'wine lakes' of the EC. This is particularly likely when a strong farmers' lobby can exert great pressure to set the target price and income above the equilibrium. There is also the problem of a trade-off between price and revenue stability, i.e. a scheme which completely stabilises price fails to stabilise revenue whilst, conversely, a scheme which completely stabilises income only partially stabilises price.

(d) To prevent market price falling below the agreed level, Community intervention agencies bought up what would otherwise be excess supply at the guaranteed price. This accounts for the large amounts of fruit that were 'taken off the market'. If some of this fruit were to be resold at cheap prices within the EC it would divert demand from the fruit already being sold at the target price. This decrease in demand for fruit at the target price would cause a further excess in supply. This would thus defeat the object of the scheme, i.e. to stabilise price at the target level.

(e) Subsidised food surpluses 'dumped' in markets outside the EEC divert demand away from the original suppliers of such market of forces them to lower their own prices in line with the subsidised produce. Hence, the stabilisation of EC agricultural markets through this method can have adverse effects on the agricultural communities of EC trade competitors.

(f) The major reason is that farming in the UK is different from that in most of Western Europe both in proportionate size and in produce. In particular, only 1.6 per cent of the UK workforce is employed in agriculture. This is the smallest percentage in the EC.

A second important reason is that the UK can no longer enjoy cheap food from Commonwealth countries. The high guaranteed prices of the EC are protected by a variable import levy which keeps cheaper non-EC food from competing prices down.

It should be remembered, however, that the UK has used these arguments to negotiate 'refunds' which reduce the UK's net contribution to the EC below that which it would otherwise have been.

Question 2

(a) In Fig. 6.12 on page 68 security of tenure has shifted the supply of privately rented accommodation (PRA) from SS to S_1S_1. This occurs as sitting tenants make property a less liquid asset (i.e. it is not so readily sold and hence converted into cash) and inconveniences landlords letting rooms in their own home. This effect of security of tenure is reinforced if rent controls prevent the raising of rents to sitting tenants to levels that could be charged to new tenants, i.e. the long-term return to the landlords investment is reduced.

Rent controls can be seen as imposing a price ceiling in the market for PRA. If the price ceiling is below the equilibrium price (i.e. rent) the resultant excess demand cannot be eliminated through an extention of supply and a contraction of demand. Thus, at the imposed low rent, many landlords withdraw their properties from the market or sell it in the Owner Occupier (OO) market. Note that, with security of tenure, rent controls may cause excess demand even if they are set above what would be the market price in the absence of all intervention. Hence, the final price might be above or below the free market equilibrium. It is unambiguous, however, that the amount of PRA being offered will be reduced by both security of tenure and rent controls.

The analysis of Fig. 6.13 (*see* page 69) suggests that many landlords will, as a result of intervention in the PRA sector, prefer to sell in the OO sector rather than re-let. Similarly, developers will build houses for sale rather than for renting. The result is an increase in supply in the OO market from SS to S_1S_1 in Fig. 6.13. In addition, the unsatisfied demand in the PRA market will, in part, be forced into the OO market. This causes the increase in demand in Fig. 6.13 from DD to D_1D_1. The final effect on price is indeterminate, but the amount of OO dwellings will definitely increase.

It might be argued that the increase in local authority housing of 2.36m could absorb the decrease in PRA of 2.52m without affecting the OO sector. But this would ignore the increase in the total number of households of 5.08m. In any case, the very long waiting lists for local authority housing in many areas testifies to an excess demand for such housing.

(b) So far we have looked at factors which have forced or deflected demand into the OO sector. But the data do suggest factors which have attracted **67**

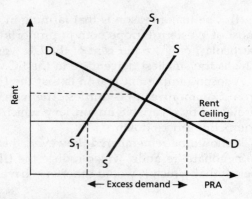

Fig. 6.12 Private rented accommodation

demand into the OO sector. In other words the growth of OO is also likely to reflect a preference for home ownership and the financial advantages enjoyed by owner occupiers.

The preference for home ownership can be analysed in terms of a normal good. Fig. 6.1 is consistent with owner occupation being a normal good and PRA being an inferior good. From the tables on page 49, we can see that, since the Second World War, there has been a substantial increase in the purchasing power of consumers. Hence, Fig. 6.1 and the tables together suggest an increase in the demand for OO dwelling and a decrease in the demand for PRA dwelling. We might also mention here that, if there is a shortage of PRA for the reasons looked at above, OO might be seen as enhancing geographical mobility and hence potential earnings.

From the tables on page 49, we can see some of the financial advantages that have been gained from property ownership. One of the tables shows that tax concessions have, in effect, greatly reduced the interest rate paid on home loans. Indeed, we can see that in the inflationary period of the seventies the real rate of interest was negative. This was because inflation, as measured by the Retail Price Index, exceeded the Net Nominal Mortgage Rate. If a negative real interest rate persists for some time this can result in borrowers paying back less, in real terms, than the amount they borrowed.

Another of the tables shows that the increase in house prices exceeded the increase in the RPI in eight of the twelve years shown. Given what we have learned from data in the other tables, it was clearly advantageous to owner occupiers to be paying in depreciating pounds for an asset which was such a reliable hedge against inflation. Indeed, it is probable that the very large increases in house prices reflect, at least in part, speculation regarding property prices *vis á vis* other asset prices/yields. The fact that the overall House Price Earnings Ratio between 1970 and 1974 rose by 50 per cent compared to a 14 per cent rise in the House Price Income Ratio for first time buyers, and that there was a real increase in house prices from 1970–74, suggests that speculation in more expensive properties did occur.

Other factors influencing the relative demand for housing, and different forms of tenure, would include changes in the size and distribution of the

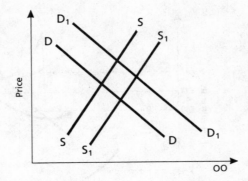

Fig. 6.13 Owner occupied housing

population. An increase in young couples is likely to increase the demand for accommodation and home ownership in particular, in that mortgages must be paid over a considerable length of time. Indeed, the number of loans to first time buyers between 1970 and 1972 rose considerably despite a sharp rise in real house prices. A more complete explanation would thus require demographic data. The participation rate of women in the labour force is another factor absent from the data provided. As there has been an increase in the number of married women entering paid employment, changes in the Price/Earnings Ratio should be considered with care as it may have a varied significance according to the source of family income. Indeed, in looking at prices in general we should resist interpreting changes in them as *causing* changes in demand, rather the change in prices will reflect changes in the variables we have mentioned.

Question 3
In the short run there are two choices:

(a) Close the factory immediately and wait until it is possible to relinquish the fixed factors of production, i.e. overheads. The result would be a short-term loss of £100 per week.

(b) Operate the factory until it is possible to relinquish the fixed factors of production. The largest surplus of revenue over operating (i.e. variable) costs will be where marginal cost equals marginal revenue. This will be an output of fifty units per week. Total revenue at this output is £550. Total variable costs will be labour costs plus raw materials cost, i.e. £500 per week. The total cost will be the sum of variable and fixed costs, i.e. £600 per week. The overall result will therefore be a short-term loss of £50 per week.

Short term decision: Do not close the factory in the short term. A surplus of revenue over variable cost (known as the contribution to fixed costs) can be obtained. This surplus can be used to offset the inevitable loss caused by the unavoidable overheads, i.e. operating the factory in the short term reduces the overall losses by £50 per week.

69

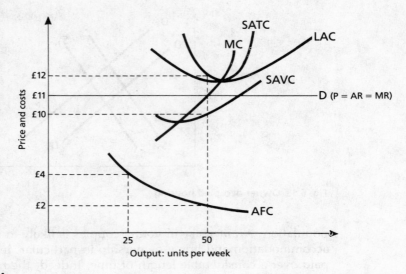

Fig. 6.14

Long term decision: If it is not possible to transfer the use of the factory to an alternative and profitable activity, then the only way to avoid a continuing loss is to close the factory. This is because, even in the long-run, achievable unit cost (i.e. long run average cost) is above price at all outputs.

Answers to multiple-choice questions

1	A		11	C
2	A		12	D
3	C		13	C
4	D		14	C
5	B		15	C
6	A		16	E
7	E		17	E
8	E		18	E
9	C		19	A
10	C		20	E

7

The theory of distribution

Questions

Essay paper

Attempt all questions. Compare your answers with those provided.

1 (Answer provided.) 'As the sexes are unequal women will always be paid less than men.' Discuss.

2 'From each according to his abilities, to each according to his needs.' Evaluate the feasibility of such a policy in the light of marginal distribution theory.

3 (Answer provided.) Why do accountants earn more than 'dustmen' (household refuse collectors) and yet many teachers earn less than some unskilled labourers on North Sea oil rigs?

4 (Answer provided.) Under what circumstances will a rise in wages lead to unemployment?

5 Why might it be considered desirable to increase labour mobility and how might this be done?

6 The rate of profit of a firm is often used as a measure of its performance. Why then do economists often condemn such profits?

7 'The high price of land for building in London has pushed house prices so high that few people can now afford to buy houses in London.' Discuss.

8 Distinguish between transfer earnings and economic rent. Why is it sometimes argued that taxes should be levied on economic rents rather than transfer payments?

9 (Answer provided.) What does an economist mean by 'normal profit'. Explain the reasons why a firm's normal profit is unlikely to be equivalent to the average rate of profit for the economy as a whole.

10 What factors are likely to cause changes in price of a company's shares? To what extent can such changes be relied upon to provide an efficient allocation of investment capital across the economy as a whole?

Data response paper

Question 1 (Answer provided.)
From the following data calculate the numbers left blank:

Labour is the only variable factor and the wage per person is £30 per week. The firm has 10 units of capital and 10 units of land. Each unit of capital has an opportunity cost of £15 per week. Each unit of land has an opportunity cost of £5 per week.

Units of labour	Total product	Marginal physical product	Total fixed cost	Total variable cost	Total cost	Average fixed cost	Average variable cost	Average total cost	Marginal cost
0	0					–	–	–	
1	10								
2	30								
3	70								
4	110								
5	130								
6	140								
7	145								
8	147								
9	148								
10	148								

Question 2 (Answer provided.)

Consider a self-employed gardener who could earn £80 per week in his best alternative job as a park keeper. He has a van which he could sell for £2000. The van costs £400 per year in tax, insurance and petrol. It is only necessary for him to use the van in his capacity as a self-employed gardener. He also uses £150 of materials in a year. His father has lent him a set of gardening tools which he could, if not a self-employed gardener, rent out for £50 per year. He has ordered a magnetic sign for the van which reads 'Rudolph C.Z. Pettigrew: Gardener to the Discerning: Tel 01-246 8026' for which he has paid £20. Rudolph expects to receive £8000 for his services during the year from garden owners.

For simplicity assume that there is no taxation, the van does not deteriorate and hence has no depreciation, no one is willing to rent the van from Rudolph and that the interest rate is zero:

(a) What is Rudolph's expected book keeping profit (i.e. incomings minus outgoings) for the year? (Ignore holidays etc, and hence use a 52 week working year for your calculations.)

(b) What is his expected profit defined as the surplus of revenue over all opportunity costs?

(c) Recalculate these two values for an expected revenue of £4000.

(d) How would a profit-maximising Rudolph react in the two situations which differ in respect of the expected revenues and how does this behaviour relate to the concepts of normal profit and economic rent?

(e) Briefly discuss how relaxing the simplifying assumptions made above would alter your calculations.

Question 3

Read the following passages concerning the impact of micro-electronic information technology on the printing industry:

Technological changes have already led to a significant shake-out among UK printing workers. Between 1967 and 1976 a total of 63 000 jobs were lost in the printing industry, reducing the overall number to 196 000. There was a decline of nearly 5% in 1976 alone. Most of the jobs that were lost were skilled craftsmen's – the direct result of new technology.
Source: CIS
The new-technology revolution in American newspapers has brought increased circulations, a wider range of publications and an expansion of newspaper jobs – in spite of reduced manning in the composing rooms ... Total newspaper employment, according to government statistics, rose from 345 000 in 1965 to 443 000 in 1984 – and that figure does not fully cover the multitude of local papers. But the Typographical Union, which formerly had a firm grip on nearly all printing jobs, has shrunk from over 100 000 in 1967 to 40 000 today.
Source: *The Sunday Times*

(a) Why is it the case that a technological innovation can lead to both job losses and job creation?

(b) To what extent are the two passages conflicting accounts of the impact of the new information technology?

(c) How are entry conditions to the newspaper industry likely to be affected by the new technology?

Question 4
Study the following two tables of data:

Changes in extent of poverty 1960–1983 (Britain)

Income in relation to supplementary benefit standard	Number in thousands			
	1975	1979	1981	1983
Below SB standard	1 840	2 090	2 610	2 700
Receiving SB*	3 710	3 980	4 840	6 130
At or up to 40 per cent above SB standard	6 990	5 500	7 210	7 550
TOTAL	12 540	11 570	14 660	16 380
	Percentage			
Below SB standard	3.5	4.0	4.9	5.0
Receiving SB*	7.0	7.6	9.1	11.4
At or up to 40 per cent above SB standard	13.2	10.4	13.5	14.1
TOTAL	23.7	22.0	27.5	30.5

* Drawn separately from supplementary benefit sample enquiry, with people drawing benefit for less than three months excluded. Thus people unemployed or sick or disabled for less than three months are counted as having the incomes they had last in employment.
(*Source*: Health Education Council)

Distribution of original, disposable, and final household income

	United Kingdom					Percentages
	Quintile groups of households					
	Bottom fifth	Next fifth	Middle fifth	Next fifth	Top fifth	Total
Original Income						
1976	0.8	9.4	18.8	26.6	44.4	100.0
1981	0.6	8.1	18.0	26.9	46.4	100.0
1982	0.4	7.1	18.2	27.2	47.1	100.0
1983	0.3	6.7	17.7	27.2	48.0	100.0
Disposable income						
1976	7.0	12.6	18.2	24.1	38.1	100.0
1981	6.7	12.1	17.7	24.1	39.4	100.0
1982	6.8	11.8	17.6	24.2	39.6	100.0
1983	6.9	11.9	17.6	24.0	39.6	100.0
Final income						
1976	7.4	12.7	18.0	24.0	37.9	100.0
1981	7.1	12.4	17.9	24.0	38.6	100.0
1982	6.9	12.0	17.6	24.1	39.4	100.0
1983	6.9	12.2	17.6	24.0	39.3	100.0

(*Source*: CSO)

(a) Summarise the trends in income distribution that are apparent from the tables above.

(b) Offer possible explanations for these trends stating what additional information would be useful.

Question 5 (Answer provided.)
EMI Cinemas plc is a wholly-owned subsidiary of EMI Film and Theatre Corporation plc. In 1983 EMI submitted the following figures to the Monopolies and Mergers Commission:

EMI Cinemas: market shares based on film hire payments

	Payments by EMI Cinemas (£'000)	Payments by all exhibitors (£'000)
1978	13 031	41 300
1979	12 841	41 000
1980	14 184	42 200
1981	13 268	41 100

EMI Cinemas: Trading results on exhibition

	1978–79	1979–80	1980–81	1981–82
Profit before interest and taxation (£m)	5.93	4.76	3.58	1.51

(a) On what grounds did the MMC justify its preparing a report on the supply of films for exhibition in cinemas?

(b) Assuming that contracts for film hire in the coming year must be signed and paid for in advance, would you have advised EMI to remain in the cinema business had the above figures been available in 1977 (i.e. through accurate forecasting) and the relevant interest rate was expected to be around 10 per cent? State clearly and in full the relevant considerations.

Multiple-choice test

Answer all questions. Time allowed: 30 minutes.

1 If as a result of the increase in size of a manufacturing plant (factory) the unit cost of production increases, then this would be an example of:

   A internal economies of scale.
   B internal diseconomies of scale.
   C returns to scale but not economies of scale.
   D external diseconomies of scale.
   E external economies of scale.

2 In Fig. 7.1 which output is the one at which this firm is the most technically efficient in the short run? Is it:

   A OJ
   B OK
   C OL
   D JR
   E KS

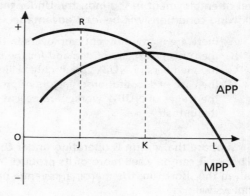

Fig. 7.1

3 If you were to undertake a course of full-time higher education, then the best description of the opportunity cost of that course would be:

   A your college fees plus your living expenses.
   B the increase in future earnings to be expected as a result of the qualifications obtained.
   C the income you could have obtained by working.
   D the cost to government of your course.
   E the benefits forgone by not undertaking other courses of study.

4 A business exists making widgetts. It can sell all the widgetts it makes at a price of £20 each. With its present workforce the business can produce 50 widgetts per week. The business then employs another worker and finds that its output has risen to 55 widgetts per week. What is the marginal physical product of the last worker? Is it:

    A 5 widgetts
    B £1100
    C £100
    D £20
    E an amount which cannot be calculated unless we first know how many workers were employed in the first place.

5 A firm operating in the short run increases its output by the employment of more labour. After a point the average physical product (APP) of labour begins to decrease. The implication of this is that:

    A profitability is declining.
    B the firm's revenue must be decreasing.
    C the marginal physical product (MPP) of the other factors will also be decreasing.
    D total output will start to fall.
    E if wages are constant then labour costs per unit of output must start to increase.

6 The NUBW is a national union which has a closed shop agreement. It wishes to increase the wages of its members but, of course, it does not wish to decrease the level of employment in the industry. Under these circumstances which of the following conditions will be *least* advantageous to the union's bargaining position:

    A there are many different employers in the industry and they are disorganised.
    B the (price) elasticity of demand for the industry's product is high.
    C the members of NUBW are highly skilled.
    D the ease of substitution of factors of production in the industry is low.
    E the wages of NUBW workers represent a low proportion of the total costs of the industry.

7 Suppose that a firm is operating under conditions of imperfect competition such that it can only sell more of its product by lowering its prices. This will mean that, in the short run, the marginal revenue product curve (MRP) for the labour it employs will:

    A be the same as the MPP curve for labour.
    B be the same as the average revenue product for labour.
    C decrease faster than the marginal revenue product curve for a firm under conditions of perfect competition.
    D not be a true indicator of wage levels.
    E be determined by the formula $MRP = MPP \times p$.

8 Study the following diagram carefully. This represents a labour market in which there is only one employer, i.e. it is monopsonic. Labour, on the other hand is not unionised. Under these circumstances we can say that the total wage bill of the employer will be less than it would be in a competitive market. This shortfall in the wages bill compared with the competitive situation can be represented by the area:

A ACDF
B BCDG
C OAFL
D BCDG + LGEM
E LGEM + ABGF

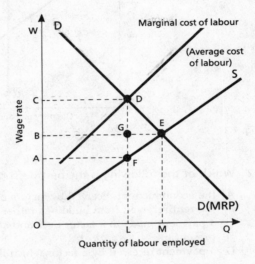

Fig. 7.2

9 Which of the following is an example of occupational mobility of labour?

A A Japanese car company establishes a factory in the North-East of England.
B A female teacher returns to work after her own children have gone to school.
C Miners from the Kent coalfield transfer to Nottinghamshire.
D Shipbuilding workers retrain as plumbers.
E A secretary takes an evening job in a pub.

10 Economic rent could best be described as the payment made to any factor of production over and above its:

A variable costs of production in the short run.
B variable costs of production in the long run.
C transfer costs.
D transfer payments.
E transfer earnings.

11 Fig. 7.3 shows the demand and supply for a factor of production. The result of the shift of the demand curve from DD to D_1D_1 will be:

A the creation of quasi-rent
B an increase in transfer earnings.
C a decrease in transfer earnings.
D an increase in economic rent.
E a decrease in economic rent.

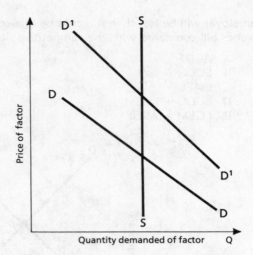

Fig. 7.3

12 Which of the following is the best description of quasi-rent. Quasi-rent is:

A the economic rent received by factors other than land.
B the rent received from buildings rather than from land.
C a payment made to a factor over and above that necessary to keep it in its present use.
D a payment received by a factor which is economic rent in the short run transfer earnings in the long run.
E factor income which is termed rent by accountants but not by economists.

13 Gravilax plc has share capital with a par value of £1 000 000, all of which has been issued and is fully subscribed. This capital consists of 800 000 £1 preference shares which pay a maximum dividend of 5 per cent. There are also 200 000 £1 ordinary shares. The present market price of Gravilax preference shares is £2.50 and the ordinary shares have a market price of £3.33.

   If Gravilax makes £250 000, all of which it distributes, then the dividend per share which each ordinary share will receive is:

A 42 pence.
B £1.05.
C £1.00.
D 5 pence.
E 25 pence.

14 An undated gilt-edged bond gives a fixed income of £1000 per year. If the present rate of interest is 12.5 per cent, what is the likely present value of the bond? Is it:

A £800
B £12 500
C £8000
D £25 000
E not possible to determine from the information given.

15 Which of the following is the best description of 'normal profit'? Normal profit is the:

A profit which is the return to enterprise and not to the other factors of production.

B payment made to enterprise to keep it in its present use.

C ruling level of profit in an industry at any particular time.

D return to a risk successfully taken.

E same thing as implicit factor returns.

Questions 16–20

Directions. Each of the following questions consists of a statement in the left-hand column followed by a second statement in the right-hand column.

Decide whether the **first** statement is true or false.

Decide whether the **second** statement is true of false.

Then answer:

A if both statements are true and the second statement is **a correct explanation** of the first statement.

B if both statements are true but the second statement is **NOT a correct explanation** of the first statement.

C if the first statement is true but the second statement is false.

D if the first statement is false but the second statement is true.

E if both statements are false

	First statement	Second statement	Directions summarised
A	True	True	Second statement is a correct explanation of the first
B	True	True	Second statement is not a correct explanation of the first
C	True	False	
D	False	True	
E	False	False	

First statement

Second statement

16 The business achieves its least cost production function for any particular output where the marginal physical products of each factor divided by their respective prices are equal to each other.

Profits are maximised where there is the greatest possible difference between total revenue and total cost.

17 Minimum wage legislation always results in more unemployment.

It is not possible to achieve perfect factor substitution.

18 One of the greatest risks to modern industries is that of obsolescence.

There is a rapid rate of technological progress.

19 A rise in interest rates will cause the price of government stock to fall.

The rate of interest and the price of financial securities are inversely proportionate to one another.

20 Profits fulfil an allocative function in a free enterprise economy.

Maximum efficiency is achieved when profit are maximised.

Answers

1 'As the sexes are unequal women will always be paid less than men.' Discuss.

Physical differences are unimportant as few jobs require strength beyond the normal reach of women. Indeed, the differential between male and female workers is higher for non-manual workers than for manual workers. Some women do earn more than some men, but on average the hourly earnings of full-time female adult workers are about three-quarters that of male hourly earnings. This does not reflect so much women being paid less for the same job, but rather the fact that women are concentrated in lower paid occupations and in the lower paid positions within occupations.

Neo-classical assumptions of competition and profit maximising predict that discrimination based on prejudice would tend to be eliminated by market forces, i.e. if woman are equally as productive as men but their wages lower, then employers could reduce costs by substituting men with women. Any employer which refused to substitute in this way would be competed out of business by their lower cost competitors. The fact that women's wages *are* lower is thus used as a criticism of neo-classical economics.

If, however, there *is* a lower return to employing women, then a sex–wage differential in favour of males does not contradict neo-classical theory. Such economists can point to the still widespread belief that it is the role of women to care for dependants. Hence, if it is anticipated that a woman is likely to drop out of the labour force in the future, then the expected long-term Marginal Revenue Product for the employer of investment in female training is reduced *vis á vis* male training. Moreover, if the woman herself plans to leave the labour force at some point, her own return to education and training (investment in 'human capital') is reduced. This investment return differential is increased by legislation prohibiting women from working over a certain number of hours per week and earlier female retirement. It should be noted that the opportunity cost to the individual of investment in human capital is not zero even in the absence of tuition fees; the major cost is usually forgone earnings.

The lower return to investment in human capital beyond school leaving age is reflected in the fact that females are less likely to possess a post 'O' level/ GCSE qualification than men, yet are more likely to hold CSE or 'O' level/ GCSE. Lack of such qualifications and training will limit career choice and progression. In addition, women who drop out of the labour force will lose seniority. Women are also disproportionately represented in small and scattered workplaces, for example, retailing. This limits scope for advancement and also makes unionisation more difficult. Women tend to take jobs from a more localised area than men, thus employers can pay wages which have to cover a lower average travelling cost and face less competition from other employers for female labour. If then the elasticities of supply of male and female labour differ it will pay the employer to wage discriminate between the sexes.

Some left-wing economists dispute the notion that employers who discriminate against women despite equal potential productivity perceive themselves to be forgoing profit. They argue instead that widespread sexism, i.e. role stereotyping, is encouraged by capitalists as it segments the labour force and can be used as an excuse for keeping female wages low across a wide range of occupations seen as 'women's work'. Hence wage competition between employers is avoided, and the weaker labour force attachment of women can be exploited to undermine union organisation. Moreover, the unpaid work of the housewife and mother reduces the financial cost of obtaining a labour force for employers as a whole.

Both schools of thought accept that lower pay and the role of females in society are linked in a way that can act to perpetuate the situation, i.e. because women on average earn less than men they are more likely to drop out of the labour force; therefore, their social role is reinforced and thus they earn less on average than men. Thus legislation or campaigns which limit the differences in social role of the power to discriminate should also reduce the wage–sex differential. It is now generally accepted that the Equal Pay Act of 1970 did reduce the wage–sex differential. Other measures which could be used include quotas, subsidisation of female training or even employment and increasing female unionisation. Clearly, a wage–sex differential is not inevitable.

3 Why do accountants earn more than 'dustmen' (household refuse collectors) and yet many teachers earn less than some unskilled labourers on North Sea oil rigs?

Demand and supply analysis is used to explain occupational income differentials. The demand for a factor is a 'derived' demand, i.e. it is demanded in order to make a product. Hence, the so called 'Marginal Productivity Theory' of neo-classical economics holds that the demand for a particular type of labour is determined by its marginal physical product (the amount added to total product by extra unit of that labour) *and* the demand for the products for which its services are an input. Thus in the short run occupational rewards will be greatly influenced by fluctuations in the demand for products and services. The storms of October 1987, for example, caused a sharp rise in the earnings of roof repairers.

In the longer run, occupational and geographical mobility will tend to reduce occupational differentials. Indeed, if all workers were concerned only with pecuniary return, were homogenous and perfectly mobile, then they would be allocated such that all units of labour earned the same wage. Rather like water finding its own level, if wages in one occupation were higher than in another, labour would leave the latter in favour of the former. Thus, downward sloping product demand curves and the law of diminishing returns predicts that the wages in the two occupations converge.

Adam Smith realised that wage differentials would persist in the real world. He argued that labour will move between different uses until there is no 'net advantage' when both monetary and non-monetary rewards are considered. Hence, the unpleasantness of working on a North Sea oil rig accounts for the higher earnings of labourers on such rigs *vis á vis* labourers on land. But a variation of Smith's theory is needed to explain why dustmen earn less than accountants.

There is probably a higher psychic income associated with being an accountant than being a dustman and yet accountants earn more. One explanation is that accountants have to forego income whilst training and therefore their higher earnings reflect the compensation for the opportunity cost of 'lost' earnings which is required to induce persons to undergo training. Chicago school economists, such as Becker, have developed a sophisticated theory of occupational choice based on treating investment in training and education like any other investment decision. Thus, such economists see investment in 'human capital', and hence occupational choice, as being determined by such things as the life profile of expected earnings, the opportunity cost of training and the rate of interest.

In its simplest form, Human Capital theory predicts that market forces will tend to equalise the expected net present value (NPV) of all occupations. The calculation of NPV involves complex discounted income flows, but it should at least be clear that a £1 in one year's time is worth less than a £1 today. The reason is that a £1 placed in a financial institution will accumulate interest. Therefore, if the interest rate is 10 per cent, £110 in a year's time is worth £100 today. Thus the accountant who defers income *vis á vis* a dustman will require more income in compensation than the earnings he could have earned as a dustman while training. Similarly, if the dustman saved part of early earnings he could raise his later income by the interest received.

Part of the difference in incomes, at any one time, might thus be explained as compensation for, and the return to investment in, human capital. If then non-monetary reward and training often go together, we may well find occupations which offer both a higher monetary and non-monetary reward, when considered at a point in time, than more unpleasant occupations. The following matrix demonstrates why, according to neo-classical theory, we can find accountants earning more than dustmen and yet teachers (who we presume enjoy their work) who earn less than North Sea labourers. The theory predicts that the lowest wages/salary will be found in the top right quadrant and that the highest will be found in the bottom left quadrant. The

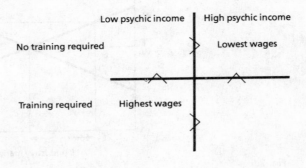

Fig. 7.4

relative earnings of the top left and bottom right quadrant, however, will depend on the precise weighting of non-monetary reward and the return/compensation of training.

In fact studies, and casual observation, reveal that the net present value of such occupations as accountant, company director, doctor, lawyer etc. are not equalised with those of roadsweepers, farm worker, porter etc. Nor is it common to find parents wavering between encouraging their children to be manual or professional workers. Socio-economic factors are the most important causes of inequality of opportunity, but to these we can add restrictions on labour mobility posed by unions and professional associations, chance and lastly inborn ability.

4 Under what circumstances will a rise in wages lead to unemployment?

Wages can be regarded as the price of labour and hence determined by the interaction of supply and demand. The demand for labour is a derived demand. It is demanded not for its own sake but for the goods and services it produces. Under perfectly competitive conditions labour will be employed up until the point at which the wage equals the marginal revenue product (MRP). This is the profit maximising equilibrium in that extra labour would add more to costs than to revenue. Therefore, the MRP curve can be considered to be the demand curve for labour. It is downward sloping because as output expands the market price of the product will fall (thus for individual firms MRP shifts inwards as industry output expands). In the short run, diminishing returns decrease MP and steepen the slope of the MRP curve. Under these conditions an increase in wages will cause a reduction in employment (*see* Fig. 7.5).

If, however, competitive conditions prevail, an increase in wages in one industry will cause a displacement of labour to others. It would require a general rise throughout the many labour markets caused by, say, minimum wage legislation to cause unemployment. It is difficult, however, to account for an exogenous increase in wages under competitive conditions, rather an increase in wages will be endogenous, i.e. caused by an increase in labour

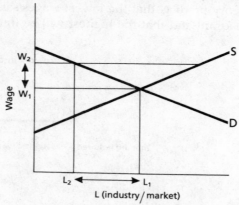

Fig. 7.5

productivity or a reduction in the overall supply of labour. As such, a new equilibrium will result in which supply again equals demand without unemployment. But if generally low wages resulted in many wages being close to or below the social security 'floor', then such an increase in wages might increase the incentive to work, resulting in a reduction in those registered as unemployed.

If a union achieved higher wages in just one firm in a competitive industry, the increase in costs would put that firm at a competitive disadvantage in relation to the other firms. This could lower the firm's profits to the extent that it closes down or reacts by dismissing unionised labour and taking on non-unionised labour. This explains, in part, the existence of 'closed shop' agreements whereby work in an industry is only made available to union members. Indeed, employers themselves often favour closed shops in that it imposes the same obligations on *all* employers in the industry. In general profit maximising theory predicts that the reduction in employment following a union-initiated increase in wages will be smaller the lower the elasticity of product demand, the lower the elasticity of factor substitution and, perhaps, the smaller the proportion of total costs represented by the wage bill.

If the employer is a monopolist in the product market and the union can control labour entry to the industry, then an increase in wages might be financed by a reduction in the employer's profit rather than causing a reduction in the amount of labour employed. The union then can 'capture' some of the firm's monopoly profit by forcing the employer to employ more labour than the profit maximising amount at a higher wage than would otherwise be the case. Indeed, if the supply curve of labour to the firm was previously less than perfectly elastic, then the union, by setting a union wage rate for the job, can reduce the marginal cost of labour to the employer by raising the average rate. As profit maximising conditions are set by equi-marginal conditions we can see in the diagram that this action raises the profit maximising level of employment as well as wages (*see* Fig. 7.6).

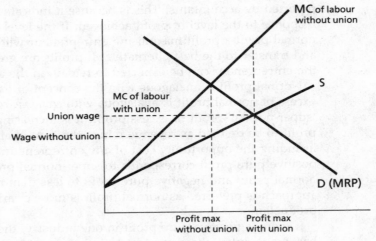

Fig. 7.6

If the increase in wages is general we must also consider macro-implications. But we should distinguish between changes in money wages and changes in real wages. If all money wages and all other prices were to increase by the same percentage, then the real wage would be unaltered. In neo-classical macro-economic theory, despite fierce problems of aggregation, the labour market as a whole is in equilibrium when the real wage is equal to the marginal (physical) product of labour. Hence, with a fixed capital stock, diminishing returns predicts that an increase in the real wage reduces employment; if union pressure is responsible this will cause involuntary unemployment, if an increase in welfare payments is responsible this will increase voluntary unemployment (*see* Fig. 7.6). In other schools of thought 'under-consumptionist' theories hold that an increase in real wages can increase aggregate demand and hence reduce unemployment.

Clearly, the relationship between wages and unemployment depends on why the variables change the initial conditions pertaining.

9 What does an economist mean by 'normal profit'. Explain the reasons why a firm's normal profit is unlikely to be equivalent to the average rate of profit for the economy as a whole.

Profit is income which accrues to the entrepreneur. For the economist this is equal to revenue minus the opportunity cost to the entrepreneur of all the other factors of production. However, the entrepreneur is likely to have opportunities to pursue alternative activities to the one he or she is presently engaged in. Thus the entrepreneur can regard part of profit as compensation for remaining in the present activity. Thus normal profit is equal to the opportunity cost to the entrepreneur in terms of the best return he or she could obtain in some alternative activity. It follows that normal profit is that profit which would just be sufficient to induce the entrepreneur to remain in his or her present activity.

The concept of normal profit is more useful to economists than the profits reported by accountants. This is because it indicates the entrepreneur's likely response to the level of profit achieved. If the level of profit is less than normal profit a profit maximising entrepreneur will discontinue the activity and transfer to the best alternative. If profits are greater than normal profit the entrepreneur can be expected to remain in the activity.

Normal profit is analogous with the concept of *transfer earnings*. Profit in excess of normal profit is analogous with *economic rent* and is called 'super-normal' profit or excess profit. It is increasingly common for pure profit to be defined as revenue minus the sum of all opportunity costs including the opportunity cost of any entrepreneurial input. In this approach positive pure profit corresponds to super-normal profit, zero pure profit to normal profit and negative pure profit to less than normal profit. This approach is preferred as normal profit is more clearly identified as a cost of production.

If there is positive pure profit in one industry, then, in the absence of barriers to entry, there must be negative pure profits in another. Thus profit maximisation predicts that there will be a reallocation of resources away from the latter towards the former. This will continue until normal profits are being made in both industries. It thus appears that once equilibrium has been reached normal, profit would correspond to the average level of profits. However, there are many problems with such an assertion.

It makes little sense to compare absolute profits; a large firm might earn more profits than a small firm and yet the rate of profit on the factors employed could be less. This then poses the problem of an appropriate measure of the *rate* of profit. In principle, this should be the return per hour on the entrepreneur's working time. This is impractical as such records are unavailable and in any case would have to quantify all past entrepreneurial effort which contributed to present profits. Moreover, the entrepreneurial input to a firm is difficult to identify. For example, in modern joint stock companies shareholders, employees and directors may all bear risk and contribute organisational skills to various degrees.

Instead of attempting to measure the return to entrepreneurial input directly, it is more usual to compare rates of return on capital advanced. If we assume that capitalists will invest their capital so as to earn the highest return, it follows that in equilibrium the rate of return on capital should be equalised across all industries. We could thus attempt to measure the rate of return on such investment that would be just sufficient to maintain it in its current use. But capital is by its nature highly immobile and cannot often be transferred to other uses should its rate of return fall. The price of capital goods is also subject to change, hence *quasi-economic rent* might be measured instead of long term profit if assets are valued according to historical rather than replacement cost. Equally barriers to entry such as economies of scale, superior cost efficiency, predatory pricing, limit pricing and non-price competition may militate against investing in some industries. Thus existing returns to capital invested can be far higher than such investments could earn elsewhere.

Clearly, barriers to entry and capital immobility can cause the return to capital to deviate from the 'normal' rate of return that would be sufficient to induce its investment in the first place. Thus average rate of profit is unlikely to be equal to normal profit. Moreover, the theoretically 'correct' measure of the rate of return involves discounting all future receipts and operating costs allowing for risk. Thus not only will observed rates of return differ according to the degree of risk, they might also differ widely from the estimated rates of profits on which the investment decisions were originally made. In practice then, it is very difficult to translate the concept of normal profit into observable variables.

Question 1

Units of labour	Total product	Marginal physical product	Total fixed cost	Total variable cost	Total cost	Average fixed cost	Average variable cost	Average total cost	Marginal cost
0	0		200	0	200	–	–	–	
		10							3
1	10		200	30	230	20	3	23	
		20							1.5
2	30		200	60	260	6.66	2	8.66	
		40							0.75
3	70		200	90	290	2.8	1.3	4.1	
		40							0.75
4	110		200	120	320	1.8	1.09	2.89	
		20							1.5
5	130		200	150	350	1.5	1.15	2.65	
		10							3
6	140		200	180	380	1.4	1.3	2.7	
		5							6
7	145		200	210	410	1.38	1.45	2.83	
		2							15
8	147		200	240	440	1.36	1.63	3	
		1							30
9	148		200	270	470	1.35	1.8	3.2	
		0							∞
10	148		200	300	500	1.35	2.02	3.4	

Question 2

(a)

Expected incomings	**Outgoings**
£8000 p.a.	£400 p.a. (petrol plus insurance)
	£150 p.a. (materials)
	£20 p.a. (sign)
	——————
	£570 p.a.

Answer: Book keeping profit = £8000 − £570 = £7430

(b)

Expected revenue	**Opportunity costs**
£8000 p.a.	£4160 p.a. (foregone wages)
	£400 p.a. (petrol plus insurance)
	£150 p.a. (materials)
	£50 p.a. (foregone rent on tools)
	£0 p.a. (sign: no alternative use)
	——————
	£4760

Answer: Abnormal or Pure profit = £8000 − £4760 = £3240
(*Note*: the £2000 selling price of the van is not an opportunity cost; see answer to (e))

(c) Book keeping profit = £3430, Abnormal/Pure Profit = − £760

(d) An abnormal or positive pure profit indicates that normal profit is more than covered. In the present case we have assumed that Rudolph has no psychic preference between the two activities, hence the normal profit is simply the opportunity cost incurred by way of the wages foregone and the foregone rent on the tools (note that a profit maximiser would not return the tools to his father if not using them himself!). Normal profit is the minimum profit necessary to keep the entrepreneur in the activity concerned, likewise transfer earnings are the minimum amount necessary to keep a factor of production in its present employment. As Rudolph is self-employed the two concepts coincide in his case and hence the abnormal/pure profit calculated above is also Rudolph's economic rent. Thus we can see that when expected revenue equals £8000 Rudolph would remain a self-employed gardener.

A negative pure profit implies that less than normal profit is being made. Thus if expected revenue is £4000 Rudolph would rent out the tools and become a park keeper.

(e) Taxation could alter the relative profitability of being self-employed or a park keeper, for example, if taxation were progressive it would tend to lower abnormal profits. Depreciation of the van should be included as an opportunity cost; if there is no depreciation then there is no loss involved in holding it as an asset (assuming the interest rate is zero). If it were possible to rent out the van, then this should be included as an opportunity cost to being self-employed. Interest rate considerations can be very complicated involving discounting cash flows by the relevant interest rate to find net present value. The most important consideration here is that, if the real interest rate is positive, then using the van incurs foregone interest on the £2000 'tied' up in the van.

Question 5

(a) The definition of a monopoly for the purposes of a reference to the MMC is a market share of 25 per cent or more. In terms of film hire payments it can be seen that EMI cinemas alone accounted for approximately 30 per cent of cinema exhibition. This, however, is but one of many ways that market share and hence concentration can be measured. The MMC might have used, for example, numbers of cinemas, audience numbers, numbers employed, box office takings etc.

(b) Taking 1977 as the starting point we can construct a time stream of costs and benefits. If we assume (as stipulated) that the films shown were paid for one year in advance, then the £13.031m for films hired in 1978 can be entered as the initial cost in 1977 of remaining in the cinema business. The £12.841m paid for films shown in 1979 can then be assumed to have been included in the costs of 1978–79. The relevant time stream would thus be:

77/78	78/79	79/80	80/81	81/82
−£13.031m	+£5.93m	+£4.76	+£3.58	+£1.51

This cannot, however, be simply summed, as income can be invested to produce greater amounts in the future. Hence a sum of money in the future is worth less than the same sum today. Thus the income stream must be discounted by the relevant interest rate stipulated as being 'around' 10 per cent. This produces the following formula for the calculation of the net present value (NPV) of remaining in the cinema business:

$$NPV = -£13.031m + \frac{£5.93m}{1.1} + \frac{£4.76m}{(1.1)^2} + \frac{£3.58m}{(1.1)^3} + \frac{£1.51m}{1(1.1)^4}$$

$$=$$

$$NPV = -£13.031m + £5.39m + £3.93m + £2.69m + £1.03m =$$
$$NPV = £9000$$

Thus as NPV is positive it does appear by this calculation that it would be worthwhile remaining in the cinema business rather than investing the initial outlay at 10 per cent.

We should note, however, that £9000 seems small in relation to the costs and revenues involved. If funds for investment were limited, profits might have been greater if the initial outlay had been invested in another business venture activity and EMI had disinvested (i.e. liquefied assets) from the cinema industry. Indeed, it might be possible to earn a higher return simply by selling off the assets tied up by remaining in the cinema business. Moreover, a slightly higher discount rate than 10 per cent would cause NPV to be negative.

We should also consider the downward trend in profits. It would have been more profitable to have operated only through 1978/79. This would mean no films would have been needed for 79/80. The NPV of this plan would have been:

$$NPV = -£13.03 + \frac{£5.93 + £12.84}{1.1} = +£4.03m$$

This is higher than the NPV in 1977 of remaining in the business until 1982, even ignoring the return to assets which would be released earlier. Of course, in the real world completely accurate forecasting is not possible.

Answers to multiple-choice questions

1	B		11	D
2	B		12	D
3	C		13	B
4	A		14	C
5	E		15	B
6	B		16	B
7	C		17	D
8	E		18	A
9	D		19	A
10	E		20	C

8

The market assessed: welfare economics

Questions

Essay paper

Attempt all questions. Compare your answers with those provided.

1 (Answer provided.) Examine the case for charging motorists by means of tolls for the use of roads.

2 (Answer provided.) Discuss the view that an unaided price mechanism ensures the best allocation of resources.

3 Demonstrate that the ability to price discriminate can lead to an increase in the output of a firm. Does price discrimination therefore increase economic efficiency?

4 Discuss whether advertising leads to an increase or a decrease in consumer welfare.

5 Examine the welfare implications of imposing a tariff on imports.

6 (Answer provided.) Discuss the relative merits of cash grants versus the subsidising of goods and services as a means of assisting the poor.

7 What are the characteristics of 'public goods' that distinguish them from 'private goods'? To what extent do these characteristics make public goods unsuited to provision through market mechanisms?

8 Explain how externalities can cause a divergence between private and social costs. What problems arise in attempting to 'correct' for the effect of externalities?

9 Examine the economic arguments for and against the State provision of education.

10 (Answer provided.) Discuss the arguments for and against using cost benefit analysis.

Data response paper

Question 1 (Answer provided.)
A non-price discriminating monopolist faces the following cost and revenue schedules:

Output (units)	0	2	4	6	8	10	12	14	16	18	20	per week
Revenue (£s)	0	18	32	42	48	50	48	42	32	18	0	per week
Cost (£s)	0	12	23	33	42	50	57	63	68	72	75	per week **91**

(a) Draw the demand curve faced by the firm.

(b) What would be the equilibrium output of a profit-maximising firm?

(c) What would be the equilibrium output of an output-maximising firm? (Ignore possible advertising campaigns.)

(d) Do either of the above two outputs you have located represent a socially efficient allocation of resources?

(e) *With reference to the above* evaluate the statement 'The privatisation of nationalised industries forces them to be efficient for unless they make a profit they are forced out of business'.

Question 2
Read the following extract from a newspaper article taken from *The Guardian*.

NCB stop critical article
by P Wintour and D Simpson

Publication of an article by five top accountancy academics criticising the internal accounting methods used by the National Coal Board to justify pit closures has been stopped after vigorous protests from NCB's director-general of finance. The article was due to appear in the current issue of *Accountancy*, the Journal of the Institute of Chartered Accountants, but may now appear in a revised form next month.

The authors argue that the NCB's internal accounting procedures 'fail to form an adequate basis for informed management decisions'.

The NCB said last night that it objected to the publication of the article because it 'contained numerous inaccuracies and privileged information'.

The article argues that the specific accountancy standard, 'F23', employed to decide whether a pit is uneconomic is 'fundamentally flawed' and would not generally be used in other industries.

Stating that F23 'does not provide a sensible basis for pit closure decisions, or public debate on them,' the authors report that it leans towards historic profit figures and makes no concessions to future projections.

Above all, they conclude that the NCB should take into account the fact that a heavy proportion of an individual pit's costs are fixed or central overheads which will not be saved should a pit be closed, but which would have to be reallocated to surviving pits.

Looking at Cortonwood Colliery, they estimate that operating costs external to Cortonwood directly were responsible for 23.1 per cent of the pit's total costs, and that this net sum of £11.7 per tonne of coal produced is not saved by closing the mine.

If these central costs are stripped out, the authors argue, Cortonwood would in 1984 have contributed a surplus of £5.5 per tonne to the NCB, rather than a loss estimated at £6.2 per tonne.

Among the costs are an allocation to pits of £2.73 per tonne of deep-mined coal for overall surface damage expenses in 1984. This the authors say, reflects not current or future costs but is based on historic costs. In the same way, pits are allocated a cost of 83p per tonne for early retirement and redundancy expenses, according to 1981–2 figures, again reflecting historic figures.

If a pit closes, the report states, the costs would probably be increased, as the aggregate cost would have to be spread among a smaller number of pits. All told, they suggest that at least £3.56 of total £6.35 costs per tonne of coal output attributed to 'other operating expenses' by the NCB would not be saved by a pit closure, but instead reallocated among surviving pits.

(a) The authors of the article referred to in the above extract claim that the accounting procedures of the NCB 'fail to form an adequate basis for informed management decisions'. Carefully explain the arguments they use relating them to the 'shut-down' conditions as identified by economic theory.

(b) Assume that the NCB is correct in its assertion that the article contained inaccuracies and that in fact many pits could not produce a revenue in excess of their operating costs as identified by accountants; would this *prove* that closing such pits is socially desirable?

Question 3 (Answer provided.)
In 1968 the 'Roskill Commission' attempted to evaluate the relative merits of four shortlisted sites for a third London airport. The following table summarises the results of the investigation:

Results of the Roskill Commission Investigation

Type of costs	Social costs (£m) Cublington	Foulness	Nuthampstead	Thurleigh
Passenger user costs[a]	1743–2883	1910–3090	1778–2924	1765–2922
Airspace movement costs[b]	1685–1899	1690–1906	1716–1934	1711–1929
Noise costs[c]	23	10	72	16
Other costs[d]	614–638	611–624	627–640	641–654

(*Sources*: DW Pearce, *Cost–Benefit Analysis*, Macmillan, 1971, and the Roskill Commission on the Third London Airport, *HMSO*. 1971)

(a) Passenger user costs refer to the costs of land travel associated with each site.
(b) Airspace movement costs refer to the social costs to passengers and airline operators of the air travel directly associated with each site.
(c) Noise costs refer to the Commission's estimation of the compensation needed to make the residents suffering from noise as well off as before.
(d) Other costs mainly include capital costs plus the costs of moving various defence establishments.

Passengers were categorised as 'business' or 'pleasure'. The value of the business person's time was taken to his or her hourly wage rate. The value of leisure time was based on past studies of road and rail travel. These studies had estimated the value of leisure time as follows: if a passenger had chosen a faster but more expensive method of travel in preference to a cheaper but slower method, then the difference in cost was taken to be the value of the time saved. No survey was actually done for air travellers.

The social costs of noise nuisance were estimated from questionnaires and estate agents' assessments of depreciation due to aircraft noise around the existing Gatwick Airport.

Forecasts of the future demand for air traffic were based on past growth rates in air traffic. In addition an individual weighting for 'attractiveness' and accessibility was given for each site.

Evaluate the accuracy of the above data and discuss the advantages and disadvantages of using it as the basis for policy choice.

Question 4
Study the following extracts taken from a newspaper article in *The Financial Times*.

REJUVENATION IS THE PRESCRIPTION AS THE NHS TURNS 40
by Alan Pike

Britain's National Health Service has today arrived alive at its 40th birthday.

The present atmosphere of financial crisis may seem a ungrateful birthday present for British society to bestow upon what remains, for many people the most significant achievement of the post-war welfare state. But nothing could be more fitting. Inaugurated on July 1948, amid bombed-out hospitals and a bombed-out economy, the NHS immediately began bursting its budgets.

The 1945–50 Labour Government of Mr Clement Attlee not only had the distinction of inaugurating the most comprehensive state health service in the western world. It also became the first to be faced with the task of deciding how to control costs within the service.

In the 40 years since July 1948, government after government has been asked the type of questions – and considered many of the possible solutions – that are contained in the latest review of health care being chaired by the Prime Minister.

The review will propose changes in the way health care is provided and managed. Mechanisms for trying to separate the financing and delivery of health care and introduce internal markets to encourage health authorities to trade with each other and the private sector have been favourite candidates for action throughout the review.

The structure of health authorities themselves will not be left completely untouched by a Government determined to make the NHS more businesslike and efficient.

Mr. Aneurin Bevan, Minister of Health in Attlee's government, who inagurated the NHS 40 years ago today, explained its introduction in terms of the highest Socialist ideals. 'A free health service is a triumphant example of the superiority of collective action and public initiative applied to a segment of society where commercial principles are seen at their worst.

Now answer the following:

(a) Why will there be a strong tendency for a free health service to exceed its budget?

(b) What arguments might be used to justify the assertion that 'commercial principles' are inappropriate to health care provision?

(c) Evaluate the proposal that the conflict between free health provision and the efficient use of resources can be reduced by the introduction of internal markets' in health provision.

Question 5 (Answer provided.)
Assume that there are two (price taking) consumers in the country. The following records their individual demand schedules for a certain good:

Price (£)	1	2	3	4	5	6	7	8	9
First consumer	9	8	7	6	5	4	3	2	1
Second consumer	20	18	16	14	12	10	8	6	4

(a) Use graph paper to draw the total demand curve on the assumption that the good in question is a private good.

(b) Also using graph paper, derive the social marginal benefit curve on the new assumption that the good in question is a pure public good.

(c) Refer to your diagram and, assuming a constant marginal cost of £8, explain why a free market would result in underproduction in the case of a pure public good.

Multiple-choice test

Answer all questions. Time allowed: 30 minutes

1 When economists speak of 'welfare economics' they mean:

A the administration of welfare benefits by the state.
B the assessment of both economic goods and economic bads.
C positive and normative questions in economics considered from the point of view of 'best' in terms of both efficiency and equity.
D input-output analysis.
E the maximisation of economic benefit in society through the reduction of inequalities caused by imperfections of the price system.

2 Which of the following is the best description of Pareto optimality? Pareto optimality means that:

A perfect competition exists in all markets.
B it must not be possible to change the existing allocation of resources in such a way that someone is made better off and no one worse off.
C there must be no government intervention of any kind in markets,
D the desired trading ratios of all goods divided by their respective prices must be equal.
E there is free trade between nations.

3 Fig. 8.1 shows the production possibility schedule of wheat and barley. The letters a–e show various combinations of wheat and barley which can be produced at the production possibility boundary and within. Under these circumstances, which of the following movements can be *definitely* said to be a Pareto improvement? A move from:

A a to b
B d to e
C e to c
D b to e
E e to d

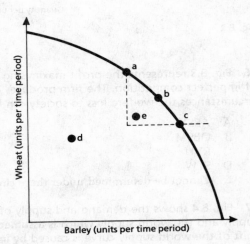

Fig. 8.1

4 If a one tonne increase in the production of potatoes requires a three tonne reduction in the output of carrots then an increase in efficiency is ensured only if:

A there is a fall in the price of potatoes
B there is a fall in the price of carrots.
C potatoes are at least three times the price of carrots.
D there is a reallocation of resources towards carrot production.
E more information is needed before the question can be answered.

5 In Fig. 8.2 SS is the supply curve for product X whilst DD is the demand curve. PMC + EMC represents the private marginal cost together with the external marginal cost of product X. The equilibrium price is OR and the equilibrium quantity OM. In order to achieve allocative efficiency in the market for X the government could:

A impose a unit tax equivalent to EMC.
B not interfere with market forces.
C subsidise producers.
D ban production of X.
E impose a unit tax equivalent to PMC + EMC.

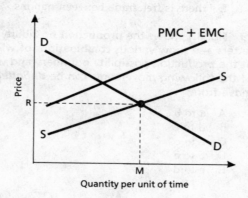

Fig. 8.2

6 Fig. 8.3 represents the profit maximising equilibrium of a firm under conditions of imperfect competition. The firm produces output OM at price OB. Under these circumstances the welfare loss to society can be represented by the area:

A ABSV
B OBSM
C RVU
D STW
E Cannot be determined under these circumstances.

7 Fig. 8.4 shows the demand and supply of product Z. It shows both the domestic supply and the world supply which is assumed to be perfectly elastic. The upward shift of the world supply curve is caused by imposing an import tariff on product Z. Domestic consumers of product Z are thus forced to pay more for imported supplies of Z.

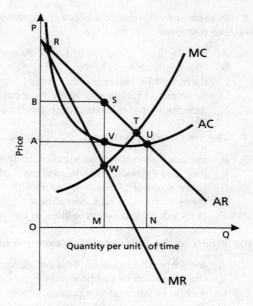

Fig. 8.3

Under these circumstances the 'deadweight' loss to society of imposing the tariff on product Z can be represented by the area:

A   GHD
B   GBCD
C   GBF
D   ECD
E   GBF + ECD

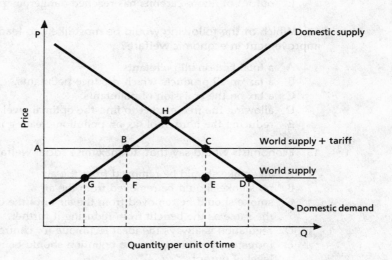

Fig. 8.4

8 In terms of neo-classical economics, monopolies are likely to result in a loss of welfare because:

A price will be in excess of social marginal cost.
B there will be less choice.
C there will be super-normal profits.
D price descrimination is likely to occur.
E monopolists can have undue political influence.

9 The free market system:

A includes all costs of production in the price of goods.
B includes external and internal costs of production in the price of goods.
C takes account of positive externalities but not negative.
D takes account of all externalities.
E does not include externalities in the price of goods.

10 Which of the following is an example of where an externality is likely to occur?

A the imposition of a unit tax on a commodity.
B the provision of public goods.
C a child is vaccinated against measles.
D government subsidy of agriculture.
E all of the above.

11 The main reason why an environmental crisis has developed is that the:

A plant life of the earth has diminished.
B social costs of production (sometimes termed externalities) have encouraged the overloading of nature because we do not have to pay for its use.
C greenhouse effect is disturbing the earth's climate.
D carbon dioxide necessary for plant growth has been reduced because of the decline in total animal life that produces it.
E output of fluoro-carbons has reached dangerous proportions.

12 Which of the following would be most likely to lead to a *long-term* improvement in economic welfare?

A a total ban on all pollutants.
B a tax on all products which produce pollutants.
C a tax on the emission of pollutants.
D allowing the free market to find the optimal level of pollution.
E reducing the burden of tax on pollution-creating industries.

13 Economists would say that, to maximise social welfare:

A all smoke should be removed from the air.
B no smoke should be removed from the air.
C smoke should be removed from the air until the cost of further reducing it is the same as the benefit from reducing it further.
D regulation is always the ideal technique for controlling smoke pollution.
E industries producing smoke pollution should be restricted to their current level of output.

14 A public good (or service) is one which:

    A is provided by the state.
    B is heavily subsidised.
    C is provided free of charge.
    D is consumed in order to impress other people.
    E if consumed by one person is still available for consumption by other people.

15 In most cost-benefit analysis a project is deemed to be socially desirable if:

    A it improves profitability.
    B most people are made better-off.
    C the monetary benefits exceed the monetary cost.
    D it improves the infra-structure of the economy.
    E the gainers could compensate the losers.

Questions 16–20

Directions. For each of the questions below, **One** or **More** of the responses given is (are) correct. Then choose

    A if 1, 2 and 3 are correct
    B if 1 and 2 only are correct
    C if 2 and 3 only are correct
    D if 1 only is correct
    E if 3 only is correct

Directions Summarised				
A	*B*	*C*	*D*	*E*
1, 2, 3	1, 2	2, 3	1	3
correct	only	only	only	

16 Negative externalities arise from:

    1 traffic jams.
    2 discharge of industrial effluent into rivers.
    3 the noise from a neighbours' hi-fi.

17 In order for Pareto optimality to exist it is necessary that there should be:

    1 perfect competition
    2 an absence of externalities.
    3 a situation where all firms are profit maximisers.

18 The benefit of using taxation to control negative externalities is that:

    1 taxation would internalise the externalities.
    2 the tax revenues would be used for ecological purposes.
    3 the taxes would benefit consumers without increasing the cost of goods.

19 Equating social-plus-private costs and benefits is the formula for:

1 maximising welfare from scarce resources.
2 controlling pollution.
3 deciding on proper public expenditure.

20 Cost benefit analysis:

1 is a branch of modern welfare economics.
2 attempt to evaluate the social costs and benefits of proposed investment projects as a guide to their desirability.
3 is only applied to public expenditure projects.

Answers

1 Examine the case for charging motorists by means of tolls for the use of roads

Road use is an example where externalities are likely to cause the free market to fail in producing a Pareto-efficient allocation of resources. A situation is Pareto-efficient if the only way to make one person better off is by making another worse off. Externalities occur when the actions of one individual directly affect the welfare of other people other than through the normal workings of the price mechanism. Externalities are positive or negative according to whether the 'spill-over' effect confers a gain or loss of welfare. In monetary terms its value is equal to what consumers would be prepared to pay to secure or avoid the externality.

Road use has a collective element which is inherent in a public good, i.e. consumption by additional consumers does not reduce the consumption of existing users, provided that the roads are not congested. As exclusion is possible it is not, however, a 'pure' public good. Nevertheless, a toll which deterred some motorists from using a particular road would cause a loss of social welfare, i.e. these motorists *could* have benefited by using the road and this would be at no cost to anyone else. Fig. 8.5 shows the loss of welfare and hence the value of the potential Pareto-improvement.

One might argue that tolls should reflect the cost of road maintenance, but the marginal cost for any road of an extra car journey is negligible. The denomination of currency would not allow the 'correct' toll. (Heavy lorries might be an exception.)

Notwithstanding the above, the building and of maintenance of roads must be financed. General taxation could be considered unfair as the burden falls upon non-motorists as well as motorists. It might be countered that motorists also pay publicly for provided pavements and footpaths and that moreover *all* consumers benefit from lower road haulage costs. But it could well be concluded that the fairest and most efficient system would be the imposition of a 'lump-sum' road tax and then unlimited road use at no extra charge. This of course is present practice.

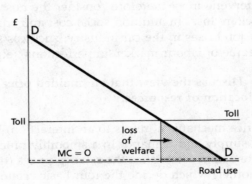

Fig. 8.5

Conversely, negative externalities, e.g. pollution, noise, threat of accident and congestion, will also cause 'social inefficiency'. This is because the motorist will consider only his or her private costs and not these wider social opportunity costs. In Fig. 8.6 the social marginal cost (SMC) is the addition of private costs and the various negative externalities at the margin. At the Q_X the marginal negative externality is equal to a+b, but the motorists' valuation of the marginal unit of travel over and above the foregone alternative is equal to a. Hence those suffering from the externality would be prepared to compensate the motorist for the loss of his marginal unit of travel and still enjoy an increase in welfare. Such Pareto-improvements could continue until Q_S is reached. Q_S therefore represents the Pareto-efficient allocation of resources.

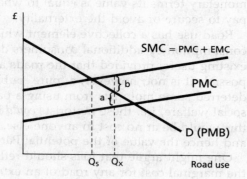

Fig. 8.6

Q_S could be achieved by charging a toll equal to the value of the negative externality. Tolls, however, will cause inconvenience. The inconvenience of the social cost of tolls could be avoided by taxing petrol or subsidising public transport. This latter method has the advantage that it could be tailored to the degree of congestion in an area. However, overall, tolls (unless perhaps automatic electronic metering proves practical) seem to be an inefficient way of correcting for 'market failure'. But any intervention would be inexact due to the difficulty of measuring the value of externalities. The decision to intervene must therefore consider the possibility of actually increasing social welfare loss. In addition social cost and equity considerations might be raised by job losses in the car industry; such costs would be greater the greater the degree of labour market 'imperfections', e.g. labour mobility.

2   Discuss the view that an unaided price mechanism ensures the best allocation of resources.

'Price mechanism' refers to an interaction, both within and between markets, of supply and demand. In a smoothly functioning free market such interaction establishes the relative prices (the price of one thing in terms of another) which decide the four basic economic (i.e. arising from scarcity and choice) questions of 'What?', 'When?', 'How?', and 'For Whom?' Price acts as a signalling device collecting information and providing incentives. Resource allocation and the distribution of product is thus determined by impersonal market forces generated by the pursuit of self interest.

A change in tastes increases the demand for some products and decreases the demand for others. The prices of the former rise and the prices of the latter fall (in the short run at least). Producers in the former industries receive increased profits, those in the latter decreased. Producers move towards the more profitable industries, bidding up the prices of factors in those industries and inducing factors to move towards producing those products. The converse will be occurring in the less profitable industries. Equilibrium is re-established when profit differentials are eliminated. The end result is that resources have moved towards satisfying consumer wants as expressed through *effective demand*.

Under the stringent conditions of the *'First Optimality Theorem* of Welfare Economics' the price mechanism would automatically produce a balance between wants, as expressed via 'money votes', and scarcity such that it would be impossible to increase the welfare of any individuals without decreasing the welfare of others, i.e. Pareto-efficiency. This result arises from the equality of the social marginal benefit of production with its social marginal cost. In the absence of externalities and ignorance, this requires that price equal marginal cost; price will equal the marginal valuation of the product and marginal cost the opportunity cost of the factors used, which in turn equals the valuation by consumers of the alternatives forgone. It can be seen that in an unaided price mechanism Pareto-efficiency requires perfect competition in all markets!

Profit-maximising monopolists equate MC and MR; hence (assuming we are not in a 'second-best' situation) SMB must exceed SMC. Externalities (when production or consumption has direct effects upon other parties) will cause a divergence between private costs and social costs. As these 'spill-over' effects are not reflected in market prices they are ignored in decisions based on private costs. This results in an over production of negative externalities such as pollution and under provision of positive externalities, as for example, in the immunisation against contagious disease. Public goods are a special case of externality where 'free-riding' results in consumer preferences not being reflected in effective demand.

Ignorance also causes market failure; producers may be unaware of opportunities and consumers may make decisions which would be changed if more information were provided. Of course, if people are prepared to pay for it, the market itself can provide certain types of information. It is also not clear that capitalism can be blamed for creating ignorance nor whether bureaucrats in a planned economy have a greater facility for correct decision-making. Moreover, it is a profound question as to how consumer wants arise in the first place.

Pareto-efficiency results from a situation in which well informed individuals are allowed to make decisions in the light of prices which truly reflect the opportunities they forego by choosing one thing in preference to another. If it is held that individuals do not know what is best for themselves, then even a **103** smoothly functioning price mechanism might be rejected. In the UK such paternalistic intervention is limited to 'merit' good, such as taxing cigarettes, banning heroin and subsidising the arts. Merit goods such as education also reflect other considerations such as externalities and equity.

Intervention may be made to alter the distribution of income and to enforce the law. Adam Smith accepted that industries strategic to defence may need protection from international competition. Keynes' version of macro-economics and the depression of the inter-war years did most to establish the belief that capitalism must be regulated through demand management if full employment is to be maintained. Much of the western world moved back towards *laissez-faire* economic policy in the eighties, but the stock market crash of 1987 reiterated Keynes' warning that uncertainty can make spending decisions volatile and that thus goverments should counter sharp changes in aggregate demand by appropriate fiscal and monetary policy.

In conclusion, an unaided price mechanism would not ensure an efficient, let alone 'best' allocation of resources. But whether alternative economic systems can increase overall welfare is a controversial question.

6   Discuss the relative merits of cash grants versus the subsidising of goods and services as a means of assisting the poor.

In neo-classical welfare economics, each consumer maximises their utility, subject to their limited income, in a world where prices truly reflect what is sacrificed, by choosing one thing in preference to another (i.e. price equals social marginal opportunity cost). Under such conditions consumers will increase their purchases of a product up until the point at which their valuation of the marginal unit is exactly equal to their valuation of what has been foregone by its production. Equilibrium therefore coincides with an efficient allocation of resources in the sense that individual welfare cannot be increased but only redistributed.

Transfer payments involving cash grants to the poor could increase the real income of the poor, and thus their welfare, without causing product prices to deviate from marginal cost. Pareto-efficiency would thus be maintained at a new set of equlibrium prices. The recipients of the grants would have spent them as they saw fit in the light of prices which reflect foregone alternatives. Hence the consumer's welfare would be the maximum that can be achieved for the consumer's given income.

Subsidies would cause the prices of products to differ from their marginal costs of production.

The subsidy, as illustrated in Fig. 8.7, has caused the market supply curve to shift vertically downward by the amount that the governments pays per unit of output to the producer. This follows from the definition of a supply curve, i.e. a supply curve shows the amount of the product that producers would wish to offer for sale at any given price, within a specified time periods, all other influences constant. If then a subsidy of so much per unit is paid producers will offer the same amount for sale as before at a new market

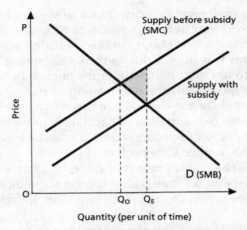

P

Supply before subsidy
(SMC)

Supply with
subsidy

Price

D (SMB)

O

Q_O Q_E

Quantity (per unit of time)

Q_O is the Pareto efficient output, where Social
Marginal Cost = Social Marginal Benefit. Q_E is
the market equilibrium after the subsidy.

Fig. 8.7

price equal to the original market price corresponding to that quantity minus
the subsidy per unit. Of course, if we do not start from perfect competition
the concept of a supply curve is not strictly applicable and hence the effect of
a subsidy less certain.

At the new equilibrium, MC exceeds market price. The true cost in terms of
resources used up, and therefore alternatives foregone, is hidden from the
consumer by the subsidy. The shaded triangle indicates the value of the loss
of welfare caused by 'over-consumption' of the subsidised product. Unlike
the situation brought about by cash grants, consumers of the product could
be made better off by a reduction in the output of the subsidised product in
favour of the best alternative(s) foregone.

In a world full of oligopoly, externalities, and ignorance, it is not logically
the case that subsidies are less efficient than cash grants. For example, a
subsidy might offset monopolistic contrived scarcity or provide medical
provision overlooked by those preoccupied with immediate essentials (in this
sense health care can be considered a merit good). Nevertheless, the common
sense of allowing people to choose for themselves how to spend their money,
rather than bureaucrats or politicians deciding for them, accords with liberal
traditions.

If one does not accept that people know their own best interest, one may
prefer the use of subsidies. For example, cash grants might be spent on white
as well as wholemeal bread, whereas subsidies could lower the price of
wholemeal bread alone. It will be pointed out that the intended effect of the
subsidy will be dissipated by the better off also benefiting from the reduced
price of wholemeal bread. Vouchers could be used but, in addition to the
administration costs, stigma might itself reduce welfare.

A subsidy might be preferred if the recipient of the cash subsidy is not the
target recipient. It can be argued, for example, that a subsidy on school meals **105**

is preferable to a cash grant to the head of the household. Another reason for preferring subsidies might be related to externalities. It is revealing to note that the first major publicly provided utility was the sewer system. No doubt this was in part due to the consideration that germs breeding among the poor do not discriminate in terms of class or social standing. Today the argument is more controversial, relating to such matters as the effects on society as a whole of the existence of inner-city deprivation. Thus some observers may wish redistribution to such areas to take the form of the direct provision or subsidy of housing, education and job provision rather than cash grants to the deprived themselves.

The relative merits of these two forms of income redistribution thus depend on the existing economic conditions, the target of the policy and one's views as to what constitutes welfare.

10   Discuss the arguments for and against using cost benefit analysis.

Cost benefit analysis (CBA) arose from the application of the theoretical prescriptions of modern welfare economics. It attempts to evaluate the social costs and benefits of proposed investment projects in order to assess their social desirability. A CBA framework could be applied to any decision but has typically been reserved for public sector projects, for example, in town planning, transport and investment by the nationalised industries. It differs from ordinary investment appraisal in that the latter considers only private cost and benefits, i.e. those that relate to private profit. Like private investment appraisal the time stream of costs and benefits must be aggregated in the form of a discounted cash flow. In short, CBA is intended to enable the decision-maker to choose between alternatives on the basis of their potential contribution to social welfare.

Major difficulties stem from the fact that, (in a world where imperfect competition, externalities and ignorance abound), market prices do not reflect true social costs and benefits. Much of CBA thus consists of estimating *shadow-prices*. These are imputed prices which are intended to reflect the true social costs and benefits of a project. For example, the value of the time saved by individuals following an improvement in transport facilities is often approximated using the average hourly wage. The Roskill Commission used the decrease in house prices around Gatwick Airport to estimate the value of the negative externality caused by aircraft noise. The valuing of human life is particularly emotive but estimates have been put forward derived from considering life insurance premiums.

The criterion of social betterment which is almost invariably adopted is that of a potential *Pareto improvement*. A Pareto improvement implies no one has lost and someone has gained. Unfortunately most economic changes in the real world do hurt someone. And even if in principle it would be possible for the gainers to compensate the losers and still be better off themselves, this is rarely done in practice. If then we were only willing to undertake projects if an actual Pareto improvement results, we would be unable to appraise the desirability of most important potential economic changes.

To compare situations in which some people gain at the expense of others we require a *social welfare function* that attaches weights to the distributional effects of a project. In practice most cost benefit analyses have avoided addressing distributional issues by deeming there to be a potential Pareto improvement if everyone affected could, by a costless redistribution of the gains, be made better off. This test of a potential Pareto improvement in known as the *Hicks-Kaldor* criterion and has been much criticised for obscuring issues of equity.

Other criticisms arise from the impossibility of correctly forecasting future values in the face of an uncertain future. The choice of the appropriate discount rate is also subject to controversy; market rates of interest may deviate from actual social time preference. The question of how to allow for the benefits and costs to future generations is unresolved. Some people have argued that a low discount rate should be used to give a high weighting to future benefits as they believe that the quality of life will decrease in the future due to resource constraints. Others argue that economic growth will make future generations better off than at present and therefore a high rate of discount should be used to weight benefits towards the present.

There are other more technical criticisms. For example, CBA often involves estimating consumer surplus, but this usually cannot be observed. Hence approximations are made, such as assuming unobservable demand curves are linear over the relevant area of change. Many observers argue that the methods used to estimate shadow-prices are artificial, arbitrary and without means of cross checking. They also feel that CBA obscures moral questions, for example in 'pretending' that it is possible to place monetary values on human life. Nevertheless, it is clear that most of us are prepared to accept the threat to life posed by many modern inventions in order to enjoy the benefits they bring. Hence we implicitly accept a less than infinite valuation of life.

CBA reflects the 'high theory' of modern welfare economics. Many observers feel that the conclusions of this theory are misleading. For example, some economists argue that observed prices are too far away from their theoretical role as a reflection of resource costs for it to be feasible to assign 'correcting' weights. CBA thus arouses much suspicion. Critics argue that it is pseudo-scientific. Cynics suspect it is used to dress up the arguments of politicians who have already privately decided on an outcome. Nevertheless, many economists defend CBA if only on the grounds that it forces into the open the differences in valuations which may lie at the root of many disagreements.

Suggested data response answers

Question 1

Note: for this answer it is easiest to first calculate average revenue, average cost, marginal cost and marginal revenue; these values can then be used to produce Fig. 8.8.

(a) In the absence of price discrimination the demand curve corresponds to the average revenue curve. The AR curve is thus plotted in Fig. 8.8.

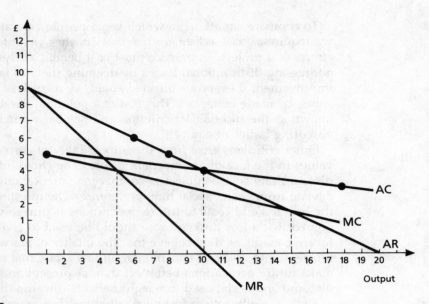

Fig. 8.8

(b) Profit maximisation occurs when MC = MR. In this case this is at an output of five units per week, as shown in Fig. 8.8.

(c) By examining the AC and AR curves in Fig. 8.8 we can see that the firm would not be covering its costs at any output above 10 units per week. The highest output the firm could thus sustain in equilibrium is 10 units of output.

(d) The term 'socially efficient' in economics usually refers to Pareto efficiency. This occurs at the output at which social marginal benefit (SMB) is equal to social marginal cost (SMC). If there is perfect competition in all other markets, no externalities and no relevant ignorance, then SMB corresponds to the demand curve and SMC corresponds to the marginal cost curve of the firm. In this case, as can been seen from Fig. 8.8, SMB would equal SMC at 15 units of output. Hence neither the profit-maximising output nor the output maximising equlibrium would appear to represent a socially efficient level of output.

(e) It can be seen that at the socially efficient level of output, i.e. 15 units per week per week, AC exceeds AR. The firm would thus be making a loss at this output. This conflict between social efficiency and financial profit arises in this case because of the significant economies of scale. As long as there are more economies of scale to exploit, AC will continue to fall as output expands. Hence MC will remain below AC. Thus, when MC = AR, AC must exceed AR. Therefore, in the absence of a subsidy a private firm could not produce the socially efficient level of output.

Many economists believe that there are almost continuous economies of scale in many industries which are or were previously nationalised. This is often due to the indivisibility of distribution networks, as, for example, in the national electric grid. Fig. 8.8 would thus suggest that privatising such industries and forcing them to make a profit would prevent them being socially efficient. Privatisation might, however, have other effects. Some economists, such as Pryke, argue that nationalised industries tend to be cost inefficient when compared with private sector enterprises. The resources thus released for alternative production might more than outweigh the economies of scale effect. Nevertheless, it should be borne in mind that profit alone is a poor indicator of efficiency. It would be relatively easy for even a cost inefficient monopolist to exploit its market power in order to make a profit.

Question 3

The most striking feature of the data is that only the social costs are listed. Cost benefit analysis (CBA), however, aids the decision-maker by comparing social costs *and* benefits in order to estimate the potential contribution to social welfare of a project. It could thus be argued that using the data to choose between the four sites ignores the possibility that none of them have positive net social benefits. It is also likely that the benefits vary between sites, a consideration reflected in the Commission's weighting for attractiveness and accessibility. Hence, choosing on the basis of costs alone might not identify the site with the largest net social benefit.

The calculation of social costs involves estimating the values of intangible externalities and other non-marketed factors. Examples from the data are noise costs and the value of time. The estimated values are known as 'shadow prices'. The data describe some of the methods used by the Roskill Commission, but there is bound to be disagreement concerning the accuracy of such estimates. Such objections include the following:

First, the wage of a businessperson is taken as a measure of the value of lost production. This is based on the assumption that wage equals marginal physical product multiplied by the price of the product in question. This assumption is invalid out of equilibrium or, as is the case, where competition in the economy is less than perfect. It might also be the case that many businesspersons travel in what would otherwise be leisure time or that they work during travel.

Second, in valuing leisure time no survey of air travellers of air travellers was undertaken. This introduces error if valuations of journey time differ according to the purpose of the journey or the mode of transport. For example, many air passengers will derive pleasure from the journey itself, it is unlikely that a holidaymaker on a plane begrudges travelling time to the same extent as a daily commuter in a car.

Third, in order to calculate figures for 'passenger costs' and 'airspace movement costs' it would have been necessary to forecast the number of passengers who would use the third London Airport. Needless to say, such estimates could be in serious error if, for example, airfares changed dramatically (e.g. following increases in fuel costs such as in the early and late 1970s), the growth of real incomes slowed, the sterling exchange rate changed significantly or if airport provision altered in other parts of the country.

Part of the argument concerning measurement would centre on the distributional or equity aspects of the proposed projects. This is particularly likely as, as can be seen, noise nuisance is given a very small value relative to the costs of the users and operators of the airlines. It could be argued that, due to the methods of valuing passengers' time, the high costs borne by air travellers reflect their high incomes. In effect, then, unless compensation is actually paid to noise sufferers, greater weight is being given to those with higher incomes.

Summing the estimates for each site suggests the following ranking of 'desirability':

	1 Cublington	2 Thurleigh	3 Nuthampstead	4 Foulness
Social Cost Estimate	Range of 4065–5443	4133–5521	4193–5570	4221–5630

It can be seen that the differences between the sites are small in relation to the magnitudes involved. Clearly different weightings and measurement of the various costs involved could affect the above ranking.

It has been seen that the final results depend upon questionable valuations of shadow prices, forecasts and social weighting of distributional effects. Moreover, the technique and rationale of CBA is an application of neo-classical welfare economics and this is itself open to many criticisms. Nevertheless, such studies attempt to make explicit the values and weights one is using and to list the various factors actually being taken into account. To this extent it can be considered an advance over less explicit or vague qualitative analysis. This is certainly not an argument for the unqualified acceptance of the 'results' of CBA studies. The point is that the explicit nature of its methods facilitates effective criticism which can, hopefully, identify the areas of disagreement.

Question 5

(a) A private good is one where there is rivalry in its consumption, i.e. each unit can be consumed by one consumer only. Thus any consumer who is not prepared to pay can be excluded from consuming it. The total or market curve demand curve is thus the horizontal sum of the individual demand curves as shown in Fig. 8.9.

(b) The social marginal benefit of each unit of the good is equal to what consumers would be prepared to pay for it. For a private good this valuation

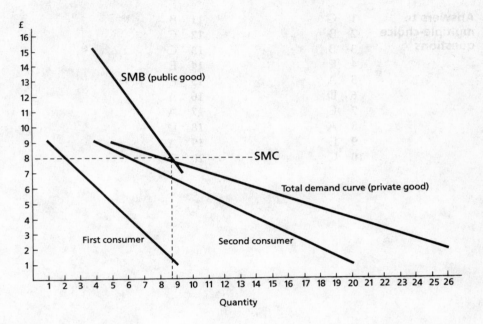

Fig. 8.9

is shown by the demand curve. But in the case of a pure public good there is non-rivalry in consumption, i.e. each unit of the good is consumed in equal volume by all consumers. Hence, for a public good the social marginal benefit (SMB) is the vertical sum of the individual demand curves as shown in Fig. 8.9.

(c) The Pareto efficient level of output is where SMC = SMB. In the diagram this occurs at about 8½ units of output. But in the case of a public good the SMB is not the effective demand curve for the good. This is due to the possibility of 'free-riding' i.e. enjoying the benefits of the goods without paying for it. For example, if the second consumer were to purchase six units at £8 each the first consumer could not be excluded from consuming these units also, even though he had not paid for them. Moreover, the first consumer would not be prepared to pay for extra units beyond the six units already produced as his or her valuation of them is below the cost of production. Hence output would remain below the Pareto efficient level even though the extra units up until this point are *collectively* valued at more than their cost of production.

In such an artificial example it should be possible for the two parties to negotiate a collective payment above the SMC until the point at which SMC equals SMB is reached. In the real world, however, millions of consumers would be involved and such a solution would not be feasible. Thus free riding means that public goods are unsuitable for market production.

Answers to multiple-choice questions

1	C	11	B
2	B	12	C
3	B	13	C
4	E	14	E
5	A	15	E
6	D	16	A
7	E	17	A
8	A	18	D
9	E	19	A
10	C	20	B.

9
The determination of national income

Questions

Essay paper

Attempt all questions. Compare your answers with those provided.

1 (Answer provided.) 'Keynes argued that consumption is a function of income.' Explain what is meant by this statement and evaluate its accuracy.

2 Explain why the relationship between the marginal propensity to consume and the average propensity to consume is likely to change over a household's life cycle.

3 (Answer provided.) What are the determinants of aggregate private investment and why is it likely to fluctuate?

4 (Answer provided.) Examine the possible consequences of the fact that saving and investment decisions are made by separate groups of economic agents.

5 (Answer provided.) 'The economy is in equilibrium when expenditure equals income. In the national accounts expenditure is always equal to income. Hence the economy is always in equilibrium.' Discuss.

6 Explain why Keynes thought that an increase in government expenditure, *ceteris paribus*, might affect the level of output. Why might problems arise from such a policy?

7 'If a recession is expected, the government should encourage people to save in order to support themselves in times to come; it should also behave responsibly by balancing the government's books.' Discuss.

8 Explain in detail what is meant by the Keynesian multiplier. What factors determine the size of this multiplier?

9 Expain how interrelationships between income, consumption and investment could cause cyclical fluctuations in the level of economic activity.

10 Evaluate the various explanations that have been put forward to explain fluctuations in the level of economic activity.

Data response paper

Question 1
Study the following chart:

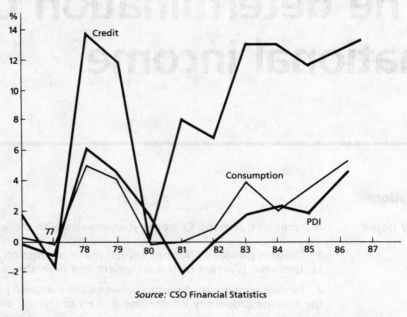

Source: CSO Financial Statistics

Fig. 9.1 Real growth in personal disposable income, consumption and consumer credit.

Now answer the following question:

Summarise the information presented in the chart and relate it to the simple Keynesian and Permanent Income Hypothesis theories of the consumption function. Indicate what other data would be helpful to your assessment of the validity of these theories.

Question 2 (Answer provided.)
In the following model of an economy there is no international trade:

Y = C + J
C = 100 + 0.8Y

Where C = domestic consumption, J = investment and government expenditure; Y = national income or real domestic output.

If the level of national income at which all resources would be fully employed is £4000 and the present level of injections is £200:

(a) What is the value of the multiplier in the above?

(b) What is the value of the inflationary or deflationary gap?

(c) Demonstrate, by application of the multiplier you have calculated, that increasing/decreasing government expenditure by the amount of the deflationary/inflationary gap will produce full employment.

Question 3 (Answer provided.)
The following table shows the allocation of Gross National income:

Gross national income	£276 000m
Direct taxes	£ 24 000m
Retained profits	£ 18 000m
Personal disposable income	£234 000m
Personal savings	£ 20 000m
Indirect taxes	£ 40 000m
Imports	£ 8 100m
Domestic consumption at factor cost	£165 000m

Assuming that additional income would be allocated in the same proportions as above:

(a) Calculate the marginal propensity to consume.

(b) Using your figure for MPC, calculate the value of the multiplier.

(c) (i) What factors determine the value of the multiplier in such a way that its value is decreased as these factors increase?
(ii) Show the values of these factors and show how they can be used to calculate the value of the multiplier.

(d) (i) If output adjusted instantaneously to changes in demand, what would be the change in Real GNP following an increase in government expenditure of £100m?
(ii) Is it likely that the increase in government expenditure would cause this increase in the volume of output in the real world?

Question 4
Read the following extracts from a newspaper article taken from *The Guardian*.

A LEADING INDICATOR OF TROUBLE
by Christopher Huhne

It is a sign of troubled times that last week's two highlights of the Chancellor's year – the autumn Statement and the Mansion House speech – should have receded so rapidly into the middle distance.

This is not meant to impugn the Treasury's judgement. It is just that what the Chancellor likes to call the 'recent events' and the rest of us call the crash is the sort of shock which computer models find hard to handle. The Chancellor had hardly let the ink dry on the forecast when he said it was subject to a 'huge' margin error and was very optimistic in the circumstances.

One number sums it up: the Treasury predicts that the growth of world trade in manufactures accelerates from 3.75 per cent this year to 4 per cent next year, despite a deceleration in real GNP growth in the major seven countries from 2.5 per cent to 2 per cent.

What this forecast is saying is that there will be no recession in the United States next year. There are a couple of good reasons why there should not be a recession in the US next year and several more good reasons why there should be.

Certainly, the administration will be reluctant to take any measures which will slow growth this side of the presidential elections next autumn. The Federal Reserve Board, in charge of monetary policy, is, however, independent and need not take account of what the White House or the Treasury think. But its instinct has quite rightly been to bring down interest rates quickly and pump liquidity into the system.

Nor is there much risk of an excessive tightening of US budgetary policy. Indeed, it would be surprising if the cuts in the deficit in the financial year which is just beginning were more than $23 billion.

The actual cut may eventually be less. Slower growth is likely to reduce projected tax revenues and raise spending on items such as unemployment insurance. So the cyclical elements in the deficit may rise even while policy changes which cut it are being enacted. In other words, the structural deficit can be reduced while the actual deficit is reacting to the cycle.

Mr Lawson laid enormous stress on the need to placate the market by taking firm political action to cut the deficit. The Chancellor's reasoning is that the US deficit is at the point at which an increase would stop acting in an expansionary, Keynesian way, and have contractionary effects via the loss of confidence in the financial markets. His evidence, of course, is the recent collapse on Wall Street.

But the Wall Street fall is more to do with the current account deficit on the balance of payments than the budget deficit. The two deficits are clearly related, but not intimately. Moreover, the US budget deficit will now suddenly begin to absorb a much smaller part of the US domestic savings, because those savings are probably heading upwards at an alarming rate to compensate for the dramatic trillion dollar loss in wealth which the American consumer has suffered due to the crash. Nor will a dampening of domestic demand through higher taxes or lower spending be needed to push resources into improving the trade deficit, since deflation is already under way from the effects of the stock market crash.

There are other worrying possibilities. President Roosevelt told Americans in 1932 that they had nothing to fear but fear itself, but it was nevertheless real. The fear of a stock market crash and slump is deep-rooted in American folk-lore, which could in turn cause a far sharper retrenchment of spending.

Now answer the following questions:

(a) Explain the reasons given for expecting an improvement in the US trade deficit.

(b) Explain the reasons given for supposing that there might not be a recession in the US.

(c) Explain why a stock market crash is likely to produce large errors in the previous forecasts generated by computer modelling of the economy.

Question 5   (Answer provided.)
Study the following data:

Year	Y (output)	C	I
1	1000	500	500
2	1000	500	500
3	1001	500	501
4	1003.5	500.5	503
5	1007.75	501.75	506
6	1013.375	503.875	509.5
7	1018.9375	506.6875	512.25

Figures will now be rounded to two decimal places

8	1021.6	509.47	512.13

The time path for the economy shown in the table on page 116
incorporates the following assumptions:
1 Autonomous investment is 500 in years 2 and 3, but thereafter is 501.
2 Investment is partly autonomous and partly determined according to the
accelerator principle.
3 MPC is constant.

Now answer the following:

(a) Continue the time path of the economy for the years 9 and 10.

(b) Explain, in words, the process and interactions which have produced the
above pattern of changes in output.

(c) To what extent does the above model represent an adequate theory of real
life trade cycles?

Multiple-choice test   Answer all questions. Time allowed: 30 minutes

1   The best definition of the marginal propensity to consume (MPC) is that it is the:

A   amount of any increase in income which is spent on consumption.
B   proportion of income spent on consumer goods and services.
C   proportion of any increase in income which is spent on consumption.
D   reciprocal of the marginal propensity to save (MPS).
E   realised level of consumer spending.

2   Suppose that the marginal propensity to consumer (MPC) is 0.75 and that the
marginal propensity to import (MPM) is 0.0834 then, assuming that there is no
government activity in the economy, the value of the multiplier will be:

A   4.0
B   1.25
C   3.0
D   1.25
E   6.0

3   The relationship between the marginal propensity to save (MPS) and the
marginal propensity to consume (MPC) is that:

A   their sum is equal to the value of the multiplier
B   their sum is equal to unity
C   together they equal the value of aggregate demand
D   they are both directly related to income
E   there is no relationship between them

4   Other things being equal, in an economy which is below the level of full
employment, an increase in the propensity to save will:

A   increase the level of national income.
B   reduce the volume of imports.
C   leave the level of saving unchanged.
D   increase the rate of investment.
E   cause an increase in the value of the multiplier.

117

5 In the diagram below the line CC represents the consumption function. Which of the marked dimensions best illustrates savings?

A OM
B RS
C MR
D ST
E MN

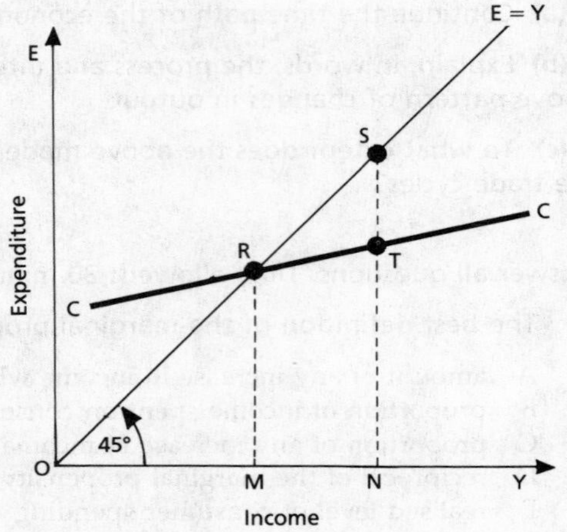

Fig. 9.2

6 The following figures relate to a hypothetical closed economy with no government intervention.

Level of Income £m.	Planned Consumption £m.	Planned Investment £m.
60 000	60 000	700
62 000	61 800	700
64 000	63 300	700
66 000	64 300	700
68 000	64 900	700

What is the value of the marginal propensity to consume (MPC) as income rises from £64 000 to £66 000?

A 0.25
B 0.30
C 0.50
D 0.75
E 1.00

7 The diagram shows an equilibrium in a closed economy with no government intervention. If we assume that the planned rate investment rises by 50 units and that the situation is such that APS = MPS, what will be the new equilibrium level of income?

A 500
B 1000
C 1050
D 1500
E 2000

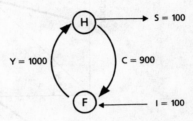

Fig. 9.3

8 Which of the following is the most satisfactory statement of the paradox of thrift?

A People tend to save more at lower levels of income.
B Following any autonomous rise in the size of the MPC there is likely to be a rise in the level of savings in the economy.
C A rise in the level of savings is likely to cause a rise in the level of investment.
D Contractual savings tend to vary inversely with the level of discretionary savings.
E An increase in the planned level of savings may bring about a fall in the level of savings.

9 Of the following formulae, which yields the most accurate value of the multiplier (K)?

A $K = \dfrac{1}{MPC + MPG + MPX}$

B $K = \dfrac{1}{(1 - MPC) + MPM + MPT}$

C $K = \dfrac{1}{MPC + MPM + MPT}$

D $K = \dfrac{1}{1 - MPC}$

E $K = \dfrac{1}{MPS}$

10 In the following diagram the line AG represents aggregate demand and the line market W represents the withdrawals function. What amount of injections (J) is required to raise the eqilibrium level of income from OG to OH?

A   KL
B   GJ
C   JK
D   HK
E   GH

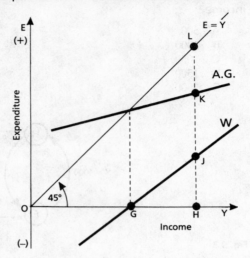

Fig. 9.4

11 Consider the following changes. Which would be most likely to cause the level of aggregate demand to fall?

A   A decrease in the level of imports.
B   A decrease in the rate of interest.
C   A decrease in the level of income tax.
D   A decrease in government expenditure.
E   A decrease in the propensity to save.

12 If, in the situation depicted by the following diagram, the full employment level of national income is represented by the distance OC, which dimension illustrates a deflationary gap?

A   GH
B   OB
C   JK
D   DK
E   FG

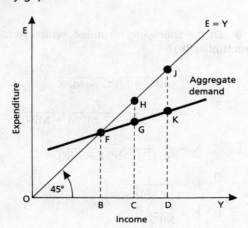

120   Fig. 9.5

13 In a closed economy with no government intervention the consumption function is as follows:

C = 50 + 0.85Y

Autonomous investment is constant at 60 units. Induced investment is:

I = 0.05Y

for all levels of income. Under these circumstances what will be the equilibrium level of national income (Y).

    A   100
    B   985
    C   1000
    D   1100
    E   1500

14 Which of the following is most likely to impose a limit on the ability of an economy to expand its output in the long run?

    A   The level of aggregate demand.
    B   The 'crowding out' of investment by government expenditure.
    C   The supply of factors of production.
    D   The money supply.
    E   The level of savings.

15 Of the following factors which would be *least* likely to produce inflationary pressure in the economy?

    A   An increase in the standard rate of VAT.
    B   An increase in the standard rate of income tax.
    C   An increase in excise duty.
    D   An increase in council house rents.
    E   An increase in government defence expenditure.

Questions 16–20

Directions. For each of the questions below, **one** or **more** of the responses given is (are) correct. Then choose:

    A   if 1, 2 and 3 are correct.
    B   if 1 and 2 only are correct.
    C   if 2 and 3 only are correct.
    D   if 1 only is correct.
    E   if 3 only is correct.

Directions Summarised				
A	*B*	*C*	*D*	*E*
1, 2, 3	1, 2	2, 3	1	3
correct	only	only	only	only

16 Which of the following statements is/are correct?

1 APC + MPC = 1
2 APS + APC = 1
3 MPS + MPC = 1

17 In a closed economy with no government intervention with a constant MPC of 0.75 the:

1 value of the multiplier(K) will be 4.
2 consumption function will be a straight line.
3 proportion of income devoted to savings will decrease with the level of income.

18 If in a closed economy with no government intervention the consumption function is given by the expression C = 40 + 2/3Y and investment (I) is constant at 50 units then:

1 the economy is in equilibrium at 270 units.
2 the value of the multiplier(K) is 3.
3 any increase in the level of income will lead to an increase in the size of the APC.

19 Other things being equal the 'balanced budget multiplier hypothesis' predicts that

1 a balanced budget has a neutral effect on the equilibrium of national income.
2 only a balanced budget is neither inflationary nor deflationary.
3 given equal increases in taxes and government expenditure the ultimate result will be a change in national income equal to the original change in government expenditure.

20 The national income is in equilibrium when

1 I + G + X = S + T + M
2 J = W
3 Y = C + G + I + (X + M)

Answers

1 'Keynes argued that consumption is a function of income'. Explain what is meant by this statement and evaluate its accuracy

Consumption refers to the using up of goods and services. A consumption function is a mathematical description of the relationship between expenditure on consumption and other economic variables. As part of the analysis of the 'General Theory', J.M. Keynes identified current disposable income (i.e. income minus direct taxes) as the major determinant of consumption. Keynesian economists believe that output and employment can be constrained by lack of aggregate demand. As consumer spending is by far the largest component of aggregate demand it has attracted much research effort.

Keynes believed that, on average, one's consumption increases with one's income but not by as much as this increase in income. He also argued that the gap between income and consumption would widen with increases in income. This is often taken to mean that the marginal propensity to consume (MPC = the fraction of additional income that is spent on consumption) declines as income rises. But in fact the following consumption function also satisfies Keynes' specifications:

$$[C = a + b.Y]$$

In this equation 'a' represents autonomous consumption, i.e. the level of consumption that would take place even if income were zero (this implies dissaving). The coefficient 'b' is the MPC and is the slope of this consumption function, hence consumption in excess of 'a' is income-induced or endogenous. Diagrammatically:

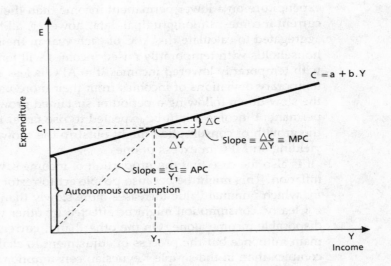

Fig. 9.6

Because of the intercept 'a', the APC is less than MPC. It is also clear that at higher levels of income the slope of the dotted line would fall, i.e. APC falls with increases in income even though MPC is constant.

Empirical evidence suggested that this simple consumption function should be modified. Firstly, consumption functions estimated from cross-sectional data (i.e. across households in the same time period) gave a far lower MPC than consumption functions estimated from long-run time series data. Secondly, year to year changes in disposable income quite often gave a figure for MPC greater than one!

Two types of explanation have attracted most attention. The first type consists of Friedman's 'Permanent Income Hypothesis' and Modigliani's 'Life Cycle Hypothesis'. The second type is Duesenberry's 'Relative Income Hypothesis'. In Duesenberry's explanation one's consumption is heavily influenced by previous income and by the consumption patterns of other people.

In the permanent income and life cycle hypotheses it is changes in expectations of long-term income that affect consumption rather than current income. Short-run changes in current disposable income are evened out by borrowing and saving.

These hypotheses can explain why the cross-section consumption function is flatter than the long-run. In a cross section survey of household income we will observe only the current income of households. Thus, in terms of the permanent income hypothesis, below the average income we will have a disproportionately large number of households with temporarily depressed income. As these households base their expenditure on a 'normally' higher income they will seem to have a high APC when this expenditure is compared with their current income.

Similarly, when we observe households above the average income the APC of the sample will be lowered by those households which base their expenditure on a lower permanent income than their temporarily higher current incomes. In longitudinal data, however, all household income is aggregated to calculate the APC of each year in the sample. As those households with temporarily raised incomes will tend to cancel out those with temporarily lowered incomes, the APC is less effected by these temporary deviations of incomes from their more usual values. Equally, in the slow-down following a period of sustained growth, the level of permanent income might be expected to rise faster than it actually does. Thus the growth of consumption might outstrip the growth of current income, yielding an MPC in excess of one.

It is also the case that the proportion of income saved often rises in times of inflation. This might be because people act to restore the real value of assets for which nominal value increases more slowly than the rate of inflation.

Clearly, consumption might be affected by other variables than current disposable income alone. On the other hand, current income could be the main influence but the process of adjustment to changes is simply more complex than in the simple Keynesian consumption function.

3 What are the determinants of aggregate private investment and why is it likely to fluctuate?

In everyday parlance, investment refers to any current sacrifice made in order to gain benefits later. In economics the term investment refers to capital goods. Private fixed investment consists of private sector expenditure on new buildings, plant and machinery. Depreciation is deducted to calculate net investment. Changes in the level of stocks or inventories are usually categorised as investment.

In simple models investment is often represented as a stable function of the rate of interest. The argument is that if the return to money invested in capital is greater than the opportunity cost of the necessary finance then the capital project will be undertaken. The return from investing in capital can be compared with the interest rate by two methods: the 'net present value' (NPV) method and the 'internal rate of return' (IRR) method.

Both methods involve discounting the expected future flow of income (i.e. yearly benefit minus costs). NPV uses the interest rate to discount this flow, IRR involves calculating an 'artificial' rate of discount which produces a zero figure for the discounted flow and this rate of discount is then compared with the relevant market rate of interest. In both cases a reduction in interest rates will tend to increase the level of investment. With NPV this occurs because the later benefits are not so heavily discounted as before. In principle the NPV technique is superior but IRR is more widely used. Indeed, other less rigorous methods of investment appraisal are common and hence the level of investment can be influenced by the quality of entrepreneurs.

If one were to plot interest rates and the level of investment one would find little correlation. But one should not be surprised at this; capital projects have a long gestation period and therefore we should not expect immediate responses to changes in interest rates. But, more important, the relationship will be overlaid with many other influences. Hence econometric methods are needed to isolate individual relationships. Many econometric investigations find long-term interest rates to be a significant determinant of private investment but a great deal of the variability is explained by other factors.

Keynes emphasised 'animal spirits' as a cause of investment volatility. In an uncertain world the returns to investment can only be estimated. These estimates will be affected by expectations as to the future levels of demand, stocks, costs, competition and technology. Thus investment will tend to be higher in periods of optimism.

Samuelson developed the 'accelerator hypothesis' of investment. Firms are assumed to wish to maintain a constant ratio of capital stock to output. Hence investment will takes place when the actual K/Y ratio falls below the desired K/Y ratio. This is likely to occur when the level of demand increases. Thus the prediction is that investment is a function of *changes* in GDP. A similar principle can be applied to investment in stocks. In fact there is a correlation between changes in GDP and manufacturing investment. This does not prove causation, but there is evidence that the level of capital utilisation is an important determinant of investment.

The majority of investment is financed by retained profits. Hence current profitability is likely to be a major determinant of private investment. But again, correlations do not prove the direction of causation as profits will tend to be high when aggregate demand is stimulated by investment! The cost of the capital goods is likely to affect this relationship but will also affect the estimated return to investment. This will be offset if the new capital is expected to have a higher productivity than the old.

Technological change will cause investment as firms seek to match or improve upon the efficiency of their competitors. Firms will also invest when new markets are created by product innovations. Strategic motivations might lead to deliberate investment in over-capacity; a firm might build up spare capacity as a response to the threat of new firms entering the industry. This demonstrates commitment on the part of the incumbent firm and suggests to potential entrants that the post-entry price is likely to be substantially below the pre-entry price. Thus changes in the threat of competition can lead to changes in investment.

Clearly there are many determinants of the level of investment. Forecasting models have tended to include profits, interest rates and accelerator type influences as determinants. But there seems to be a wide margin of error in predicting future levels of investment. This may well be due to the difficulty of modelling expectations.

4 Examine the possible consequences of the fact that saving and investment decisions are made by separate groups of economic agents.

Saving involves the postponement of consumption, for example, the purchase of an interest bearing asset such as a bond or building society deposits. Investment, however, is the act of adding to the productive potential of the economy, for instance the adding to 'physical' capital such as the building of new industrial plant. It is case that much investment is financed directly from retained ('ploughed' back) profits which might be considered analagous to household saving. But, as Keynes pointed out, households and firms act for different reasons and thesefore the savings decision of the former may not correspond to the investment decisions of the latter.

In simple Keynesian models the major determinant of household saving (and hence consumption) is current (disposable) income. Investment is often assumed constant or determined by the interest rate and the marginal efficiency of capital (e.i. the internal rate of return to capital investment). Clearly, in such models a change in autonomous investment is not immediately matched by a corresponding change in savings of the same direction. Instead it is the level of income which adjusts withdrawals to match injections. This contrasts with 'Say's Law' and the 'Loanable Funds' theory which asserts that saving and investment are equilibrated through changes in the interest rate. In Say's model, which Keynes termed the 'classical' model, saving could only be for the purpose of investment. Thus Say assumed that

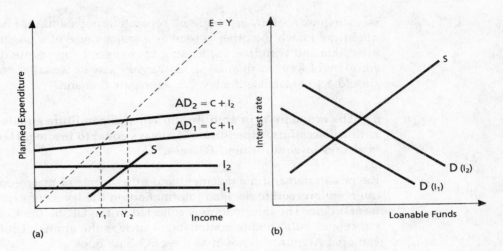

Fig. 9.7 (a) Keynesian adjustment process
(b) Classical adjustment process

saving and investment are equal at any level of income. A disparity between them could not occur to cause fluctuations in aggregate demand.

Keynes emphasised expectations and uncertainty as the reason for the volatility of private investment. He stressed that the perceived return to investment is greatly influenced by expectations. Thus, even if interest rates fell to very low levels, it could not induce businesspersons to invest if they believed they would not be able to sell the resulting product. Again, a sharp loss of business confidence could cause a decrease in investment; this would not necessarily be matched by a decrease in saving, nor an extension of investment as interest rates subsequently fell. Indeed, as the economy plunges into recession, saving could initially increase as households prepare for the future (Keynes' paradox of thrift). Moreover, businesspersons will further cut back investment in the light of falling sales.

In Keynesian models adjustments to fluctuations in aggregate demand take place via changes in quantities rather than prices. Thus a fall in aggregate demand results in a fall in sales causing businesspersons to cut back production rather than lower prices. Likewise workers are laid off rather than wages reduced. This process is seen by Keynesians as leading to a multiplier process: aggregate demand falls (perhaps because of a loss of confidence brought about by a stock market crash), leading to a loss of sales, production is cut back leading to a loss of employment, as employment and incomes fall consumption also falls, leading to a further loss of sales and so on. In this way, initial changes in injections and/or withdrawals are magnified in effect.

Clearly, Keynes' central message was that an unregulated capitalist economy could be subject to large fluctuations in aggregate demand. There would therefore be periods of depression (low output and high unemployment), and also periods of boom (high levels of economic activity and employment but also inflation and balance of trade deficits). The fact that saving and investment decisions are made by separate groups and that hence the one might not match the other is seen as a major cause of a possible disparity of injections and withdrawals, leading to changes in aggregate demand. The corollary of Keynesian analysis, as Keynes saw it, was that governments should act to stabilise the level of aggregate demand.

5 'The economy is in equilibrium when expenditure equals income. In the national accounts, expenditure is always equal to income. Hence the economy is always in equilibrium.' Discuss.

Keynesian demand management and other forms of macro-economic intervention require detailed information on the levels of expenditure, output, taxation etc. The information is collected in the UK by the Central Statistical Office and published in compilations such as the annual 'United Kingdom National Accounts' (known as the CSO Blue Book).

In compiling the statistics the following accounting identity is used:

[National Expenditure ≡ National Income ≡ National Product]

Identities hold by definition, hence for any time period the monetary value of spending *must* equal the amount received which *must* in turn equal the monetary value of what has been sold. Clearly, in terms of the actual (i.e. *ex post*) transactions which have been made, these three measures are simply different ways of looking at the same monetary transactions.

In terms of these *ex post* identities expenditure must always equal income. We can also use a Keynesian saving investment macro model to demonstrate that *ex post* savings must equal investment. Income arises from the sale of goods and services for consumption or for investment, hence the value of income in any time period must equal the value of consumption and investment, thus:

$$Y \equiv C + I$$

Income received is either spent or not spent, thus:

$$Y \equiv C + S$$

Thus: $\quad C + I \equiv C + S$

Therefore: $\quad I \equiv S$

As it is an imbalance between injections and withdrawals which causes changes in income in Keynesian models it would appear from the accounting identities that the economy can never be in disequilibrium!

The confusion is caused by failure to distinguish between planned (i.e. *ex ante*) behaviour and what actually results ex post. In the national income accounts expenditure and income are defined in a way which ensures they must equal each other, but there is no reason why planned expenditure should equal the income received from any year's output.

One way of ensuring that *ex ante* differences between saving and investment appear as *ex post* equalities is to include changes in the level of stocks as changes in investment:

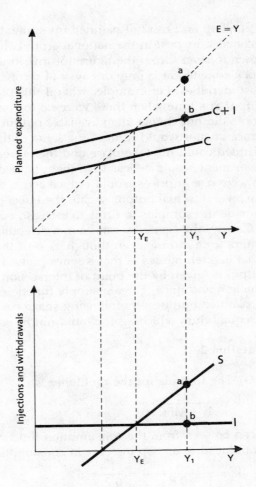

Fig. 9.8

In the diagram equilibrium income is at Y_E. At Y_E planned expenditure is equal to the value of output produced i.e. income. As can be seen from the lower part of the diagram this results from the fact that planned investment is equal to planned saving. At Y_1, however, planned expenditure falls short of the value of output by the amount ab; this is because planned saving exceeds investment by this amount. As planned injections differ from planned withdrawals this is clearly a disequilibrium situation. In terms of stock adjustment there will be an increase in stocks by the amount ab, i.e. by the amount by which output has exceeded expenditure or saving exceeded planned investment. If this unintended increase in stocks is included as investment then:

[Actual (*ex post*) I ≡ Planned (*ex ante*) I + Unplanned Investment ≡ S]

It would also be this failure to sell all that has been produced which causes firms to cut back production thereby reducing output and income in the direction of its eventual equilibrium at Y_E.

Similary an excess of planned investment over planned saving could be reconciled *ex post* in the national acounts by deducting an unintended run down in stocks from the figure for investment. But in this case it is clear that stock adjustment is only one way of reconciling *ex ante* differences with *ex post* identities. For example, what if this planned expenditure exceeded output at a time when there were no (or insufficient) stocks to run down? If prices did not change then available output would not meet demand and hence queues would form. Thus some of the consumption and investment planned could not take place and therefore actual consumption and investment would be less than that planned. More likely prices would adjust, hence a rise in prices would reduce actual consumption and investment to the level of actual output. Again the effect of queues or rising prices might provide the stimulus to firms to increase output to a higher equilibrium.

Clearly, the economy can be in a disequilibrium where planned expenditure differs from income even though *ex post* these must be identically equal. But what is often missed is that Keynes himself emphasised that the volume of output is 'given by the point of intersection between the aggregate demand function *and* the aggregate supply function' (my emphasis). Hence changes in planned output, e.g. following sharp cost increase, can also cause a disequilibrium which again would not be seen in *ex post* identities.

Suggested data response answers

Question 2

(a) The formula for the multiplier is

$$k = \frac{1}{1 - MPC}$$

It can be seen from the consumption function that a £1 increase in income would lead to an 80p increase in consumption. Hence MPC = 0.8. Thus

$$k = \frac{1}{1 - 0.8} = \frac{1}{0.2} = 5$$

The value of the multiplier is thus 5.

(b) At Y = 4000 the level of aggregate demand would be:

$$C + J = 100 + 0.8 \times 4000 + 200 = £3500$$

The value of the deflationary gap is thus £500.

(c) If government expenditure is increased by the value of the deflationary gap income will increase by

$$5 \times 500 = £2500$$

If this increase in income is to produce full employment then the present equilibrium level of income should be £1500. This can be checked by substituting for Y in the equilibrium condition of the model:

$$Y = C + J = 100 + 0.8Y + 200 = £1500$$

We have thus demonstrated that increasing government expenditure by the value of the deflationary gap will bring the level of income up to its full employment level.

Question 3

(a) The marginal propensity to consume (MPC) is the proportion of any addition to income that is spent on consumption. This definition is complicated in practice by taxes which cause a difference between income and disposable income and by consumption expenditure that is leaked from the circular flow, i.e. indirect tax and imports. These complications do not arise in the present case as additional income will be allocated in the same proportions as at present. Hence domestic consumption at factor cost will be a constant proportion of GNP. This also implies that MPC = APC. Thus the MPC in terms of income-induced consumption on domestic goods and services is:

$$MPC = \frac{\text{Domestic Consumption at Factor Cost}}{\text{Gross National Income}}$$

$$= \frac{165\ 600}{276\ 000} = 0.6$$

(b) The formula for the multiplier is

$$k = \frac{1}{1 - MPC}$$

Therefore, in our example, the value of the multiplier is 2.5.

(c) (i) The size of the multiplier will be determined by the magnitude of the withdrawals from the circular flow of income. In the above, the relevant factors are:
- The proportion of any addition to income that is allocated to savings i.e. the marginal propensity to save (s).
- The marginal rate of taxation (t).
- The proportion of any addition to income that is allocated to imports (m).

(ii) From the table, again noting the assumption that average equal marginal propensities:

$$s = \frac{\text{Retained profit} + \text{personal saving}}{\text{Gross national income}}$$

$$= \frac{18\ 000 + 20\ 000}{276\ 000} = 0.14\ \text{(approx)}$$

$$t = \frac{\text{Direct taxes} + \text{indirect taxes}}{\text{Gross national income}}$$

$$= \frac{24\ 000 + 40\ 300}{276\ 000} = 0.23\ \text{(approx)}$$

$$m = \frac{\text{Imports}}{\text{Gross national income}}$$

$$= \frac{8\ 100}{276\ 000} = 0.03 \text{ (approx)}$$

The multiplier can be calculated from the 'alternative' formula:

$$k = \frac{1}{w}$$

Where w is the marginal propensity to withdraw. As

$$w = s + t + m$$

we have

$$w = 0.14 + 0.23 + 0.03 = 0.4$$

Thus the multiplier is

$$k = \frac{1}{0.4} = 2.5$$

This demonstrates the equivalence of the two formulae for the multiplier.

(d) (i) From the definition of the multiplier the change in income will be 2.5 times the change in injections. In our example, the change in injections, is an increase in government expenditure of £100m. Therefore, under the condition stated, the increase in output will be:

$$k \times 100m = 2.5 \times £100m = £250m$$

(ii) The answer is no. Modifying factors must be taken into account. These include:

- Time lags i.e. the time taken for the multiplier to work through the various rounds of spending.
- The fact that different types of spending can have different multiplier effects as the MPCs of income recipients will vary.
- Fiscal drag e.g. the progressive nature of the tax system whereby any rise in income will tend to increase the proportion of income paid in tax.
- Long-term feedback effects through trade links with other countries.
- The possibility that at least part of the increased demand is absorbed in higher prices.
- The offsetting effect on investment expenditure and consumption of durables caused by interest rates increasing in the face of an increased transactions demand for money.

Question 5

(a) Inspection of the data reveals that: consumption in any period is equal to half the income (Y) of the previous year; investment (I) in any year is equal to autonomous investment plus twice the difference between the previous year's output and the output of the year before that. Continuing this pattern results in:

Year	Y (output)	C	I
9	1017.13	510.8	506.33
10	1000.63	508.57	492.06

(b) The pattern revealed in the data is that of a multiplier–accelerator process. In year 3 an increase in autonomous investment has caused income/output to rise. This in turn causes consumption in year 4 to rise according to MPC = APC = 0.5. But the increase in income/output between years 2 and 3 now causes induced investment in year 4. This investment is a function of the change in income. In the present example capitalists are attempting to maintain a ratio of 2 of induced capital to output minus 1000. In year 4 income/output rises by both the increase in consumption and induced investment. This is turn causes further increase in consumption and induced investment and thus income/output continues to rise.

Note, however, that the cycle peaks in year 8 even though the multiplier and the accelerator coefficient are still equal to 2. The reason is that the induced investment is a function of *changes* in output. Although income/output rises to year 8 the amount of increase is decreasing from year 6. Hence the level of induced investment begin to fall which subsequently causes income/output and thus consumption to fall. The process thus continues upon a downward path until the amount of decrease lessens and induced investment thus begins to increase again.

(c) The data demonstrate that it is possible to generate income/output cycles. The model thus appealed to some of the followers of Keynes who wished to develop theories of instability and thus reinforced Keynes' message that governments must act to stabilise the level of economic activity.

In practice it has been very difficult to find convincing evidence of such a process. This, however, is not surprising as in real life there are a myriad of other factors to consider. In the simple model above depreciation has been ignored; depreciation not only complicates the relationships but means allowance must be made for the actual composition of the capital stock. In practice the capital–output ratio is likely to be flexible according to changes in expectations and technology. Investment can take place for many reasons such as in response to innovations, a changed composition of aggregate demand or significant changes in interest rates. The degree of fluctuation is subject to the capacity constraints of the economy, for example output cannot rise above its full employment level. A real economy is also subject to many exogenous shocks, changes in the cost of imported raw materials, for instance, and the effects of the domestic policies of other nations impinging upon one's own economy.

It should also be noted that the time path produced by such models can vary according to changes in MPC and the accelerator coefficients. It is possible to produce time paths in which fluctuations quickly disappear or the level of output simply rises to a ceiling or falls to a floor. The model also ignores possible constraints on the fluctuations in investment and output. The demand for money and loanable funds will also tend to rise with increasing output. If the money supply is constant, increases in interest rates will tend to choke off further increases in investment and output.

Perhaps the most damning criticism of the model is that it seems to ignore the possibility that businesspersons will learn from experience. In practice they will tend to anticipate future stages of the cycle. Thus they are unlikely significantly to increase capacity on the strength of one year's orders. Conversely, if demand is dropping, they might be willing to increase their inventories against a rise in demand in subsequent years.

In conclusion, we do have reason to doubt that the multiplier–accelerator hypothesis is valid. Even if it does encapsulate part of the dynamics of the real world it cannot be considered as a comprehensive theory of fluctuations in economic activity. Nevertheless, when businesspersons do react to changes in demand by increasing investment this *will* have further repercussions throughout the economy. The model is thus a useful demonstration of how simple assumptions generate complex interrelationships and a reminder of the even greater complexity of the real world.

Answers to multiple-choice questions

1	C	11	D
2	C	12	A
3	B	13	D
4	B	14	C
5	D	15	B
6	C	16	C
7	D	17	A
8	E	18	B
9	B	19	E
10	A	20	B

10
Monetary theory and practice

Questions

Essay paper   Attempt all questions. Compare your answers with those provided.

1 'Money is like a myth; it requires only imagination for its creation but faith for its effectiveness.' Explain this statement making reference to the functions and various measures of money.

2 Discuss whether there is any limit on a private sector bank's ability to create credit.

3 Assess the ability of the Bank of England to control the money supply in the light of recent experience with monetary targets.

4 'Monetary policy has a more powerful influence on the economy than fiscal policy' Discuss.

5 (Answer provided.) 'Real things are determined by real things.' What is meant by this statement when monetarists use it to refer to the determination of the level of employment?

6 Examine the difficulties involved with the compilation and interpretation of the Index of Retail Prices (RPI).

7 (Answer provided.) Explain what is meant by financial intermediation and its benefits to borrowers and lenders. Illustrate your answer by reference to commercial banks and building societies in the UK, or another country with which you are familiar.

8 Assess the possible effects of increased government borrowing on the money supply and long-term interest rates.

9 (Answer provided.) What is meant by the terms 'the discount market' and 'the parallel money markets'? To what extent is it possible or meaningful to distinguish between the two?

10 (Answer provided.) Explain how the monetary authorities might seek to influence the quantity of money in the economy. Describe how the monetary authorities have gone about this task since 1979.

Data response paper

Question 1
The following twenty items contain all the information to construct the various measures of the money supply which came into operation in 1987. Rearrange the items to produce the correct presentations of MO, Nib M1, M2, M3, M3c, M4 and M5.

1   Building society holdings of bank deposits and bank certificates of deposit and notes and coin

2   M3c

3   Private sector holdings of sterling bank certificates of deposit

4   M2

5   UK private sector interest-bearing sight bank deposits.

6   M1

7   Private sector interest-bearing retail sterling bank deposits

8   Notes and coins in circulation with the public

9   Private sector holdings of building society shares and deposits and sterling certificates of deposit

10   Private sector holdings of foreign currency bank deposits

11   Holdings by the private sector (excluding building societies) of money-market instruments (bank bills, Treasury bills, local authority deposits) certificates of tax deposit and national savings instruments (excluding certificates, SAYE and other long term deposits)

12   M5

13   M3

14   Private sector holdings of retail building society shares and deposits and national savings bank ordinary accounts

15   Private sector sterling time bank deposits

16   Nib M1

17   M4

18   Bankers' operational deposits with the Bank of England

19   UK private sector non-interest bearing sight deposits

20   M0

Question 2 (Answer provided.)

The following information relates to the Index of Retail Prices (RPI). It gives the 14 categories of the RPI when the index was recast in January 1987. Column I gives the base values (i.e. 100), column II gives the index for each category in April 1988 and Column III gives the weights used in 1988.

	Column I Jan 13 1987	Column II April 18 1988	Column III Weight 1988
Food	100.0	104.4	163.0
Catering	100.0	108.5	50.0
Alcoholic drink	100.0	106.1	78.0
Tobacco	100.0	103.2	36.0
Housing	100.0	109.9	160.0
Fuel and light	100.0	99.1	55.0
Household goods	100.0	105.0	74.0
Household services	100.0	105.7	41.0
Clothing and footwear	100.0	103.1	72.0
Personal goods and services	100.0	106.0	37.0
Motoring expenditure	100.0	107.0	132.0
Fares and travel costs	100.0	105.8	23.0
Leisure goods	100.0	103.9	50.0
Leisure services	100.0	108.3	29.0

(a) From this information calculate the value of the RPI on April 18 1988. Demonstrate how you arrived at your answer.

(b) What difficulties are encountered in interpreting RPI figures.

(c) In 1988 Chancellor Lawson said that he thought that it would be better to take mortgage payments out of the index. Why did he say this? Do you agree with him? Explain your answer.

Question 3 (Answer provided.)

The information below gives all the figures which are necessary for the presentation of Cardinal Bank Plc's balance sheet. Cardinal is a recognised bank and is a member of the Clearing House. The distribution of its assets is in accordance with monetary-control provisions of 1981.

CARDINAL BANK Plc
[Recognised as a bank by the Bank of England]
Items in the balance sheet as at 1 April 1989

	£ millions
Advances	5747
Other bills*	241
Coins and notes	180
Money at call and short notice*	260
Certificates of deposit*	292
Loans to UK banks*	212
Investments	1575
Operational balances with the Bank of England*	225
UK Treasury bills*	130
Sight deposits	3969
Local authorities*	111
Time deposits	5051
Non-operational deposits with the Bank of England	47

(a) Present these figures as a balance sheet laid out in the conventional manner for a bank and determine the overall balance for Cardinal Plc.

(b) If the whole of the items marked * are regarded as liquid assets for control purposes, determine the liquidity ratio on which Cardinal is operating. Assume that all liabilities marked * are eligible liabilities.

(c) Outline the factors which determine the distribution of a bank's assets and liabilities.

(d) Examine the consequences of their being a significant decrease in the required liquidity ratio.

(e) To what extent does the balance sheet of Cardinal differ from those of a typical clearing bank?

Question 4 (Answer provided.)
The following information summarises all the transactions which take place in an economy in one period of time:

> 490 loaves sold at 70p each
> 10 pairs of shoes sold at £15 each
> 5 coats sold at £100 each
> 48 shirts sold at £20 each
> 75 train journeys at £2 each
> 297 pints of beer at £1 each

This economy has a money stock of £600.

(a) Under these circumstances determine the value of the velocity of circulation (V) and explain how you arrived at your answer.

(b) Explain what would happen if the money stock were to increase to £1000 but the number of transactions were to remain the same.

(c) What factors determine the velocity of circulation in a modern society?

Question 5
Study the following graph:

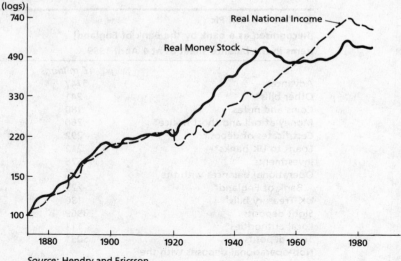

Source: Hendry and Ericsson

Fig. 10.1

Now answer the following questions:

(a) Interpret the information shown in the graph.

(b) To what extent is this information consistent with the monetarist theory of inflation?

Multiple-choice test

Answer all questions. Time allowed 30 minutes.

1 It would be difficult to use diamonds as money because they are:

A   not durable
B   unstable in conditions of supply
C   non-homogeneous
D   not easily portable
E   their supply is largely controlled by two countries.

2 With a reserve (or liquid asset) requirement of 20 per cent, additional deposits of £1 million in a commercial bank will allow *it* to make additional loans of:

A   £800 000
B   £1 000 000
C   £4 000 000
D   £5 000 000
E   £10 000 000

3 Which of the following is *not* a correct statement about 'money at call'? Money at call is:

A   an asset of the clearing banks
B   an interest bearing asset
C   usually lending to discount houses
D   highly liquid
E   money called for by the Bank of England

4 Which of the following best describes maturity transformation? The way in which:

A   a Treasury bill is automatically repaid (liquidates) after 91 days
B   the yield on a financial asset varies in relation to its term to maturity
C   the Bank of England converts short term gilts into longer term gilts
D   banks convert short term liabilities into longer term assets
E   building societies are now allowed to become PLCs

5 Which of the following would *not* result in an increase in the size of the M3 measure of the money stock? An increase in:

A   notes and coins in circulation
B   private sector non-interest bearing sterling sight deposits
C   private sector sterling time deposits
D   private sector building society sterling deposits
E   private sector holdings of sterling certificates of deposit

139

6 The Bank of England often sells gilt-edged securities through a firm of London stockbrokers. Which of the following functions of the Bank could this be an example of? Its function as:

A   lender of last resort
B   operator of monetary policy
C   issuer of notes
D   manager of the Exchange Equalisation Account
E   bankers' bank

7 Consider an undated government security which was sold in 1970 for £10 000 with a nominal interest rate of 5 per cent. The market price of this bond is now £4000. Under these circumstances we can conclude that the yield on this bond is:

A   5%
B   10%
C   12.5%
D   15%
E   £200

8 The graph marked Z in Fig. 10.2 shows a situation where there is an expectation that interest rates are likely to:

A   fall
B   rise
C   remain constant
D   remain constant for a while and then rise
E   impossible to determine

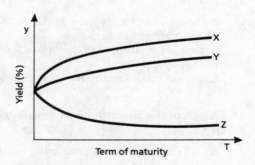

Fig. 10.2

9 Figure 10.3 demonstrates that:

A   the demand for money, i.e. erratic
B   wage earners have a smaller demand for money but bring about a higher velocity of circulation
C   wage earners have a greater demand for cash
D   salaried employees stimulate a higher velocity of circulation than wage earners
E   the demand for money is inversely proportionate to the rate of interest

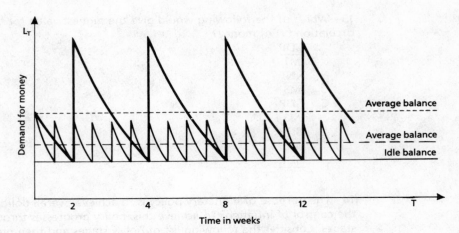

Fig. 10.3

10 An upward shift in the liquidity preference schedule is likely to cause a rise in the interest rate unless:

    A   there is an increase in the money supply
    B   the country is functioning below the level of full employment
    C   the Bank of England calls for Special Deposits
    D   the government runs a budget deficit
    E   there is an incomes policy in force

11 Keynes' liquidity preference theory of interest differed from the flow of funds explanation in that Keynes':

    A   did not accept the transactions demand for money
    B   maintained that the price of securities and the rate of interest were inversely related to one another
    C   suggested that people would never wish to hold money for its own sake
    D   believed that disequilibrium was possible between savings and borrowing
    E   suggested that the rate of interest was determined by the real net productivity of capital

12 In the portfolio balance theory, monetarists say that money is:

    A   a close substitute for a range of financial assets
    B   an alternative to holding all other assets be they financial or physical
    C   only the high powered money stock (H) of the economy
    D   left in idle balances when the interest rate is low
    E   anything readily acceptable in payment of a debt

13 Which of the following would give the highest value for the velocity of circulation (V) of money?

A $\dfrac{GDP}{M1}$

B $\dfrac{NNP}{M3}$

C $\dfrac{GDP}{M3}$

D $\dfrac{GDP}{M5}$

E $\dfrac{GDP}{M0}$

14 The purpose of monetary policy is to achieve overall policy objectives, such as the control of inflation. To achieve this, policy progresses through a number of stages. Consider the following list of policy stages and then place them in the correct order from start to finish.

1 Operating policy targets
2 Instruments (weapons) of policy
3 Actual effect on aggregate demand
4 Intermediate policy targets
5 Overall objective of policy

The correct order is:

A 1, 2, 4, 3, 5
B 2, 1, 4, 3, 5
C 2, 4, 3, 1, 5
D 3, 2, 1, 4, 5
E 1, 2, 3, 4, 5

15 If the Bank of England were to undertake open market sales of securities of £5 million this would immediately reduce the volume of commercial bank deposits with the Bank of England by £5 million. Supposing that the banking sector was working on a reserve requirement of 5 per cent, what then would be the maximum possible *additional* contraction in the money supply which could result from banks adjusting their assets and liabilities to maintain the ratio. Is it:

A £100 million
B £95 million
C £20 million
D £15 million
E £10 million

Questions 16–20
Directions. For each of the questions below, **one** or **more** of the responses given is (are) correct. Then choose

A if 1, 2 and 3 are correct
B if 1 and 2 only are correct
C if 2 and 3 only are correct
D if 1 only is correct
E if 3 only is correct

Directions summarised				
A	B	C	D	E
1, 2, 3	1, 2	2, 3	1	3
correct	only	only	only	only

16 Keynes put forward a theory of liquidity preference. In this he argued that the 'transactions demand' for money would be determined by the:

    1   level of consumers' income
    2   speculation on the future rate of interest
    3   price of bonds and other fixed income securities

17 Which of the following are included in the M_1 measure of the money stock:

    1   notes and coins in circulation with the public
    2   cheques
    3   sterling certificates of deposit held by the private sector

18 Which of the following measures are consistent with a contractionary monetary policy?

    1   increased sales of gilt edged securities
    2   a rise in short term interest rates
    3   conversion of short term government debt into long term government debt

19 An increase in which of the following is likely to cause an increase in the index of retail prices?

    1   a rise in the rate of VAT
    2   an increase in house prices
    3   raising the rate of income tax

20 The calculation of the TPI (Taxes and Prices Index) involves measuring the effects of which of the following?

    1   the level of retail prices
    2   rates of direct taxes
    3   social security benefits

Answers

5 'Real things are determined by real things.' What is meant by this
statement when monetarists use it to refer to the determination of the level
of employment?

Monetarists tend to believe in the notion of the neutrality of money, i.e.
although money facilitates the working of the economy it does not, in the
long run at least, affect anything 'real' in the economy. Real things refer to
such things as the level of output, investment, employment and relative
prices. In contrast to relative prices are nominal prices and the aggregate price
level. For example, if the nominal price of a cow is £100 and that of a pig £50
then the relative or 'real' price of a cow is two pigs. If all nominal prices were
to double real prices would remain unaltered. For example, if money wages
doubled and the prices of all goods and services also doubled then the real
wage would be unaltered, i.e. in terms of real goods and services the reward
to labour would be unaltered. A rational worker would thus not be affected
by this inflation in his decision of how many hours to work.

In neo-classical/monetarist theory, in the absence of government
interference, the level of employment is determined by the size of the
population, human nature, technology and the size of the capital stock
according to the mechanics of the marginal productivity theory of distribution.
For simplicity we shall assume that there is only one labour market, in
'reality' there are many inter-related markets each with its own equilibrium
real wage.

The real wage is measured by the money wage divided by some index of
the prices of goods and services, i.e.

$$\frac{\text{Money wage}}{\text{Prices}} = \frac{W}{P}$$

This is a measure of the actual purchasing power of the worker's wage. It is
this real amount rather than consideration of the money wage which induces
a worker to work.

The concept of price-taking is a major building block of monetarist theory.
The labour market is assumed to be perfectly competitive and hence for each
employer the wage that must be paid to attract workers is also the marginal
cost of employing labour. In short, the supply of labour to each employer is
perfectly elastic and hence employers are price takers. Equally, each worker
has no market power and is thus a price taker.

Under the above assumptions a supply curve for labour can be drawn as a
function of the real wage. We shall assume that this is upward sloping but it
is not important for the theory if income effects offset substitution effects
such as to cause a slightly backward bending aggregate supply curve. The
precise position of the supply curve is determined by the size and composition
of the population and human willingness to work. These are taken as given.

At any time the capital stock is assumed more or less fixed i.e. investment
is insignificant in relation to the existing capital stock. The 'law' of eventually

diminishing marginal returns thus implies a downward sloping marginal physical product (MPP) curve.

From elementary microeconomic theory we know that labour will be employed until the money wage is equal is equal to the marginal revenue product of labour. In perfectly competitive conditions this can be expressed mathematically as follows:

$$W = MPP \times P$$

But, by dividing through by P, this can be expressed in real terms:

$$\frac{W}{P} = MPP$$

Thus, in equilibrium two real variables are equated, i.e. the real wage and the MPP of labour (see Fig. 10.4).

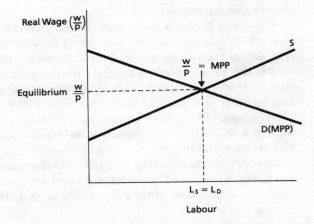

Fig. 10.4

In conclusion, the level of employment is determined by human choice in the face of the opportunities offered by the capital stock and existing technology.

7 Explain what is meant by financial intermediation and its benefits to borrowers and lenders . Illustrate your answer by reference to commercial banks and building societies in the UK, or another country with which you are familiar.

The everyday meaning of the word intermediary is that of a 'go-between.' This is a very important function of banks and building societies channelling funds from surplus units in the economy to deficit units, i.e. from borrowers to lenders. This we can summarise in diagrammatic form as in Fig. 10.5. However, it is important to realise that financial intermediaries are more

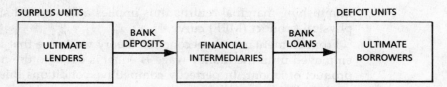

Fig. 10.5 **Financial intermediaries, such as banks, channel funds from surplus units in the economy to deficit units**

than go-betweens. They do act like employment agencies placing one lot of people in touch with another, but other more important functions are involved. This was summarised by the Wilson Committee in 1976 as follows:

'When a financial institution intermediates it not only passes funds from lenders to borrowers, it usually changes their terms and conditions. By aggregating small amounts of funds obtained from each of a large number of savers it is able to on-lend in larger packets, and often to transform *risk* and *maturity* characteristics.'

As well as the *go-between* function of financial intermediation, we now have two others namely *maturity transformation* and *risk transformation*. To illustrate this, let us take an example. People deposit money in their current accounts which the bank promises to repay on demand – it then lends the money to a customer for, say, three years. Maturity transformation has taken place. However, if you were to lend your money directly to a friend to buy a new car you would be taking a great risk. However, by taking many such risks and by knowledge of its business the bank greatly reduces the risk. This is risk transformation.

Maturity transformation and risk transformation are two of the main advantages bestowed on borrowers and lenders by financial intermediaries. There are, however, other advantages such as the transmission of money by banks.

Financial intermediaries need to be convenient and accessible so that we find a range of institutions with whom lenders can deposit funds at a suitable rate of return and for periods of time of the lender's choosing. On the other side of the equation financial intermediaries are also a convenient source of funds for borrowers. As explained above, borrowers are able to borrow in larger amounts and for longer periods than if they treated with the ultimate lender. The Wilson Committee, commenting on this, said that in reconciling the differing requirements of borrowers and lenders intermediaries also 'usually facilitate a higher level of saving and investment'. This is particularly well illustrated by the case of financial intermediaries such as insurance companies and pension funds where investors are enabled to diversify their investments in a way they would be unable to do so on their own.

Two of the main forms of financial intermediary in the UK are banks and building societies. We can learn more of the processes of financial intermediation by examining the ways in which they conduct their business.

The liabilities of building societies consist mainly of share accounts and deposits which are almost entirely from the private sector. Many of these funds are sight deposits and most of those which are not are withdrawable at short notice. The assets of building societies consist mainly of mortgages which are loans for periods up to 25 years. In 1988 about 75 per cent of the assets of building societies consisted of mortgages whilst only about 20 per cent were in near liquid or readily saleable forms such as gilts. By contrast on the other side of their balance sheet 85 per cent of their liabilities were in the form of share accounts and other deposits. Obviously, therefore, considerable maturity transformation takes place. Risk transformation also takes place as the building societies risk the non-repayment of mortgages. The building societies, of course, limit this risk by prudent lending policies such as limiting the size of mortgages to a multiple of consumers' incomes, insisting on the borrower providing at least 10 per cent of the purchase price and so on.

The assets and liabilities of the commercial banks also show maturity and risk transformation characteristics. In 1988 the clearing banks had sterling deposits of £160 billion, of which about 50 per cent consisted of sight deposits. In contrast only about £45 billion was in liquid assets which ranged from till money to short-dated gilts whilst the remainder was in advances and other longer term assets. Thus, since most sterling deposits are withdrawable on demand or very short notice but advances and mortgages are likely to be for considerable periods of time the maturity transformation is readily apparent.

The banks also have much non-sterling business where we would also see risk and maturity transformation in these assets and liabilities as well. In Eurocurrency markets, however, maturity transformation is noticeably less.

Banks like building societies seek to minimise their risks by vetting loans and by taking security such as mortgages over property. We can summarise the business of maturity transformation by saying that banks and building societies borrow short and lend long. As far as risk transformation is concerned we see the perennial clash between prudence and profitability. By this we mean that the bank must exercise prudence to ensure that it always has adequate liquidity but lend for long enough to gain a high enough interest rate to satisfy its shareholders.

9 What is meant by the terms 'the discount market' and 'the parallel money markets? To what extent is it possible or meaningful to distinguish between the two?

The discount or classical money market refers to the institutions and arrangements which exist between the discount houses (and certain recognised money brokers), the money trading departments of the clearing banks and the Bank of England for the discounting of Treasury bills and commercial bills of exchange. The parallel markets such as the local authority market developed initially out of the inadequacy of the discount market to serve the needs of banks, local authorities, commercial companies and others.

The function of the discount market is to buy and sell bills of exchange. By purchasing commercial bills of exchange the discount market provides short term finance to industry. This is done by buying the bills at a discount. This **147** is the way in which the interest is formed on the bills and from which the market gets its name. The discount market also finances the government's short-term debt by agreeing to purchase all the Treasury bills issued by the Bank of England on behalf of the government. In order to finance these operations the discount houses borrow money at *call* and *short notice* from the clearing banks.

The parallel markets are the other money markets, apart from the discount market and the foreign exchange market. The institutions involved are often the same the difference lies in the type of business conducted. The first parallel market was the *local authorities market* which began in the 1950s out of the need of local authorities to borrow for short periods of time. The *inter-bank market* is the short term borrowing and lending between banks for periods between one day and three months. The *certificates of deposit (CD) market* is concerned with the buying and selling of CDs and originated in the 1960s with the issue of dollar CDs. CDs are now issued in many currencies. The *finance houses* market is concerned with short term borrowing by the finance houses (hire purchase companies). The *inter-companies market* is concerned with the direct borrowing and lending of funds to each other. It thus presents an interesting example of disintermediation. The *eurocurrency market* is concerned with short term borrowing and lending in eurocurrencies, notably the dollar.

The traditional view of the discount market is that it provided a way by which fluctuations in government expenditure and receipts could be evened out. This was done by the sale and purchase of Treasury bills. It also provided a mechanism whereby indebtedness between the clearing banks and the government could be settled. It was also the mechanism through which the Bank of England acted as lender of last resort by re-discounting bills of exchange and undertook open market operations both to influence interest rates and the volume of money. It was, after all, the Bank's setting of re-discount rate on first class bills which set interest rates for the banking system. The discount market was also the way in which inter-bank liquidity was adjusted and liquidity assured. Banks lent money to discount houses at call or short notice. The discount houses in turn on-lent this money by purchasing bills of exchange for periods up to 91 days but the bank was able to get its money back more or less on demand. If a bank was forced to call in its loan from a discount house the most likely reason for this was its indebtedness to another clearer. Under these circumstances the discount house simply moved its borrowing to the creditor bank and thus liquidity in the system adjusted. In the event of a general lack of liquidity the discount houses would be forced to borrow from the Bank of England paying its penal interest rate. For these reasons it was the practice to regard the discount (or classical) money market as a distinct entity. However, the rise of the parallel markets has called this separate identity into question. Today we might, for a number of reasons, regard the markets as unified.

All the money markets deal in short term borrowing and lending (periods up to three months). The activities of the discount houses also blur the distinction between the markets because they are active in several of the parallel markets, for example, dealings in the local authority market. Since the discount houses borrow unsecured from the clearing banks and lend to other institutions in the monetary sector they can be said to be involved in the inter-bank market. The discount houses also buy and sell CDs in large quantities. The blurring of distinctions between the market is further advanced by the activities of the banks. Similarly the banks no longer have to rely on the discount houses to ensure their short term liquidity because they can borrow on the inter-bank market. The banks are also active in the discount market because they deposit secured and unsecured money with the discount houses and they buy and sell bills. At the same time they are also active in the parallel market such as the CD market. For these reasons the discount and parallel markets may be regarded as similar.

On the other hand, significant differences do exist. These distinctions are largely based on the borrowers involved and on the purposes of borrowing rather than on the lenders. First, the discount market remains the only market in which bills of exchange are bought and sold. The major borrowers in this market are commercial organisations wishing to sell (discount) commercial (or trade) bills. Second, the government still uses the discount market to borrow short-term by selling Treasury bills. Third, the discount market is, as we saw above, important in the operation of government policy. Open market operations are responsible for the setting of short term interest rates. Fourth, the Bank of England's lender of last resort function is also operated through the discount market. This not only involves the Bank underpinning institutions in trouble but on a day-to-day basis the Bank ensures that there is always enough liquidity in the banking system through the sale and re-purchase of Treasury and commercial bills of exchange. For these reasons it is still useful to distinguish the discount market from the parallel market.

10 Explain how the monetary authorities might seek to influence the quantity of money in the economy. Describe how the monetary authorities have gone about this task since 1979.

Monetary policy may be said to be the direction of the economy through the supply of and price of money, i.e. through control of the money supply and interest rates. Since 1979 in the UK and other western economies there has been great emphasis on control of various measures of the money supply such as M3. In the first part of this answer we will consider the broad range of instrument (weapons) of policy available to the monetary authorities. In the second part we will consider how this policy was pursued in the UK in the 1980s.

Part 1 Since all measures of the money supply, except M0, consist mainly of the liabilities (deposits) of the banks we can say that action to control the money supply is, essentially, action to control the size of banks' balance sheets. The monetary authorities usually impose some *cash or reserve assets ratio* on banks, requiring them to maintain a minimum proportion of their assets in cash or liquid form. An increase in the size of the ratio would bring **149** about a multiple contraction in bank deposits by decreasing the size of the credit creation multiplier. For example, if banks were working on a ratio of five per cent, then each £1 of liquid assets would guarantee £20 of liabilities. If the ratio were raised to 10 per cent then £1 of liquid assets would be needed for each £10 of deposits, thus raising the ratio contracts banks' ability to lend. Conversely lowering the rate increases their ability to lend.

In practice the monetary authorities change the ratio only occasionally. In the UK ratio was lowered from 28 per cent to 12½ per cent in 1971 and in 1981 was abolished. This does not mean that no ratios exist, rather that the Bank of England demands a ratio which is appropriate to each individual bank. Although the monetary authorities are unlikely to move liquid asset ratios around as an instrument of policy other instruments of policy work upon the existing ratio. For example, the Bank of England can call for *special deposits*, whereby banks are required to make additional deposits at the Bank which may not be classed as liquid assets. In effect, a call for special deposits is like a temporary raising of the liquid assets ratio, in which case a direct control is placed on credit growth and the money supply.

Central banks have the power to issue *special directives* to the banks on their lending, for example a recent Bank of England directive that mortgages should only be made for the purposes of house purchase or improvement (rather than realising equity to buy a new car or a chateau in France). The Bank of England has ceased to issue directives on the quantity of bank lending. Central banks can exert *moral suasion* on the banks to restrict their lending. The government could also exert direct pressure on credit lending by placing greater restrictions on hire purchase or credit instalment agreements.

The measures we have considered so far may be referred to as *portfolio constraints*. They are aimed in a direct way at the banks' portfolio of assets and in particular at the balance between advances, investments and liquid assets.

Let us now turn to the price of money – *interest rates*. There is thought to be a connection between the level of interest rates and the volume of borrowing and thereby the growth of the money supply. It should be said that the linkage is by no means clear or immediate. If rates are made sufficiently high they must eventually affect the ability to borrow. However, in 'normal' ranges it is very difficult to demonstrate any simple linkage.

The monetary authorities have techniques to control the rates of interest, especially short-term rates. The techniques which the Bank of England uses are *open market operations* and exercise of its function as lender of last resort.

Open market sales should have the effect of increasing the rate of interest as increased sales depress the price of securities and, therefore, put up the rate of interest. Open market sales also affect the volume of money directly as they act upon the banks' liquidity ratios in a similar way to special deposits. However, the efficacy of open market sales is affected by who buys the securities sold and how near the banks are to their required liquidity ratios. If securities are sold to the banks then they are not as effective as if the sales are to the general public. This is because the banks are able to use the securities as liquid assets thus leaving their ratios largely unaffected. For maximum effect it is necessary that the securities be purchased by the general public. Also if the banks are operating well above their liquidity ratios it would be necessary for open market sales to be immense before there would be any multiple effect upon banks' lending. Open market purchases have the reverse effect to sales.

The central bank is able to to set short term interest rates because it is lender of last resort. Banks and discount houses will not let their interest rates drop far below the central bank's prime rate in case they are forced to borrow from the central bank when they would then lose money. There would obviously be no point in banks operating above the central bank's rate. If banks do let the rate drop below that desired by the central bank it can make its rate effective by indulging in open market sales until the banks and discount houses are forced to borrow from it.

There is a link between the PSBR and the growth in the money supply. If the PSBR is financed by government borrowing from the banks, there is likely to be an increase in the money supply because the banks are able to use the securities as assets to lend against. If the government wishes to control the money supply it is, therefore, necessary either to reduce the size of the PSBR and/or finance the PSBR by borrowing from the non-bank private sector.

Part 11. Let us now turn to recent British experience of attempts to control the money supply. At the beginning of the 1980s, the UK monetary authorities abandoned portfolio constraints as ineffective. The government believed that the banks found ways to get round them. This was well illustrated when the 'corset' was abolished in 1979 and there was an immediate surge in £M3 as assets 'came out of hiding'. The 1981 Monetary Control-Provisions, however still specifically retain the right to call for special deposits. The Bank of England has statutory duties (the Banking Act 1979 and the Banking Act 1987) to police the monetary sector and ensure that banks maintain adequate liquidity. However, we may now regard this duty as independent of efforts to control the money supply.

The 1980s saw a change towards using interest rates as the method of controlling the money supply and also as the preferred anti-inflationary measure. As explained above there is no clear or immediate connection between short-term interest rates and the growth of the money supply. However, the government believed they might be effective because the Bank of England can exert a powerful influence on short-term interest rates whereas it believed the banks might evade other weapons of policy. There were few occasions when the Bank operated as lender of last resort by lending through the 'discount window'.

In the UK when the Bank of England lends, it does so by purchasing (discounting) first class bills of exchange from the discount houses. Discount houses are a unique feature of the UK system. The Bank can lend (rediscount) at interest rates of its own choosing but its rates must show market realism. Because the discount houses were only occasionally 'forced into the Bank' it was through open market operation that the Bank's interest rates were made effective.

Great attention was also paid to the PSBR. This was done both by restricting the size of the PSBR and by overfunding. The government at first aimed at reducing the size of the PSBR as a percentage of GDP and later reducing it in money terms. In this, at least, the government was successful so that by 1988 it was possible to speak of Public Sector Debt Repayment rather than PSBR. Overfunding is the practice of borrowing more from the non-bank private sector than is actually necessary to finance the PSBR. Overfunding reduces the size of M3. Overfunding was abandoned in 1985 because it was recognised that efforts to control the broad money supply were not as critical as had been thought. Continued efforts to control the PSBR were more to do with the government's desire to reduce its role in the economy than its desire to control the money supply.

If the monetary authorities are judged by their achieving the targets in control of the money supply which they set themselves then it must be said that they failed. Targets for M1 and M3 were continuously overshot. By 1988 the government had abandoned all targets for money supply except that for the broad monetary base MO. This was the only aggregate which seemed to behave itself. However, once its control became an object of policy it too proved to be unruly. Perhaps this is an illustration of Goodhart's Law that 'any statistical regularity will tend to collapse once pressure is put on it for control purposes'.

By the late 1980s the government was relying on interest rates to achieve nearly all its objectives of policy. By 1989 short-term rates had been so high for so long that long term rates such as mortgage rate inevitably followed. The government reasoned that this would take money out of people's pockets thus leaving them less to spend so that the expansion of credit would be controlled. It was also relying on this instrument to redress the current account deficit and to restrain inflation. It was great deal for one instrument to achieve.

Suggested data response answers

Question 2

(a) The index for April 18 1988 is arrived at by taking the value for each of the 14 categories in April and multiplying it by its respective weight (column 11 × column 111). The weights are derived at from the Family Expenditure Survey. These values are then totalled and divided by the sum of the weights. This is illustrated below and in the table on page 153.

$$\frac{105809.7}{1000} = 105.8$$

Thus the value of the RPI on April 18 1988 was 105.8, i.e. prices were 5.8 per cent higher than when the index was created in January 1987.

(b) There are of course many problems associated with compiling an index of prices but even when these have been dealt with there remain the problems of interpretation. These we may summarise as follows:

	Column I Jan 13 1987	Column II April 11 1988	Column III Weight 1988	Column II × Column III
Food	100.0	104.4	163.0	17017.2
Catering	100.0	108.5	50.0	5425.0
Alcoholic drink	100.0	106.1	78.0	8275.8
Tobacco	100.0	103.2	36.0	3715.2
Housing	100.0	109.9	160.0	17584.0
Fuel and light	100.0	99.1	55.0	5450.5
Household goods	100.0	105.0	74.0	7770.0
Household services	100.0	105.7	41.0	4333.7
Clothing and footwear	100.0	103.1	72.0	7423.2
Personal goods and services	100.0	106.0	37.0	3922.0
Motoring expenditure	100.0	107.0	132.0	14124.0
Fares and travel costs	100.0	105.8	23.0	2433.4
Leisure goods	100.0	103.9	50.0	5195.0
Leisure services	100.0	108.3	29.0	3140.7
			1000.0	105809.7

(*i*) It is difficult to compare price changes accurately over more than short periods of time, say up to five years, because the weighting of the index changes so much. The change of the index in 1987 illustrates this problem. Comparisons of prices over many years, for example, today with 1900 are all but meaningless.

(*ii*) Very high rates of inflation make the index numbers themselves difficult for the average citizen to understand. For this reason we tend to use year-on-year percentage rates calculated from the index.

(*iii*) The index cannot reflect changes in the quality of goods, only changes in prices.

(*iv*) Peoples' cost of living is influenced by government actions, some of which affect the index and some of which do not. For example, changes in the rate of VAT will affect the index but changes in income tax will not. Similar problems are encountered with subsidies and benefits. It was for this reason that the government introduced the Taxes and Prices Index (TPI) in in 1979.

(*v*) Although the index may give a good guide to how prices have changed for the mass of the population it may be less accurate for those whose incomes or expenditure patterns are greatly different from the average. Examples of such groups of people are the very rich, the very poor and those with large families.

(c) Mortgage payments are included in the RPI but the price of houses is not, nor is there an imputed charge for the occupation of owner-occupied houses. Rents on the other hand are included in the index. The Chancellor argued that mortgage payments should be excluded because rises in these are more the result of government monetary policy than a reflection of inflationary pressures. He also pointed out that in many comparable economies, France for example, mortgage payments are not included in the index. The Chancellor was stung into this line of argument because as a result of his need to restrain the economy he raised interest rates the result of which was an immediate increase in the RPI. The house purchaser is also becoming the owner of a rapidly appreciating asset thus, for example, the housebuyer may pay out £3000 a year in mortgage payments but finish the year with an asset which is worth £10 000 more than it was at the beginning of the year. It would also be possible to argue that increases in mortgage payments only affected a minority of the population because many people own their houses without the need for mortgage.

Comparisons with our neighbours such as France are especially difficult in the area of house prices because the majority of people in that country live in rented accommodation, which does show up in the index, whereas in the UK the majority of people live in owner-occupied houses the price of which does not. To exclude the cost of housing from the index would be to exclude a major component of the cost of living. We can see from the weights used in the index that housing was the second most significant form of household expenditure (16 per cent in 1988). Thus some method of including the cost of buying a house should be included in the index. A house buyer with a mortgage of £30 000 (the average in 1988) who found payments £150 a month higher as a result of interest rate rises in 1988 would hardly like to be told that the cost of living was not really increasing. The fact the the Chancellor advanced this argument as a temporary political expedient can be gauged from the fact that it was only one year after a major re-weighting of the index when the argument on mortgages had been examined by the CSO and rejected. Perhaps the Chancellor would not have been so keen on this line of argument if interest rates were falling.

Question 3

(a)

CARDINAL BANK Plc
Balance sheet as at 1 April 1989

	£ millions
Liabilities:	
Sight deposits	3969
Time deposits	5051
Total Liabilities	9020
Assets:	
Cash and balances with the Bank of England:	
Coins and notes	180
Operational balances with the Bank of England*	225
Non-operational deposits with the Bank of England	47

Market loans:	
Money at call and short notice*	260
Loans to UK banks*	212
Certificates of deposit*	292
Local authorities*	111
Bills:	
UK Treasury bills*	130
Other bills*	241
Investments	1575
Advances	5747
Total assets	9020

(b) Operational balances with the	
Bank of England*	225
Money at call and short notice*	260
Loans to UK banks*	212
Certificates of deposit*	292
Local authorities*	111
UK Treasury bills*	130
Other bills*	241
Total of liquid assets	1426
Eligibility liabilities	9020

The liquidity ratio is the ratio of liquid assets to eligible liabilities. Thus, in the case of Cardinal it is 15.8 per cent.

(c) For a bank the distribution of its assets is a matter of reconciling prudence with profitability. That is to say the bank must act prudently to ensure that it always has sufficient liquidity to meet calls for withdrawals by its depositors, while at the same time lending out enough money to earn profits to satisfy its shareholders. Depositors like to be able to withdraw their deposits more or less on demand. On the other hand, the bank can only make profits by lending out the money for periods of time which in some cases may be as long as 25 years.

The banks reconcile this conflict by the structure of the assets in their balance sheet. They keep cash in hand (till money) and deposits at the Bank of England to meet immediate demands for cash by customers and other banks. They then keep a percentage of their assets in highly liquid form such as money lent to the discount houses. These assets can rapidly be turned to cash if required but they bear a relatively low rate of interest. The banks then have money in gilt-edged and similar securities which are is referred to in the balance sheet as investments. The remainder of their assets are overdrafts and loans to customers which are shown in the balance sheet as advances.

The ratios of these various items are very important and are arrived at both through the banks' own experience and through the action of the monetary authorities imposing ratios on them. At the moment there is no one specified ratio for all. The Bank of England judges the liquidity of each bank according to the type of business it is doing. The failure of Johnson Matthey Bankers in 1984 shows that it still possible for both banks and the Bank of England to make mistakes.

(d) If the required liquidity ratio were to be decreased significantly the result would be a large increase in the ability of the banking system to lend. This was illustrated in 1971 when the 12½ per cent reserve assets ratio replaced the 28 per cent liquid assets ratio.

The required ratio determines the size of the bank multiplier. Thus before 1971 the multiplier governing the amount of deposits in the system was as follows:

$$D = \frac{1}{0.28} \times \text{the amount of liquid assets}$$

Whereas after the change it was as follows:

$$D = \frac{1}{0.125} \times \text{the amount of liquid assets}$$

Suppose that the amount of liquid assets in the banking system were £10 000. Then before the change the size of the banks' balance sheet could not exceed £35 714 but after the change it could be as great as £80 000. Small wonder that this massive increase in the money stock was followed by the high rates of inflation of the mid-1970s.

(e) The principle difference is that Cardinal's business is entirely in sterling whereas all the clearing banks in the UK do substantial foreign currency business. Also its liquidity ratio is high compared with that of most British banks. However, in the layout and distribution of its assets it is essentially similar to other banks.

Question 4

(a) In order to determine the velocity of circulation we need to apply the quantity formula of $MV = PT$.

The value of M is given in the question as £600. By totalling the number of transactions in the left hand column we arrive at a value of 1000 for T. The total value of these transactions is £2400 which gives P the general price level (£2400 ÷ 1000) of £2.40. These values are given below:

490 loaves sold at 70p each	£343
10 pairs of shoes sold at £15 each	150
5 coats sold at £100 each	500
48 shirts sold at £20 each	960
75 train journeys at £2 each	150
297 pints of beer at £1 each	297
1000	£2400

Rearranging the formula we obtain:

$$V = \frac{P \times T}{M}$$

This gives:

$$V = \frac{£2.40 \times 1000}{£600}$$

Therefore:

$$V = 4$$

(b) If the money stock were to increase to £1000 and the number of transactions remain constant it would be impossible to determine an exact answer unless we also know what happens to the value of V. To get round this difficulty let us, first of all, assume that V is also constant. Using the MV = PT formula we would obtain the following:

$$£1000 \times 4 = P \times 1000.$$

From this it is obvious that in order to balance the equation P (the general price level) must rise to £4, i.e. we experience inflation in exact proportion to the change in size of the money stock.

Here we are dealing with one of the fundamental monetarist propositions that increases in the money stock must cause inflation. This is based on the contention that V is constant or at least stable and predictable. It is also argued by monetarists that the T is constant, i.e. that the economy tends towards a full employment equilibrium in the absence of government intervention.

If we drop the assumption that V is constant then the answer becomes indeterminable. The Radcliffe report of 1959 held that changes in V were as likely to offset changes in M as they were to complement or augment it. This rather extreme conclusion is now rejected by most economists.

Over the past decade they have been changes in V. The Vs calculated from M1 and M3 have steadily declined whilst the V calculated from M0 has increased significantly. Thus the extreme monetarist proposition is flawed. However, there are not dramatic month-to-month changes so that there is a short term stability to the value of V.

If we also drop the assumption that T is constant we then become involved in arguments on the whole nature of the macroeconomy.

(c) The velocity of circulation is determined by the pattern expenditure and incomes in a society. It depends upon factors such as how people are paid – what proportion are paid weekly and what proportion are paid monthly and so on. A higher proportion of weekly payments means a smaller demand for money but a higher velocity of circulation. It also depends upon the proportion being paid in cash and the proportion being paid by credit transfer. Velocity also depends on people's patterns of expenditure, i.e.

whether they pay their bills weekly, monthly or annually. It is also influenced by the proportion of people having bank accounts because this influences the way in which they are paid and the way in which they spend.

As mentioned above monetarists support the view that V is constant, or at least stable and predictable. This, it is said, is because the pattern of payments and receipts is stable. This indeed is true but also as mentioned above there have been significant changes in the various measures of V. It only takes a relatively minor change in V to have rather massive effects on the size of money national income.

Answers to multiple-choice questions

1	C	11	D
2	A	12	B
3	E	13	E
4	D	14	B
5	D	15	B
6	B	16	D
7	C	17	D
8	A	18	A
9	B	19	D
10	A	20	A.

11
International economics

Attempt all questions. Compare your answers with those provided.

Essay paper

1 (Answer provided.) J S Mill said that the benefits of international trade are a more efficient employment of the productive forces of the world. Explain what are the benefits of international trade and who receives them.

2 To what extent can the creation of the single Eurpean market in 1992 be said to be a victory for the principles of free trade?

3 (Answer provided.) Explain how a nation might seek to rectify a deficit on the acount of its balance of payments.

4 (Answer provided.) To what extent can the balance of payments be controlled by manipulation of interest rates?

5 Examine the the view that rapid changes in the exchange rate are damaging to the UK economy.

6 To what extent have international economic organisations played a role in improving the economies of developing countries?

7 What is meant by the purchasing power parity theory of exchange rates? To what extent does this theory provide a satisfactory explanation of the pattern of exchange rates?

8 (Answer provided.) What is meant by the problem of international liquidity and how does the IMF help to overcome it?

9 How did the problem of Third World debt arise and what are its implications for the future development of the world economy?

Data response paper

Question 1 (Answer provided.)

The following information contains all the figures that are needed to calculate a summary balance of payments statement for country X.

	$ million
Services	+2 435
Exports (fob)	55 565
Net increase in external assets	30 831
Transfers	−1 809
Net increases in external liabilities	28 569
Interest profits and dividends (net)	+1 078
Imports (fob)	53 234

(a) From this information prepare country X's balance of payments statement to show:

(i) Visible balance

(ii) Invisible balance

(iii) Balance of current account

(iv) Transactions in external assets and liabilities

(v) Balancing item

(b) Do these figures suggest that country X is a developed or a less developed nation? Give reasons for your answer.

Question 2 (Answer provided.)

Read the following article which is taken from *The Observer* of 27 November 1988.

Trade Deficit Poised to Hit £16 Billion
William Keegan *Economics Editor*

The government now expects the balance of payments deficit for this year to reach £16 billion, compared with the official Treasury forecast of £13 billion unveiled less than a month ago.

The shock decision to raise interest rate to 13 per cent was taken because Government advisers decided that they would lose credibility if they announced the record £2.4 billion balance of payments deficit for October and insisted that the the economic strategy was still on course for the year.

Both the Treasury and Bank of England want to keep the pound high to counter inflationary pressures.

The recent speech by Robin Leigh-Pemberton, Governor of the Bank of England, was fully approved by Chancellor Nigel Lawson, who appears to have shifted significantly from his position earlier in the year, when he wished to hold the pound down against the Deutschmark and join the European Monetary System.

It is understood that a full autumn Budget to raise taxes was briefly considered by the Treasury at an official level, but ruled out because it was not politically acceptable to the Chancellor.

Economic policy now is to keep interest rates and the pound high in order to hold down inflation.

But with another increase in mortgage rates on the cards, the Government runs the risk of making inflationary expectations worse, not better, with the prospect of a raise to 8 per cent in the annual figure for the Retails Prices Index early next year. This is bound to affect bargaining position in the next round of wage negotiations.

One City analyst commented yesterday: 'In order to control the price level, they are raising the rate of inflation.'

A new analysis by former Treasury official Simon Briscoe, senior financial economist at Greenwell Montagu Gilt-Edged, questions the Chancellor's forecast that the balance of payments will improve in 1989, and states that 'the Government's policy of maintaining high interest rates and high sterling exchange rates for the foreseeable future is damaging the trade position'.

It says that the Confederation of British Industry data shows that it is not just excess dema in the UK that is limiting export orders. 'By far the most common reason given by companies of all sizes and types is lack of price competitiveness.'

Briscoe also takes issue with the view that machinery imports presage an investment boom. 'Very rapid import growth has been associated with the car industry', he says. 'But we do not consider this to be investment, even if many cars are being bought by companies.'

(a) Explain fully the reasons why the Chancellor raised the interest rate. Outline the mechanism by which the increased interest rate is supposed to alleviate the situation.

(b) What is the European Monetary System (EMS)? By what methods other than joining the EMS might the UK seek to stabilise the exchange rate of the pound?

(c) What alternative policies (other than interest rates) did the UK government pursue in order to attempt to produce a satisfactory balance of payments?

Question 3 (Answer provided.)

The Table below gives an example of comparative costs. In this example there are only two countries (Britain and Australia) and only two commodities (food and clothing). The upper part of the Table shows the situation before any trade takes place. The lower part of the Table shows the situation after complete specialisation has taken place. It assumes an international trading ratio of 10:6 and assumes figures for the amounts of exports and imports. There are no other countries or commodities involved in the example.

BRITAIN AND AUSTRALIA.
SPECIALISATION AND TRADE (All figures in million units)

Area Compared	Exchange ratio of food for clothing Pc/Pf	Food production	Food consumption	Food exports (+) or imports (−)	Clothing production	Clothing consumption	Clothing exports (+) or imports (−)
SITUATION BEFORE TRADE.							
Australia	10.3	30	30	0	21	21	0
Britain	10.8	50	50	0	80	80	0
World	None	80	80	0	101	101	0
SITUATION AFTER SPECIALISATION AND TRADE.							
Australia	10.6	100	40	+60			
Britain	10.6	0	60	−60	120		
World	10.6	100	100	0			

(a) Based on the assumptions stated you are asked to complete the Table.

(b) Construct a production frontier (production possibility curve) diagram to illustrate how specialisation and trade has benefited Britain.

(c) (i) Considering the modern British economy (i.e. not the hypothetical one in the example), state one product in which you think Britain has a comparative advantage and give your reasons for this.

161

(ii) Similarly state a product in which you think Britain has no comparative disadvantage and give your reasons for this.

(d) Comparative advantage may change from time to time. Give examples of three industries in which Britain's comparative advantage has declined or disappeared since the 1939–45 war.

(e) Suggest reasons why one country may wish to trade with another even there is no comparative advantage involved.

Question 4

Study the figures contained in the Table below which present information of the foreign indebtedness of selected nations.

The World Debt League

	Country	Popu-lation (millions) 1985	GDP/ head ($) 1985	Debt in $ billion 1982	1987	Debt/Exports ratio 1982	1987	Discount at which debt is sold cents in the $ 1988
1.	Mexico	80.0	1973	88	103	3.1	3.7	56
2.	Nicaragua	3.3	770	3	7	7.0	21.0	98
3.	Bolivia	6.4	470	3	6	3.6	9.0	90
4.	Argentina	30.5	2767	43	59	4.3	6.1	79
5.	Brazil	135.6	1640	92	117	3.9	3.2	57
6.	Poland	37.2	2050	25	42	1.8	3.1	66
7.	Yugoslavia	23.1	2070	20	24	1.0	1.5	54
8.	Nigeria	99.7	800	13	30	1.0	4.4	78
9.	Sudan	21.9	300	7	11	7.0	16.0	98
10.	Zaire	30.6	170	5	9	2.8	4.5	80
11.	South Korea	41.1	2150	37	40	1.3	0.7	–
12.	Singapore	2.6	7420	3	4	0.09	0.1	–
13.	Philippines	54.7	300	24	30	2.9	3.2	51
14.	Indonesia	162.2	530	26	55	1.2	2.7	N/A

Sources: World Bank; Amex Bank; Salomon Bros; Rodger and Huhne.

(a) Which of the countries in the Table are likely to find their overseas debts most onerous and why?

(b) Explain the term 'Debt/Exports ratio'.

(c) The last column of the Table shows the discount at which some of the international debt has been sold. Nicaraguan debt, for example, has been sold at only two cents on the dollar. How and why does this process take place?

(d) Explain the origins and development of the world debt crisis.

(e) Why is it in the interests of the creditor nations to attempt to alleviate the debt burden on debtor nations?

Question 5

The Table below shows the GDP per head of the various EC nations in 1970 and 1985. In each year the EC average is 100 and the two columns give the GDP per head for each country as index numbers based on the average.

GDP PER HEAD (AVERAGE OF ALL EC = 100)

	1970	1985
Denmark	129.3	156.9
Germany	122.7	152.7
France	111.4	133.1
Netherlands	97.5	128.9
United Kingdom	88.2	119.0
Belgium	105.1	116.2
Italy	75.3	91.1
Ireland	52.9	65.8
Spain	37.4	58.8
Greece	36.1	50.4
Portugal	22.7	28.0

Source: The Regions of Europe, *Pub EC* and World Development Report, *Pub IBRD*

(a) Based on these figures describe the changes which have taken place in the GDP per head over the period shown.

(b) (i) Which nation experienced the greatest relative increase in its GDP per head?
(ii) Which nation experienced the smallest relative increase in its GDP per head?

(c) What effect did the accession of Greece, Spain and Portugal have upon the figures?

(d) Does the fact that the index for the UK rose from 88.2 to 119.0 mean that income per head in the UK rose by 35 per cent? Give reasons for your answer. What other information would you need to know to give a more definite answer?

(e) To what extent do the figures illustrate a North-South divide in the EC? What other information would it be useful to know in order to evaluate the relative living standards of the various EC members?

Multiple-choice test

Answer all questions. Time allowed 30 minutes.

1 Consider the following measures which might be employed in an attempt to rectify a balance of payments deficit on current account. Which one of these items might be described as expenditure reducing rather than expenditure switching?

A devaluation or depreciation of the currency
B import quotas
C exchange control regulations
D imposition of an import tax
E increasing Excise duty

2 If a country is operating a system of fixed exchange rates and it experiences a balance of payments deficit which of the following will be the most likely consequence?

    A   reserves of foreign currency rise
    B   net outflows on capital account increase
    C   a tight fiscal policy
    D   a fall in interest rates to encourage investment
    E   the Exchange Equalisation Account sells pounds.

3 Both a regime of freely floating exchange rates and the gold standard are said to bring about an automatic rectification of a balance of payments deficit. However, they differ in that:

    A   with the floating exchange rate there is no change in the level of the country's foreign currency reserves
    B   on the gold standard the domestic purchasing power of the currency rises whilst with the floating exchange rate the external purchasing power of the currency falls
    C   only the gold standard is independent of changes in the interest rate
    D   with the floating exchange rate the level of unemployment will rise whereas with the gold standard employment will be maintained
    E   there is no scope for government intervention with the gold standard

4 If the exchange rate of sterling were to depreciate from £1 = $1.40 to £1 = $1.20 and as a result of this the volume of exports to the USA were to increase by 20 per cent then, *ceteris paribus*, the elasticity of demand for exports would be:

    A   1.40
    B   0.71
    C   0.83
    D   0.20
    E   impossible to determine from these figures

5 The J-curve effect shows that:

    A   any surplus on the balance of payments overall must, at some time, be followed by corresponding deficits
    B   there tend to be regular fluctuations between deficit and surplus on the balance of payments
    C   following measures to eradicate a balance of payments deficit, such as devaluation, there tends to be an immediate further deterioration in the balance before subsequent recovery
    D   it is necessary for expenditure reducing measures to be taken before expenditure switching methods are used as a means of improving the trade balance.
    E   Japanese trade surpluses have an adverse effect on the balance of payments of Japan's trading partners.

6 When monetary authorities interfere to influence the determination of a floating exchange rate, this is known as:

A   monetary intervention
B   exchange equalisation funding
C   a dirty float
D   destabilisation
E   mercantalism

7 Which of the following is an example of exchange control?

A   government intervention in foreign exchange markets by purchasing foreign currencies
B   maintenance of a fixed exchange rate
C   the Bretton Woods Agreement
D   a premium imposed on foreign currencies purchased for the purpose of overseas investment
E   devaluation

8 Special drawing rights (SDRs) are:

A   an international unit of account created by the IMF
B   rights to draw on extra credit *tranches* at the IMF
C   mutual aid given by central banks of the Group of Seven (G7) nations
D   World Bank (IBRD) aid to Third World countries
E   provisions to support the exchange rates of European Monetary System (EMS) members

9 The purchasing power parity theory suggests that:

A   freely fluctuating exchange rates will always move towards equilibrium
B   the exchange rate between two currencies depends upon their relative domestic purchasing power
C   exchange rates are determined by the balance of payments situation
D   a nation's purchasing power is determined by relative movements in exchange rates
E   fixed exchange rates are harmful to the balance of payments

Questions 10 to 11 are based on Fig. 11.1 which shows the quantity of pounds sterling demanded and supplied on the foreign exchange market. The initial supply and demand curves are shown by the DD and SS lines. The broken lines show the situations which might occur after various changes have taken place.

In each question, starting from the original equilibrium exchange rate, and presuming that only the changes stated occur, determine whether the new equilibrium point will be A, B, C, D or E.

10 American tourists spend more money in the UK

11 The UK purchases Trident missiles from the USA and there is a fall in demand for UK exports

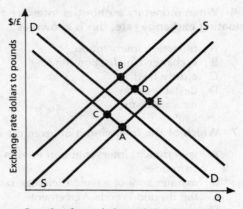

Fig. 11.1

12 This question is based on Fig. 11.2 which shows the exchange rate of the £ against the Deutschmark and the quantity of pounds sterling supplied. The slope of this particular supply curve is the result of the fact that the:

A British demand for imports is elastic
B British demand for imports is inelastic
C supply of DM's is limited
D government has interfered with the exchange rate
E supply of pounds is inversely proportionate to the DM/£ exchange rate

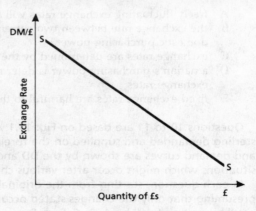

Fig. 11.2

13 If two non-trading countries become a single market unit, then the production possibility frontier:

A increases for one country and falls for the other
B falls for both countries
C rises for both countries
D remains unchanged
E is not affected in real terms

14 Consider two countries, one of which can produce every product more efficiently than the other. The efficient country should trade:

    A   all products
    B   no products
    C   only those goods in which its efficiency advantage is the greatest
    D   only those goods in which its efficiency advantage is the least
    E   only those products in which it possesses an absolute advantage

15 The supply of yen to the United Kingdom goes up when:

    A   the UK imports from Japan
    B   Japanese travel in the UK
    C   Britain invests in Japan
    D   profits are paid to Japanese who have invested in the UK
    E   the pound is devalued

Questions 16–20

Directions. Each of the following questions consists of a statement in the left-hand column followed by a second statement in the right hand column.
    Decide whether the *first* statement is true or false.
    Decide whether the *second* statement is true or false.
Then answer:

    A   if both statements are true and the second statement is a correct explanation of the first statement
    B   if both statements are true but the second statement is **not** a correct explanation of the first statement
    C   if the first statement is true but the second statement is false
    D   if the first statement is false but the second statement is true
    E   if both statements are false

	Directions summarised		
	First statement	*Second statement*	
A	True	True	2nd statement is a correct explanation of the first
B	True	True	2nd statement is **not a correct** explanation of the first
C	True	False	
D	False	True	
E	False	False	

First statement	**Second statement**
16 Devaluation will always increase a nation's earnings from foreign trade.	Devaluation increases the demand for a nation's exports.

17 Tariffs are usually opposed by economists.

Tariffs are a subsidy to inefficient producers.

18 The IMF is unable to deal with the world debt crisis.

The IMF has insufficient reserves of international liquidity.

19 A rise in interest rates will usually improve a nation's balance of payments.

Investment in manufacturing industry is influenced by the cost of borrowing.

20 The Single European Act will increase the possibility of the UK to benefit from the principle of comparative advantage.

The benefits of the creation of a free trade area may be offset by the trade diversion caused by the existence of common external tariff.

Answers

1   J S Mill said that the benefits of international trade are a more efficient employment of the productive forces of the world. Explain what are the benefits of international trade and who receives them.

We see throughout the subject of economics how specialisation and exchange lie at the heart of increasing productivity and prosperity. When we reach the subject matter of international trade we see how these principles apply to nations no less than to individuals. Thus it makes no more sense for a nation to aim to produce all the goods and services which it needs than it does for an individual.

The explanation of the benefits of international trade was first put forward by David Ricardo and was subsequently developed by John Stuart Mill. Ricardo's explanation is known as the doctrine of *comparative advantage* and it is the basis of the case for free trade between nations.

Trade between nations has existed for thousands of years, but this was usually understood in terms of *absolute advantage*. Absolute advantage is said to exist when one nation can produce a product more efficiently than another in terms of factor inputs. This may arise, for example, out of different geographical conditions. Thus the diversity of conditions between nations has long been regarded as a reason for trade.

What Ricardo demonstrated was that trade will be mutually beneficial to nations even when a nation possesses no absolute advantage. It is only necessary for comparative advantage to exist. Ricardo explained this by taking an example of two nations (Portugal and England) and two products (wine and cloth). In order to illustrate comparative advantage we will follow through Ricardo's example.

	Labour hours required to produce	
	1 Gallon Wine	*1 Yard Cloth*
Portugal	80	90
England	120	100

Portugal has an absolute advantage in the production of of both cloth and wine because it takes less hours of labour to produce each. However, Portugal has a comparative cost advantage in wine because the ratio of Portugese to English wine costs is 80:120 which means that wine can be produced *comparatively* more cheaply than cloth where the ratio is 90:100. If Portugal specialises in wine and trades for cloth then, for every yard of cloth she does not produce she can gain 1⅛ gallons of wine because both cost 90 hours of labour. England similarly gains because for every gallon of wine which she ceases to produce 120 hours of labour will be set free to make one and a fifth yards of cloth which can be converted by trade to one and one fifth gallons of wine. Thus both countries have benefited.

169

Ricardo's example assumed a one-to-one trading ratio of cloth to wine. It was left to J S Mill to explain that the trading ratio would be determined by the forces of demand and supply in international markets. This principle is know as the *law of reciprocal demand*. Modern theory is no longer reliant on Ricardo's labour theory. It is now established that the only necessary condition for the possibility of gains from trade is that the opportunity ratios should differ between countries.

To complete our look at the benefits of international trade it is necessary to consider various extensions and qualifications to the theory of comparative advantage. First we may extend the theory by going beyond Ricardo's two countries and two commodities. If we bring more countries into the theory then, in fact, it works better with multilateral trade increasing the possibilities of comparative advantage. Also a wider pattern of international trade increases the possibility of matching international demands and supplies. Also bringing more commodities into the picture makes the mathematics more complex but does not destroy the basic principle.

The benefits of international trade are also increased by the possibility of economies of scale and decreasing costs. If as a country specialised in a particular product it were to gain increased economies of scale in the production of that good, then this would increase the benefit to itself and the world from that specialisation. Indeed, the possibility of economies of scale may be an argument for international specialisation and trade even when no comparative advantage exists. The creation of the single European market in 1992 provided examples of this. On the other hand it must be admitted that the possibility of diseconomies of scale and increasing costs also exists.

Transport costs also present a limitation on the benefits to be gained from international trade. The cost of getting a product from country A to country B may completely offset comparative advantage. Tariffs also prevent a country from taking full advantage of international trade. There are, of course, today many other methods by which protectionism exists and prevents nations from fully benefiting from international trade. Exchange controls and non-tariff barriers such as discriminatory safety regulations provide examples of this. The immobility of factors of production may also limit the extent to which a nation may benefit from international trade.

Addressing ourselves to the second part of the question it should be apparent that a nation will benefit from free trade except where it is prevented from doing so by such things as transport cost and tariffs. The Heckscher-Ohlin factor price equalisation hypothesis suggests that, as a result of international trade the prices of factors of production in different countries will tend to move towards each other. In our original example, therefore, the wages of those in the wine industry in Portugal will rise as will those of clothworkers in England. This will, obviously, be to their benefit. On the other hand as trade opens up between the two countries clothworkers in Portugal will go out of business as will wine makers in England. Thus international trade will not have benefited them. This phenomenon was well illustrated in the late nineteenth century in England when the opening up trade with the New World bankrupted thousands of British farmers. However, in the long run the whole economy benefited from cheaper food prices. It could even be argued that in the long run those that remained in agriculture benefited as the productivity of remaining farms (hence wages etc) had to improve to compete with imports.

3 Explain how a nation might seek to rectify a deficit on the current account of its balance of payments.

The correct measures to rectify a current account deficit will depend upon its cause and upon the exchange rate regime in force. A short-term deficit might be dealt with by running down the nation's reserves of foreign currency or by borrowing from other central banks or international agencies such as the IMF. Raising interest rates will bring money flowing into the country on capital account and offer a temporary respite but will not rectify the underlying problem unless it be that higher interest rates have a deflationary effect upon the domestic economy.

If there is a continuous and serious deficit on current account other policies will have to be considered. The current account is principally made up of the nation's overseas sales and purchases of goods and services. Thus measures must seek to increase our sales overseas and/or decrease our consumption of imported goods and services. We can divide measures to rectify the imbalance into *expenditure-reducing* and *expenditure-switching*. Expenditure-reducing measures such as domestic deflation aim to rectify the imbalance by reducing domestic expenditure and thereby the nation's consumption of imports. Expenditure-switching methods such as import controls are aimed at switching demand from imports to domestically produced goods. The two types of measures need not be regarded as alternatives but rather as complements. For example, the government might reduce domestic expenditure in order to create spare capacity in the economy prior to taking expenditure-switching measures.

One of the most common methods of dealing with a current account deficit in the UK has been to deflate the economy through tight fiscal and monetary policies. This is, therefore, an expenditure-reducing method. It may appear indirect to reduce the whole level of demand in the economy in order that the demand for imports be restrained. However, this was the most common form of policy in the UK in the period 1947–72 and again in the late 1980s the government was relying on dear money policies to rectify the imbalance. (See also the answer to question 4 in this section.) There are a number of reasons why a government might favour this type of policy. First, if the government was committed to a fixed exchange rate regime, as was the case in the UK 1947–72, then domestic deflation might recommend itself. Second, protectionary measures such as import tariffs are illegal under the terms of the GATT treaty and, as far as the UK is concerned, would conflict with the Treaty of Rome. Third, protective measures invite retaliation which might leave you worse off than before. deflation might have a secondary expenditure-switching effect if the domestic rate of inflation is reduced below those of the nation's trading partners, thus giving its exports a price advantage.

Using deflation to rectify a current account deficit is subordinating the needs of the domestic economy to its external needs. The cost of such a policy may be high in terms of unemployment.

A nation may take protective measures to rectify its deficit. Protective measures include tariffs, quotas and exchange control. As was mentioned above increasing tariffs or imposing quotas conflicts with the GATT treaty. The UK has no exchange controls as they were abolished in 1979 but many other countries do. The Mitterand government in France, for example, imposed exchange controls to protect its balance of payments. The Single European Act meant that by 1992 all such controls became illegal within the EC. In recent years, however, there has been an increase in protectionism worldwide according to recent reports of GATT and the IBRD. New forms of non-tariff barriers have been exploited, for example, imposing safety regulations which favour domestic methods of production but discriminate against imports – the Japanese are masters of this method.

Protection is an expenditure-switching method. The danger is that such measures do little to cure the underlying causes of the deficit but work simply by cutting off imports. The efficacy of tariffs as a method of restricting imports is affected by the elasticity of demand for import. If demand is inelastic then, although the balance of payments may benefit consumers' expenditure will be greater for a smaller quantity of goods.

An alternative policy is the devaluation or depreciation of the external value of the nation's currency. This has the effect of making the nation's exports cheaper to foreigners while making imports dearer. The term devaluation is normally used when a country is operating a fixed exchange rate regime. For example, the UK devalued from £1 = $2.80 to £1 = $2.40 in 1967. If a country has a floating exchange rate and it allows or contrives that the external value of its currency decreases this is usually referred to as depreciation. These methods are expenditure switching. In order to assess the efficacy of devaluation and depreciation it is necessary to consider the elasticities of demand for exports and imports.

A P Lerner in his book *The Economics of Control* applies Alfred Marshall's ideas on elasticity to foreign trade. Devaluation will improve total export earnings only if the demand for exports is price elastic. Similarly expenditure on imports will only decrease as a result of devaluation if the demand for imports is price elastic. Therefore we have to consider the elasticities of demand of both exports and imports. The Marshall-Lerner criterion states that that devaluation will only improve a country's balance of payments if the sum of the elasticities of demand for exports and imports is greater than one. If this condition is not fulfilled, we arrive at the rather startling conclusion that a nation could decrease its balance of payments deficit by *revaluing*.

Since most of the years since the 1939-45 war have been years when Keynesian ideas on the economy have ruled it is not surprising that the key to the balance of payments problems was understood as ensuring the appropriate level of aggregate demand in the economy. Rearranging the familiar demand equation we can arrive at:

$$X - M = Y - (C + I + G)$$

This suggests that the balance of payments will be in deficit if total domestic expenditure (TDE) is greater than national income. From this we could argue that any devaluation of the currency will only be successful if TDE does not absorb the whole of national income, i.e. that there must be spare capacity in the economy. The effect of any depreciation in the currency, even if there is spare capacity, will be reduced by the multiplier effect on national income from any increase in the demand for exports. This *absorption effect* therefore points to the need to take expenditure-reducing measures prior to taking expenditure-switching policies.

The monetarist approach to the balance of payments sees any deficit or surplus as a monetary phenomenon. The supply of money is the result of that created domestically plus any net inflow resulting from a deficit. According to this view, a too rapid increase of the money supply will cause a payments deficit because the money supply will exceed the amount of goods that can be produced domestically and will therefore be spent on imports. If there is a fixed exchange rate regime then the government will be forced to buy up its currency on the foreign exchange markets to prevent the exchange rate falling, which can only be a temporary expedient. The monetarist prescription for a satisfactory balance of payments is, therefore, a regime of floating exchange rates coupled with tight control of the money supply.

What is undoubtedly true is that the best prescription for improving the balance of payments on current account is to increase the productivity of industry. In this way the nation's exports will become more competitive. A neo-classical or supply-side prescription would lay emphasis on any measures which do this, thus we might see supply side measures such as trade union reform and the sweeping away of restrictive practises as being aimed (amongst other things) at improving the balance of payments.

By the late 1980s, the government was grappling with the biggest current account deficit ever recorded. It was relying on the supply-side measures which it had been taking to increase productivity sufficiently to improve the situation. Its other active policy measure was high interest rates which were supposed to choke off demand in the high streets and therefore restrain the demand for imports. High interest rates however have the effect of attracting foreign investors and therefore pushing up the exchange rate and thus making exports uncompetitive. The government feared however that lowering interest rates would increase inflation. It thus found itself trapped between competing ends of policy as so many of its predecessors.

Question 4   To what extent can the balance of payments be controlled by the manipulation of interest rates?

The balance of Payments records payments to, and receipts from the rest of the world. These flows are expressed in sterling values. The account has two sections. The 'Current Account' records the flows of expenditure and income generated by trade in goods and services. The 'Transactions in External Assets and Liabilities' section (which replaced the previous 'Capital Account' and 'Official Financing' sections) records capital flows and the movement of 'Official Reserves'.

An interest rate is the price of borrowed money or the return to lending money. Particular interest rates will differ but arbitrage ensures that, usually, all interest rates tend to move in the same direction. Thus if the Chancellor of the Exchequer 'tightens monetary conditions' (for example, by raising the discount at which the Bank of England will buy bills) this will lead to a general rise in interest rates.

In simple 'elasticities' models the exchange rate brings into balance the demand for and supply of a nation's currency. If the exchange rate of, say, sterling is above its equilibrium (i.e. sterling is temporarily worth more in terms of foreign currencies, then the supply of sterling will exceed demand. This will cause a 'depreciation' of sterling; UK imports become more expensive to domestic citizens and UK exports become cheaper for foreigners. As producers ultimately require payment in domestic currencies, this should decrease the supply of sterling as imports decline and increase the demand for sterling as exports increase (subject to the Marshall-Lerner condition). This continues until the supply of pounds is equal to the demand and hence the balance of payments balances without the need for accommodating flows of official reserves. The process is reserved when the exchange rate below the equilibrium.

In these models the exchange rate adjusts so as to maintain purchasing power parity. Changes in the exchange rate are thus predicted to reflect changes in comparative advantage and/or divergences in inflation rates, eventually restoring equilibrium when the two currencies can buy the same amounts of internationally traded goods in each country

Although the above theories may have some validity as long-term determinants of the exchange rate, exchange rates also fluctuate for other reasons. Underlying changes in competitiveness may, in the short-run, be overwhelmed by other forces acting upon the Balance of Payments. Undoubtedly the most potent causes of short-term fluctuations are the flows of so called 'Hot Money'. This refers to the volatility of short-term speculative capital flows. These largely consist of the 'Eurocurrency Market; i.e. currencies owned by other than the nation states of origin. The sums involved are vast having been built up from past US deficits and the surpluses of OPEC countries. These stocks of currency are placed in order to exploit temporary differences in interest rates and expected changes in exchange rates rather than as an investment which reflects the economic performance of a country.

The inflow of hot money increases the demand for the domestic currency. Thus, faced with a long-term decline in international competitiveness, a government can protect the value of its currency by raising interest rates. Indeed, this action will itself tend to reassure speculators that the government does not intend to allow its currency to weaken and thus further increase demand. Clearly, interest rates can be used to cause an inflow on the Transactions section of the account to 'contain' a deficit on the current account.

Despite exhortations that exchange rates be left to market forces, Mrs Thatcher's government used changes in interest rates to influence the exchange rate. Often the fear was that by increasing the price of imports, a falling pound would precipitate an inflationary wage-price spiral. Such a policy, however, may also be seen as device for containing a current account deficit in terms of the 'absorbtion approach'. Basically the argument is that increased interest rates will decrease consumer demand and investment spending. Thus aggregate demand falls and hence imports also.

Whatever the merits of a rise in interest rates as an anti-inflation device, its virtues as a method of controlling a current account deficit are doubtful. First, the consequent rise in the exchange rate will tend to worsen the deficit, particularly in the longer term when elasticities of demand increase. Second, the cut back in investment may in the long-term exacerbate the problem by further eroding the competitiveness of UK industry and its capacity to absorb domestic expenditure. Nevertheless, most econometric models suggest the short-term effect of a rise in interest rates is to move the Balance of Payments towards surplus. The danger is that this action reduces the nation's longer term productive potential.

8   What is meant by the problem of international liquidity and how does the IMF help to overcome it?

International liquidity refers to the assets which may be used as liquid assets in the settlement of international debts. International liquidity consists of those reserves held by the monetary authorities – central banks, and international institutions such as the IMF – for this purpose. As such they consist of reserves of foreign currency, gold and Special Drawing Rights (SDRs).

Not every foreign currency is able to function as a *reserve currency*. Reserve currencies are those foreign currencies which central banks commonly hold for the purposes of defending exchange rates and settling balance of payments deficits. Only those currencies which are generally acceptable in settlement of international debts should be included in a nation's stock of foreign exchange and thus be part of the reserves of international liquidity. The most important reserve currency is the US dollar. Other important reserve currencies are the Deutschmark, yen and sterling.

The problem of international liquidity is that the official reserves are inadequate for the needs of international trade. World trade has expanded much more rapidly than have official reserves so that there now is a situation that the combined weight of the leading central banks and the IMF is too small to cope sufficiently with the problems which now afflict international settlements. This is because there is another aspect to international liquidity and this is the unofficial liquidity. Most international liquidity comes not from the monetary authorities but from commercial banks. The result of massive lending by commercial banks in the 1970s is that there is now a world debt crisis with many of the poorer nations unable to pay the interest on their debts let alone repay them. The size of these debts is now so great that the monetary authorities cannot bail out the debtor nations even if they wanted to.

Little problem exists between the richer nations, with traders able to switch pounds to dollars, dollars to Deutschmarks with little difficulty. As far as the worldwide situation is concerned, the major institution which attempts to grapple with the problem is the International Monetary Fund (IMF).

The aim of the IMF is to provide financial support to countries with temporary balance of payments deficits. It finances this with quotas of currency drawn from members. In order to supplement quotas it created SDRs in 1970. SDRs are an international unit of account whose value is based on a basket of the leading currencies. Each member was given an allocation of SDRs and thus the IMF could be said to have 'created', or added to, the stock of international liquidity. The other reserves which the IMF possesses are not its creation but an acknowledgement that member countries have contributed some of their reserves to the IMF.

In assessing the success of the IMF in helping to deal with the problem of international liquidity, we must address ourselves to two questions. First, to what degree have the Fund's reserves (SDRs and other quotas) contributed to make-up of official reserves? Second, to what extent has the Fund been able to help out countries with payments difficulties especially those afflicted with massive overseas debts?

The IMF has in fact only had a minor effect on the total stock of international liquidity. The vast majority of official liquidity (about 95 per cent) is the reserves of foreign currency and gold held by central banks. SDRs have added very little in proportionate terms either to the Fund's reserves or the reserves of central banks. The IMF has tried to increase the stock of SDRs but this is subject to the approval of members. There are periodic reviews of the quotas but big increases tend to be resisted. This is because those with large quotas such as the USA and the UK oppose increasing their contribution both on grounds of expense and because they fear that increasing the international money supply will increase inflation worldwide. The latest quota review is that of 1989.

All IMF transactions are now denominated in SDRs and it was the intention of the Fund to establish the SDR as the leading reserve 'currency'. It was as part of this process that the Fund demonetised gold in 1976. However, member countries have refused to give up gold as a reserve asset and the there is no great desire to hold SDRs despite the IMF offering higher rates of interest to holders of SDRs.

As mentioned above, the amount of lending by the IMF is completely dwarfed by the lending of commercial banks. Many of these indebted poor countries can no longer afford their debts and there is a danger of default. The ability of the IMF to deal with this problem is limited by its own lack of funds and by the reluctance of many debtor nation to accept the conditions imposed by the loan. The IMF usually demands rigorous austerity programmes to rectify payments imbalances. Austerity is hardly likely to recommend itself to nations which may already be on the verge of starvation.

However, although the quantity of IMF lending is small by comparison with that of commercial banks it does have some importance. Commercial banks when granting loans now often insist that the debtor nation also borrows from the IMF and accepts the IMF's lending conditions. For the desperately poor nations it is often only the IMF that will lend to them. Thus though the loan may be comparatively small it may be vital to the survival of that nation. The IMF is also an important forum for discussions on the re-scheduling of

Third World debts and for discussion of international financial problems generally e.g. the Baker plan of 1986. Thus, its importance may be greater than the size of its lending suggests.

Thus we may conclude that while the IMF has been relatively unsuccessful in creating more international liquidity its role both in lending and debt re-scheduling problems is not insignificant. The problem of Third World debt continues to grow in magnitude and it is probably only in an international forum such as the IMF that any concerted effort to deal with it can be co-ordinated.

Suggested data response answers

Question 1

(a)

The balance of payments of X	
	$ million
Current Account	
Visible trade	
Exports	+55 555
Imports	−53 234
Visible balance (balance of trade)	+2 331
Invisibles	
Services	+2 435
Interest profit and dividends	+1 078
Transfers	−1 809
Invisible balance	+1 704
Current Account Balance	+4 035
Transactions in external Assets and Liabilities	
Net increase in external assets	−30 831
Net increase in external liabilities	+28 569
Net transactions	−2 262
Balancing item	−1 773

(b) Country X is undoubtedly an advanced nation. There are many pointers to this in the figures. First of all, the size of the items such as exports in tens of billions of dollars suggests an advanced economy. It could be a poor but very large economy, such as India, but the rest of the information does not support this view.

The fact that there is a surplus on services also suggests an advanced economy, this possibly represents the sale of banking, insurance and transportation services of foreigners. The surplus on interest, profits and dividends provides conclusive proof that this is an advanced economy. It clearly is wealthy enough to have substantial investments in other people's

177

economies. This view is supported by the information in the capital movements part of the account.

The deficit on transfers suggests contributions to international organisations or immigrants sending money home, both of which again suggest an advanced economy.

When we turn to the capital section of the account we find that the net increase in overseas assets (i.e. investments abroad) is greater than inward investment (i.e. net increase in external liabilities). Country X, therefore, is a creditor nation investing overseas. In view of this and the other evidence we may conclude that country X must, therefore, be a developed nation.

(In fact the figures are taken from the UK's balance of payments in the early 1980s with the £s changed to $s.)

Question 2

(a) There were two main problems with which the rise in the interest rates was supposed to deal. First was the over-heating in the economy, demand was expanding at an unsustainable rate leading to fears of increased inflation. It is ironic, as the article suggests that the direct effect of raising interest rates was in fact to increase the rate of inflation by pushing up the cost of mortgages. Second was the desire to rectify the deficit on the balance of payments. It is also possible to say that the reason why interest rates were increased is that the Chancellor had abandoned almost all other forms of policy. Committed to market forces, he rejected other forms of monetary intervention such as special deposits preferring to rely on the price mechanism implicit in interest rates. The other main alternative would be fiscal measures but he was ideologically disinclined to take those especially after making such a fuss over the cutting of tax rates in the Spring.

The rise in interest was therefore designed to accomplish two objectives but the control of inflation was most important to the government in the Autumn of 1988. This was based on the belief that increased interest rates would discourage the growth of credit which was fuelling the high street boom. High interest rates would also keep the pound high by encouraging the inflow of speculative money. This would have the effect of keeping the balance of payments in balance by generating a surplus on capital account. The Chancellor also believed it to be anti-inflationary. Speaking to the CBI the Chancellor said: 'I shall not allow the exchange rate to depreciate, to bail out British firms who do not keep their costs under control . . . . . inflationary pressure arising from pay awards has to be neutralised in the only possible way, through higher interest rates'.

The way by which higher interest rates were supposed to rectify the current account deficit was indirect. Higher mortgage payments would leave a section of consumers with less disposable income. They would, therefore, be able to to spend less, inevitably some of this drop in spending would be imports not bought and in this way the deficit would be rectified. It was in many ways a throwback to the old stop-go policies but reliant entirely on one instrument – the interest rate. Many people feared, at the time, that it might stop the whole of the economy and plunge it into depression.

(b) The EC countries operate a system of exchange rates designed to limit the fluctuations in the value of their own currencies. However, the EC currency 'snake' is allowed to depreciate and appreciate in terms of other world currencies. The EMS was established on 13 March 1979. All the members of the EC joined it except the UK. The UK government decided that, at a time when exchange rates were highly volatile, it was not in its interests to join. The EMS is based on a newly devised unit of account called the European currency unit (ECU). The value of one unit is determined by taking a weighted basket of all member currencies. The value of each weight is determined by the size of the member's GDP. Sterling was included in the calculation even though it did not belong to the EMS. This was because the UK is a member of the EC and all EC transactions are now denominated in ECUs.

The value of members' currencies is allowed to fluctuate by plus or minus 2.25 per cent of the central rate established by the value of the ECU (the lira was allowed to fluctuate by six per cent).

By 1988 the EMS may be judged to have been relatively successful. The ECU had remained stable against other world currencies – in contrast to sterling.

Despite not being a member of the EMS the UK tried to stabilise the value of sterling as is illustrated by the references in the article to the value of the pound in relation to the Deutschmark. In fact, this was part of a much wider attempt by the leading industrialised nations to stabilise exchange rates. The Plaza Agreement 1985 (so called after the Plaza Hotel, New York) was an agreement by the monetary authorities of the G5 nations to bring about an orderly decline in the value of the dollar which was then considered overvalued.

The Louvre Accord 1987 (so called because it was arrived at in Paris) was an agreement among the G7 nations to stabilise variations in their exchange rates within certain limits. These limits were not published. However, they could, at least partly, be deduced from the actions of central banks. For example, in March 1988 it become obvious that the Bank of England was committed to holding the pound below the level of £1 = DM3. As can be seen from the article this was not possible.

These semi-official methods of stabilising the exchange rate for the UK having failed the UK was reduced to relying on domestic policies such as that of manipulation of the interest rate discussed in the article.

(c) In the end, the best remedy for balance of payments difficulties on current account is to improve productivity in exporting industries. In this way we may improve our comparative advantage compared with other countries. The Conservative government, therefore, argued that its chief effort to improve the balance of payments was the general supply-side measures to improve productivity in the economy at large. These measures included trade union reform and deregulation in the economy.

By the end of the 1980s the government was able to claim substantial increase in productivity. It could also claim that investment was rising. However, as the National Institute of Economic & Social Research pointed out: 'Capacity fell substantially through most of the Eighties, as investment

179

remained depressed. This worsened both inflation and the balance of payments.' It is true that productivity, measured strictly in terms of output per person employed, improved. However, productivity should also be related to the total level of output. During the Sixties, output in manufacturing rose by nearly 40 per cent, whereas the Conservative's productivity achievement over the Eighties saw output in manufacturing rise by less than four per cent. Meanwhile, the growth in manufacturing output amongst the UK's principle competitors averaged 25 per cent.

It was the government's failure to to increase the output of the economy which was the principle cause of the horrendous balance of payments deficit.

Question 3

(a)

**BRITAIN AND AUSTRALIA
SPECIALISATION AND TRADE**
(All figures in million units)

Area Compared	Exchange ratio of food for clothing Pc/Pf	Food production	Food consumption	Food exports (+) or imports (−)	Clothing production	Clothing consumption	Clothing exports (+) or imports (−)
SITUATION BEFORE TRADE.							
Australia	10.3	30	30	0	21	21	0
Britain	10.8	50	50	0	80	80	0
World	None	80	80	0	101	101	0
SITUATION AFTER SPECIALISATION AND TRADE.							
Australia	10.6	100	40	+60	0	36	−36
Britain	10.6	0	60	−60	120	84	+36
World	10.6	100	100	0	120	120	0

(b) *See* Fig. 11.3

(c) (i) Banking services. Britain possesses a historical advantage in this area, having for many years been a leading banking nation. It possesses the institutions and the know-how in a highly specialised area. It also benefits from the lack of restrictions placed on the movement of money in and out of the UK.

(ii) Agriculture. Basically land is too scarce and expensive in the UK. It does present an interesting case in that agriculture in the UK is *technically* extremely efficient in terms of output per worker and output per hectare but this still leaves the UK at a comparative disadvantage because of the high price of the factor inputs land and labour.

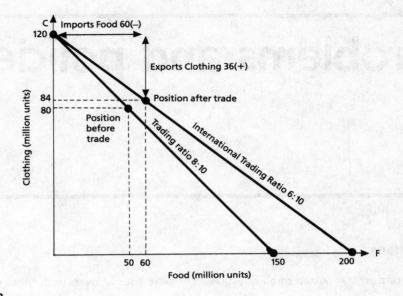

Fig. 11.3

(d) Motor vehicles, steel and textiles.

(e) Differences in taste or demand, strategic reasons and to obtain economies of scale.

Answers to multiple-choice questions				
	1	E	11	A
	2	C	12	B
	3	B	13	C
	4	A	14	C
	5	C	15	B
	6	C	16	D
	7	D	17	A
	8	A	18	A
	9	B	19	B
	10	D	20	B

12

Problems and policies

Questions

Essay paper

Attempt all questions. Compare your answers with those provided.

1 (Answer provided.) What is meant by 'fiscal demand stabilisation policy' and what problems arise with its implementation?

2 (Answer provided.) 'Supply-siders argue that if the poor have more they work less but if the rich have more they work harder'. To what extent is this statement a fair representation of the arguments of supply-side economists?

3 (Answer provided.) 1988 saw the replacement of the Public Sector Borrowing Requirement with the Public Sector Debt Repayment. Explain these terms and assess their significance.

4 Evaluate the argument that interest rates are the key instrument in the macro economic management of the economy.

5 (Answer provided.) Examine the view that the unemployment figures are not facts but rather they reflect economic theory.

6 Economic policy making is made more difficult by the conflicts which exist between the major objectives of policy. Explain why this is so.

7 'Trade is better than aid when it comes to helping developing countries'. Discuss.

8 Evaluate the statement that 'inflation is always and everywhere a monetary phenomenon'.

9 Assess the arguments for the replacement of rates by the Community Charge (poll tax) as a method of financing local government.

10 Why do the rates of economic growth between nations differ?

Data response paper

Question 1 (Answer provided.)

(a) Account for the relationship shown in the following diagram and explain its implications for economic policy making.

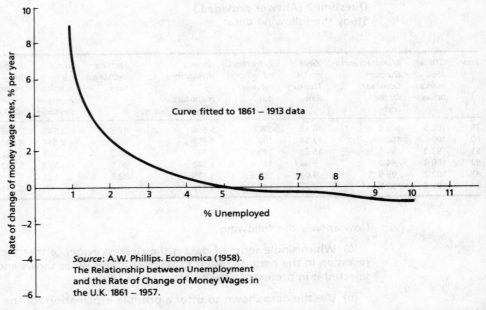

Source: A.W. Phillips. Economica (1958). The Relationship between Unemployment and the Rate of Change of Money Wages in the U.K. 1861 – 1957.

Fig. 12.1 The relationship between unemployment and the rate of change of money wages in the UK 1861–1957
(*Source*: Economica (1958) A W Phillips)

(b) Use the following data to assess the diagram's applicability to recent experience. Comment on your findings.

(Data Rounded to ½%)

	Prices percentage increase on year earlier	Unemployment percentage of working population (1987 basis)
1973	8.5	2
1974	16	2
1975	24	3
1976	15.5	4.5
1977	16	5
1978	8.5	4.5
1979	13.5	4.5
1980	18	5
1981	12	8
1982	8.5	10
1983	4.5	11
1984	5	11
1985	6	11.5
1986	3.5	11.5
1987	4	10.5

Question 2 (Answer provided.)
Study the following data:

Year	GDP at 1980 market prices	Manufacturing Output: Constant factor cost	Yield on UK Treasury Bills	Extraction of mineral oil and gas	Gross investment by manufacturing (£m, 1980 prices)	Sterling exchange rate	Value of physical increase in stocks	Employment in manufacturing industry (000's)	Unemployment in UK (000's)
79	102.5	109.5	16.49	98.7	5 555	87.3	2 547	7 259	1 235
80	100	100	13.58	100	4 959	96.1	−2 844	6 940	1 513
81	98.9	94	15.39	110.3	3 723	94.9	−2 489	6 220	2 395
82	100.4	94.2	9.96	125.6	3 648	90.5	−1 127	5 897	2 770
83	103.7	96.9	9.04	137.6	3 775	83.2	681	5 605	2 984
84	106.4	100.8	9.33	147.1	4 436	78.6	− 50	5 517	3 030

Now answer the following:

(a) Which single series of data is the clearest evidence that the UK suffered a recession in the period shown? Explain what this series shows and why you have selected it in preference to the other series of data.

(b) Use the data shown to offer a possible explanation for the recession.

(c) What other explanations might there be and what further evidence would be needed to investigate them?

Question 3 (Answer provided.)

Read following statement carefully:

"Amalgamation under public ownership will bring great economies in operation and make it possible to modernise production methods ... Public ownership ... will lower charges, prevent competitive waste, open the way for co-ordinated research and development ... Only if public ownership replaces private monopoly can industry become efficient."

(Labour Party Manifesto 1945)

"Privatisation is bringing about a fundamental change in the operation and efficiency of key sections of the UK economy. Its success .. is self-evident ... Privatisation liberates managers and allows them to reach their full potential ... Privatisation increases productive efficiency whether or not a monopoly is involved."

(Financial Secretary to the Treasury 1985)

Now answer the following questions:

(a) Explain the arguments put forward in each statement.

(b) Use your knowledge of economics and the 1979-? Conservative Government's privatisation programme to shed light on the validity of these statements.

Question 4
In 1988 the National Institute for Economic and Social Research estimated the effects on inflation and the balance of payments, for the year following, of changes

in income tax and interest rates. The figures show the NIESR's forecasts as comparisons with what was forecast to happen in the absence of changes in income tax and interest rates:

	Prices	Balance of payments
The effect of a 3p cut in income tax	+1.95	−£3012 m
The effect of a 4% point rise in interest rates	−2.8	+£3648 m

(a) Explain the links in the economy which could account for these relationships.

(b) Evaluate the desirability of a policy of low income tax and high interest rates.

Question 5
Read carefully the article on page 186 which is taken from *The Guardian* of 27 December 1988. Then answer the questions which follow.

(a) With the aid of the information in the article and other examples with which you are familiar explain what is meant by hyperinflation.

(b) What is the effect of inflation on the functions of money?

(c) What methods are used in Brazil to get round the adverse effect of inflation on the functions of money?

Multiple-choice test

Answer all questions. Time allowed 30 minutes

1 Which of the following provides the best description of the term 'the marginal rate of tax'?

    A $\dfrac{\text{Taxes paid}}{\text{Total income}}$

    B The amount of tax paid once allowances have been made

    C The rate of tax which which is the most efficient in terms of tax paid per person

    D A special tax on higher incomes

    E $\dfrac{\text{Change in tax paid}}{\text{Change in income}}$

2 Unemployment benefits and social security payments tend to:

    A go up as GDP goes up
    B go up as GDP goes down
    C go down as GDP goes down
    D be unaffected by changes in GDP
    E become discretionary

3 Fiscal drag occurs because inherently:

    A tax collections go up faster than GDP
    B tax collections go up slower than GDP
    C government expenditure goes up faster then GDP
    D government expenditure goes up slower than GDP
    E welfare payments are index-linked.

Life with inflation at 1,000 per cent

Jan Rocha in Sao Paulo

LIKE EVERY Brazilian I have become an amateur mathematician, perpetually calculating rates and percentages, and knowledgeable about all the inflation indices that now rule our lives here. Brazilians have adjusted to living with a monthly increase in their cost of living of 25, 26, or 28 per cent without panic. This means a yearly rate of nearly 1,000 per cent.

Inflation is made tolerable by indexation; one could almost say hyperindexation. Everything, wages, prices, tariffs, rents, school fees, is indexed.

We do not have to cart our money around in wheelbarrows or even carrier bags, because the mint simply prints new bank notes of higher and higher denominations.

The only problem is the lack of national heroes to illustrate them — Brazil's most famous painter, composer, writer, president, and scientists have all been featured already.

A typical day in inflationary Brazil goes something like this: In the morning I offer the usual 80 Cruzados for the trolley bus fare. The conductor points to the new notice glued to the window behind him: 120 Cruzados.

When I get off in the centre and go to buy the paper, the newspaperman rejects my proffered 250 Cruzados. "It's gone up. 320 now." Walking down the street I decide to stop for a *cafezinho* at a coffee bar. I haven't been in here for over two weeks, so I've no idea how much it will be. 80? 100? "It went up on Saturday," says the boy behind the bar handing me my small cup of strong black coffee. It's 180 now."

Outside, a woman holding a sleeping child sits on the pavement begging. In the bowl beside her are five 10-Cruzado coins. Beggars do badly because people still give the same small change although it is worth a fraction of what it was.

In the office I look at the paper. The headline is "Sarney government's inflation totals 17,903 per cent". That is in just three years and nine months. A quick glance at the page called "Your Money" — advice on how to beat inflation, or at least how not to lose too badly.

The lunchtime television news shows the official inflation rate for November — 26.9 per cent — and the indexed adjustments that automatically follow. Rents go up 258 per cent for a six-month contract, 816 per cent for an annual contract. In fact it has become impossible to rent a flat or house in Sao Paulo, because owners do not want to risk losing out if inflation continues to rise at this rate.

On the way home I post a letter and notice that the stamp no longer carries the Cruzado price but instead says "national postal tariff". As postal charges now go up at least once a month it saves having to produce new stamps. Then on to the supermarket which echoes with the steady clicking of price-labelling pistols.

At home my 16-year-old daughter asks for a cheque to pay her guitar teacher who, though vaguely hippy, has long ago given up charging in Cruzados and instead charges one OTN (adjustable Treasury bond) a lesson. I look at the price of an OTN in the paper. At least he is charging in monthly adjusted OTNs and not the so called fiscal OTNs, which are adjusted every day.

My 6-year-old daughter then asks for her pocket money to buy something at the school tuck shop. When I try to fob her off with a pink 50-Cruzado note, her favourite colour, she says scornfully, "That won't buy anything. I need a green one." (500 Cruzados).

Fig. 12.2 (*Courtesy* The Guardian)

4 Other things being equal, an increase in the size of the PSBR is likely to lead to:

    A   a fall in the rate of interest
    B   an increase in note issue
    C   a decrease in the rate of inflation
    D   a fall in the price of securities
    E   all of the above

5 Which of the following presents the best method of decreasing the level of aggregate demand in the economy?

    A   Increasing the rate of income tax.
    B   Cutting the highest band of tax
    C   Increasing government expenditure
    D   Lowering the rate of interest
    E   Running a balanced budget.

6 The relief of structural unemployment must come chiefly from:

    A   fiscal policy
    B   monetary policy
    C   prices and incomes policy
    D   reform of trade union legislation
    E   education and training

7 Labour saving technology can offset the unemployment it gives rise to by:

    A   reducing costs
    B   reducing prices so much that people can afford to buy more goods
    C   inducing additional investment
    D   reducing restrictive practices
    E   all of the above

8 Supply-side measures to reduce unemployment include all of the following except:

    A   improvement of training schemes
    B   abolition of closed shop legislation
    C   privatisation
    D   the strengthening of Wages Councils
    E   cutting Corporation Tax.

9 Which of the following is **not** likely to give rise to cost-push inflation?

    A   Strong trade unions
    B   A decline in the exchange rate
    C   An increased budget deficit
    D   Mark-up pricing policies amongst producers
    E   Cartelisation of oil supplies

10 The following diagram shows the expectations augmented Phillips curve. Curves P_0, P_4 and P_8 represent short-run curves based upon various expectations of inflation. The long-run Phillips curve occurs at OU level of unemployment which is the 'natural rate of unemployment'. Given the above condition what will be the effect, in the long run, if the government attempts to reduce unemployment to OZ?

A   Inflation of 8 per cent
B   Inflation of 4 per cent
C   The natural level of unemployment increases
D   The natural level of unemployment decreases
E   None of the above

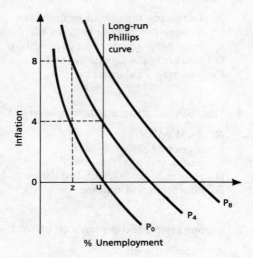

Fig. 12.3

11 Milton Friedman stated that: 'Inflation is always and everywhere a monetary phenomenon'. If we assume that this view is correct which of the following could be the cause of inflation?

A   An increase in the velocity of circulation
B   An increase in note issue
C   A rise in the number of transactions in the economy
D   All of the above statements are true
E   None of the above statements are true

12 Which of the following situations is most likely to give rise to inflationary effects?

A   The effect of new investment in the economy has a greater effect upon output than upon income
B   The income effects of new investment are greater than the output effects
C   The marginal capital/output ratio is very high
D   There is a large withdrawals function
E   There is a high acceleration factor

13 Balanced growth requires that:

A additions to savings should be equal to additions to output and income
B new (net) investment should give rise to equal additions to output and income.
C there should be a marginal capital/output ratio which is equal to the marginal propensity to save
D the multiplier produces rises in income equal to additions to investment
E investment be divided between the private and public sectors.

14 An advantage which poorer countries possess in pursuing development development is that they have:

A the possibility, as latecomers, to benefit from the experience of pioneers in the advanced nations
B many spare resources
C a plentiful supply of cheap labour
D easy access to the markets of the development world
E all of the above advantages

15 If we compare the rich nations of the world with the poor, which of the following statements is an accurate reflection of their relative situations?

A The gap in wealth between the rich and the poor is narrowing
B The gap between the rich and the poor is narrowing
C The rich are growing richer and the poor are either standing still or becoming poorer.
D The growth rate is higher in poorer countries than it is in the rich.
E The poor are only sustained by large net transfers of funds from the rich.

Questions 16–20
Directions. For each of the questions below, **one** or **more** of the responses given is (are) correct. Then choose

A if 1, 2 and 3 are correct
B if 1 and 2 only are correct
C if 2 and 3 only are correct
D if 1 only is correct
E if 3 only is correct

Directions summarised

A	B	C	D	E
1, 2, 3	1, 2	2, 3	1	3
correct	only	only	only	only

16 The poverty trap arises because

1 flat rate benefits may be lost as income rises
2 the tax system is regressive
3 VAT puts a disproportionately large burden on the poor

17 Neo-classical economists argue that the 'natural' level of unemployment in the economy may be reduced in the long run by

1 boosting aggregate demand through expansionist fiscal policies
2 retraining schemes
3 policies to reduce imperfections in the housing market

18 Other things being equal, the Public Sector Borrowing Requirement (PSBR) is likely to fall if

1 the price of gilt-edged securities falls
2 the aggregate level of unemployment falls
3 VAT rates are increased as a result of the Single European Act

19 Cost-push inflation can come from

1 higher wage costs per unit
2 higher profits per unit
3 decreases in productivity

20 Inflation during the 1980s was consistent with

1 the decrease in the M3 velocity of circulation
2 the decrease in the M1 velocity of circulation
3 increases in the money stock

Answers

1 What is meant by 'fiscal demand stabilisation policy' and what problems arise with its implementation?

Fiscal policy is that part of government policy which is concerned with raising revenue and deciding the level and distribution of public sector expenditure. The level and pattern of the public sector's budget turnover, surpluses and deficits has been used extensively in the past (following the 'Keynesian Revolution') in attempts to control the level of aggregate demand in the economy and through this important 'macro' target variables, i.e. unemployment, inflation, the balance of payments and economic growth.

Keynesian theory suggests that unemployment can be reduced by increasing government expenditure and reducing taxation. This initial increase in aggregate demand works through a 'multiplier' effect as income received is passed on in the circular flow thereby creating further income. Output is increased in response until equilibrium is reached at a higher level of output and, through derived demand, a higher level of employment. Similarly, a reduction in government expenditure and an increase in taxation can be used to control inflation by bringing demand into line with the 'full employment' level of output.

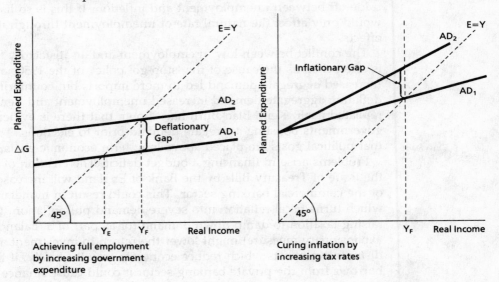

Achieving full employment by increasing government expenditure

Curing inflation by increasing tax rates

Fig. 12.4

In practice problems arise: for example, there may be conflicts between policy targets. Within Keynesian theory and forecasting models these conflicts usually take the form of trade-offs. For most of the 1960s there was thought to be a stable trade off between unemployment and inflation. This was based on the 'Phillips Curve' which resulted from empirical research by A W Phillips.

191

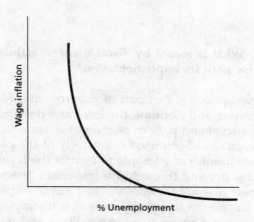

Fig. 12.5

Since the mid 1970s the Phillips relationship has been seen to be unstable. Some economists emphasised cost push factors, but the assertion of the monetarists that there is no long-run trade-off between inflation and unemployment gained greater political influence. Indeed, the rational-expectations school of monetarism argues that the effects of demand management will be anticipated. Thus, there would not be even a temporary trade-off between unemployment and inflation. If this is so fiscal policy would only affect the natural rate of unemployment through its supply side effects.

The conflict between low unemployment and a satisfactory balance of trade is often cited as the cause of the 'stop-go' policy of the 1950s and 60s. Increased aggregate demand led to more imports but countering this by deflating aggregate demand increased unemployment and hence the cycle repeated itself. Keith Blackburn had shown that there is evidence of some governments boosting aggregate demand prior to elections. The worry here is that political goals are placed above long term economic goals.

Problems arise in financing a budget deficit. The creation of new money or the issue of Treasury Bills by the Bank of England will increase the liquidity of the commercial banking sector. This could result in monetary expansion which turns fiscal reflation into severe demand pull inflation. Conversely raising taxation to damp down demand (or as part of a 'balanced budget' expansionary measure) might lower the return to investment and have other disincentive effects which reduce economic growth. Lastly, if the government borrows from the private banking sector it could cause finance to be diverted from the private sector thus 'crowding' out private sector activity. If the crowding out effects of fiscal policy are large, perhaps because of an interest inelastic demand for money, then the intended demand effects of fiscal policy may be negated.

Lack of knowledge of the precise workings of the economy also poses a problem for effective demand stabilisation, as do unforeseen changes in investment, consumption, the volume of world trade and industrial disputes.

Time lags mean that conditions in the economy can change between the formulation of a policy and its effect. Because of such difficulties some economists argue that stabilisation policy often has destabilising effects.

Few economists now argue that it is now possible to 'fine tune' the economy. But many economists, such as Godley of the Cambridge School, argue that broad adjustments to the level of output and employment can and *must* be made in order to prevent chronic recessions. Monetarist economists argue the exact opposite. Hence controversy rages not only over whether 'active' demand management has been successful but also over whether it is necessary.

2 'Supply-siders argue that if the poor have more they work less but if the rich have more they work harder'. To what extent is this statement a fair representation of the arguments of supply-side economists?

Supply-side economists place policy emphasis on aggregate supply rather than aggregate demand. They tend to be monetarist and believe that 'real things are determined by real things'. Thus, they believe in freedom of choice in the face of the resource constraints of the economy as embodied in market forces. They do not see fiscal policy as an important influence on aggregate demand other than through its indirect monetary effects. Nevertheless, fiscal policy is seen as greatly affecting the performance of the economy through the incentive effects of taxation and by changing the ratio of the size of the public to the private sector. Supply-siders believe that taxes erode work effort and individual freedom and that the private sector is superior to the public sector in almost all spheres of economic activity.

The quote reflects Galbraith's observation that supply-siders invariably advocate a reduction in welfare payments and taxation. They argue that welfare payments allow the idle to live off taxpayers and that many low-paid workers find it more lucrative, or almost as lucrative, to be unemployed. Conversely, they argue, low taxes mean that the better off will be able to keep more of the rewards of their efforts and hence will remain in this country and work harder, thereby creating greater wealth for all of the nation. Investment will also be encouraged in that the 'reward for abstinence' will be greater.

Clearly, the receipt of a transfer payment cannot cause a substitution effect away from leisure. On the contrary, it is likely to cause an income effect towards leisure as it can be expected that leisure is a normal good. Moreover, if the transfer payment is means tested then the income from work for the low-paid can be subject to an extremely high effective rate of taxation as state benefits are withdrawn. This situation is known as the 'poverty trap'. In a recent survey, however, Nickell found that of those who would be better off unemployed than at work nine out of ten were in work.

Economic theory is ambiguous regarding the effect of a reduction in taxation for those in work. On the one hand a reduction in taxation increases the marginal reward for work, as this makes the opportunity cost of leisure greater we can expect workers to substitute away from leisure by working longer hours. On the other hand the average return to work is increased, thereby increasing the take-home pay from any given amount of work. This will have an income effect (strictly speaking a wealth effect) away from work towards more leisure.

Supply-siders argue that, ultimately, everyone can benefit from a reduction in taxation. Art Laffer pointed out that total tax revenue would be zero at a tax rate of zero or one hundred per cent. (At one hundred per cent, post tax income would be zero and hence there would be no incentive to earn income at all.) Laffer drew the following curve:

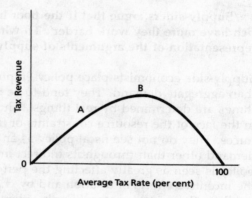

Fig. 12.6

Until point A substitution effects are insignificant and hence tax revenue increases proportionately with the tax rate. Between points A and B, substitution effects become more pronounced and hence tax revenue rises less than proportionately with tax rates. After point B the substitution effect clearly dominates as tax revenue actually falls as tax rates are increased. Another consideration is that tax avoidance and evasion might increase with the tax rate.

Empirical research by Beenstock of the London Business School using total tax revenue suggested that the UK laffer curve peaked at a tax rate of around 60 per cent. Research by Dunnett at Ealing College of HE, using direct personal taxes, found no evidence of peaking. Recently, research at Stirling University also failed to find any significant disincentive effects. It was also pointed out in this study that many workers simply do not have the option of varying their hours of work as these are set by employers, legislation or collective agreement.

The quote is not a fair summary of the supply-sider's case. Nevertheless the weight of empirical evidence appears to be against the supply-sider's arguments regarding taxation and welfare payments. It should be borne in mind, however, that supply-side policies also encompass the reduction of union power and the breaking up of restrictive practices.

3   1988 saw the replacement of the Public Sector Borrowing Requirement with the Public Sector Debt Repayment. Explain these terms and assess their significance.

The PSBR is the expenditure of the public sector minus its income. In 1987/88, this income exceeded expenditure and thus Mr Lawson quipped that the PSBR should be renamed the PSDR as this surplus reduced the outstanding debt of government (i.e. the 'National Debt').

The public sector comprises central government, local authorities, and the nationalised industries. Thus expenditure consists of public expenditure programmes, the expenditure of the nationalised industries, and the gross debt interest of the public sector. Income consists of central government taxation and royalties, national insurance, local taxes, the revenue from public corporations and other miscellaneous public sector revenues. Recently, the privatisation programme has had a major effect on reducing the PSBR because of the peculiar practice of regarding the sale of these assets as negative current expenditure!

The reduction of the PSBR was part of the 'Medium Term Financial Strategy'. It was to be reduced to control the money supply and to free resources for the private sector. But controlling government expenditure proved difficult; government expenditure as a percentage of GDP is still expected to be higher in 1989/90 than 1979/80. Increased taxation, would be against the advice of supply-siders on the role of incentives and contrary to the election pledges. Nevertheless, revenues from taxation as a percentage of GDP have risen when compared with 1978.

The PSBR has fallen dramatically. This is not, however, entirely the result of efforts to control public expenditure combined with buoyant (particularly corporate) tax revenues. Indeed, although in 1987/88 the PSBR was minus £3bn it should be noted that the proceeds from privatisation and North Sea tax/royalties were £10bn.

The PSBR can be financed through the sale of debt to the public or to overseas residents, or through borrowing from the monetary sector. Monetarists regard all these methods as having undesirable 'side-effects'. They argue that borrowing by the sale of government debt diverts funds from the private sector and 'crowds out' private sector consumption and investment if, for example, interest are thereby increased. This is regarded as a 'bad' thing if the private sector is seen as more productive than the public sector.

Overseas borrowing will lead to interest payments to other countries. This is a drain on the nation's resources and one which if left unchecked could eventually cause dramatic falls in the exchange rate.

Monetarists have argued that the PSBR causes monetary expansion and thus inflation. For some years in the 1970s this argument was supported by a correlation between changes in the PSBR and the money supply. For other periods, however, the correlation is very weak. This might be because the effects of the PSBR depend crucially on how it is financed.

Borrowing from the monetary sector can be from the Bank of England or from the commercial banks. In the former, not only does this represent a direct increase in the money supply but also the Bank's debt is likely to appear as new reserve assets of commercial banks leading, under fractional reserve banking, to a multiple expansion of the money supply. Borrowing from the commercial banks also expands the money supply if the commercial banks create new deposits to purchase the government debt. In addition, if Treasury Bills are issued these may be used as commercial bank reserves of liquidity. In contrast, if gilts and Savings Certificates are sold to the non-bank private sector there will be no effect on the money supply if this money is re-spent by government. But interest rates might increase if the increased debt holding leads to an increase in the demand for money to balance wealth portfolios.

Keynesian economists emphasise the fiscal effects of the PSBR. Thus, if private aggregate demand falls the government can prevent increased unemployment by increasing the Central Government Borrowing Requirement. The effect of such a budget deficit is thus seen to maintain economic activity rather than to crowd out the private sector. Keynesians feel money supply implications are of little importance in the face of changes in the velocity of circulation or, like Kaldor, that the money supply merely responds to accommodate changes in aggregate demand and is not constrained nor boosted by changes in the PSBR. Thus Keynesians do not place emphasis on the PSBR as a problem to be tackled.

5 Examine the view that the unemployment figures are not facts but rather they reflect economic theory.

Since 1979 there have been over 20 changes to the way in which the official unemployment statistics are compiled. All but one decreased the unemployment figure. For example, since 1982 the figure has no longer been based on the numbers registered at Job Centres and career offices but instead on a computer count of benefit claimants. Thus this excluded those looking for work but not eligible for unemployment linked benefits.

In addition to changes in compilation there have been other changes which have caused a reduction in the official measure. For example, in the 'Restart Scheme' letters were sent to the long-term unemployed which may have scared many people off the register; the period over which people who become 'voluntarily' unemployed are refused benefit was extended from 6 to 13 weeks, thus deterring people from giving up jobs even if their employment conditions are poor. More recent changes have included tighter availability test for benefits and, with the introduction of a new comprehensive training scheme, the Government has announced that anyone under 18 cannot be included as unemployed.

Many observers claim that the government has been fiddling the figures. This is not surprising, for example in November 1988 the official total was 2.1 million but the Unemployment Unit estimated that had the figures been calculated in the pre-1982 way the total would have been 2.8 million. But accusations of fiddling imply that there is a 'correct' way of measuring the unemployed. In fact there are different criteria which can be used. These include those entitled to unemployment-related benefits; those seeking work; those wanting a job; and those available for work. Thus it is possible to produce a wide range of 'unemployment' totals.

An alternative to the official measure is produced by the Labour Force Survey (LFS). The LFS total is extrapolated from a survey of 60 000 adults in Great Britain. To be included as unemployed, a person must have sought work within the last week and not have done even one hour's paid work in that week. Because of the stringency of this criterion the LFS total is smaller than the total from the official count of claimants although judgements as to availability for work and effort put into work seeking can also affect one's eligibility for benefits. Recently the OECD recommended that the LFS extend its criterion to a four-week period. Obviously this produces a higher total, but one which is still below the official UK total.

The apparent 'correctness' of the various measuring criteria will reflect one's perception of what unemployment is and how it is caused. Thus D Lipsey has concluded that the 'correct' total depends on an essentially political Left-Right view: for example, the Left will tend to add to the official total those excluded by statistical changes; those on the government's special employment training schemes; those on short-term working; students on vacation unable to find work; and the 'unregistered' unemployed. The Right will tend to subtract claimants not 'really' looking for jobs; 'unemployables'; those out of work for a short time; and those claimants who are working in the 'informal' economy.

Views on unemployment are not purely party political. Indeed, for 25 years there was a Keynesian consensus across all major political parties. Keynesian economic theory suggests that the unemployed are the victims of the macroeconomic malfunctioning of a market economy. In particular, that deficient aggregate demand can severely curtail job opportunities resulting in involuntary unemployment which could be reduced by fiscal expansion.

In contrast, neoclassical theory suggests that unemployment is a rational choice made by the unemployed person. There is no malfunctioning of the economy but rather the reality of the situation. Hence, an individual will have a low market value because of their low Marginal Revenue Product. This might reflect a lack of personal qualities or a lack of skills in producing goods which are in demand. Given this low market value, the individual might well decide not to sell their labour, particularly if social security payments to the unwaged are near or above this market value. Of course, some of the unemployed might be simply 'work-shy'.

Some economists interpret Keynes as postulating that the unemployed can be 'quantity constrained' in that they are not able to sell as much of their potential labour as they wish. The Left could speculate that most people would be able to offer more if society were ordered differently and hence almost everyone is unemployed! Equally the Right might argue that if the unemployed put more effort into job seeking, the pressure of this excess supply of labour would lower wages and hence create the employment sought. Thus the very persistence of unemployment is proof that it is voluntary!

Clearly, the boundary between fact and opinion is difficult to discern.

Question 1

(a) The diagram shows the original Phillips curve fitted by Phillips himself to the data for 1861–1913. He also claimed that the curve fitted later periods up to the date of publication in 1958 quite well. It seemed as if Phillips had discovered a relationship between the rate of increase of money wages and unemployment that had been stable for some 100 years.

The article by Phillips had an enormous impact. This was particularly so as it was felt by many economists that prices were set according to a fairly stable relationship with unit costs. As the major part of costs consists of wages, the implication was that Phillips had discovered a stable relationship between unemployment and inflation in general.

The relationship seemed to support demand-pull theories of inflation. Lipsey's interpretation of the curve as indicating a Keynesian demand-pull process did much to establish the curve as a 'menu' for policy choice. It was felt that if the pressure of demand was such that the economy was run 'too near' to full employment then bottlenecks in the economy would cause wages, and other costs, to rise sharply as employers competed for the remaining resources. In contrast near price stability could be obtained by allowing unemployment to rise to around three per cent. Indeed, at what were then regarded as very high rates of unemployment, wages and prices would actually begin to fall slightly because of lack of demand.

The policy maker could thus set the position of the economy on the curve according to his priorities.

(b) A glance at the data plotted on a graph reveals that the original Phillips curve does not fit more recent experience. Indeed, it can be argued that no trade-off is apparent. For example, 1973 and 1982 saw virtually the same rates of inflation and yet the rate of unemployment was approximately five times higher for the latter period. Alternatively, it might be argued that the Phillips curve had shifted substantially to the right or at least that each level of unemployment now tends to be associated with a higher level of inflation than before. There are various theories as to why this might have happened.

Cost-push theorists had pointed out that the Phillips curve did not fit the periods after 1913 nearly as well. They argued that it reflected the more competitive capitalism of the 19th Century. As monopolistic elements and collective bargaining began to dominate cost-push forces took over with the rate of inflation being determined by the outcome of a struggle between capitalists and workers more or less independent of demand. Only at very high levels of unemployment would fear of unemployment cause a decrease in wage demands.

Other economists argue that the sharp increase in the price of oil in 1974 was a watershed in the Phillips curve relationship which significantly worsened the trade-off. Indeed, some cost-push theorists such as Beckerman argue that the decrease in inflation in the eighties is almost wholly due to a

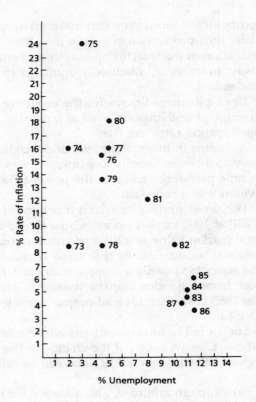

Fig. 12.7

reduction in the cost of imported raw materials rather than any aspect of government policy.

Monetarists deny that there is any long-term trade-off between inflation and unemployment. The Gradualist, or Adaptive Expectations version of monetarism argues that a temporary trade-off can occur if a sudden change in inflation causes money illusion: for example, if the unemployed are fooled by increasing money wages into thinking that real wages have risen and therefore accept jobs which they would refuse if they had anticipated the increase in the general price level. Hence, the Phillips curve shifts to the right as higher levels of inflation come to be anticipated and thus even higher rates are required to cause money illusion. In the rational expectations version, economic agents, on average, correctly anticipate inflation and hence the real wage and unemployment do not deviate even temporarily from their equilibrium. Monetarists argue that the general increase in unemployment through to the eighties has been largely due to supply-side factors e.g. the effect of welfare payments and demographic changes.

Question 2

(a) It is possible to distinguish between a rapid restructuring of the economy and a slump in overall economic activity. Thus, for example, technological innovation can make many workers redundant while at the same time production is greatly increased. Hence, the figures showing a reduction in manufacturing output and employment could be 'explained away' in terms of, admittedly dramatic, technological change and/or changes in demand.

Unemployment figures for the economy as a whole can also rise due to demographic changes as well as structural change. In addition, labour force participation rates can vary.

A decline in investment and stocks could reflect past over optimism or previously exceptionally low interest rates. It could also indicate a sharp shift in time preference towards the present. Taken alone, neither are conclusive evidence of a recession.

The series of data for which it is hardest to find alternative explanations is 'GDP at 1980 market prices'. Gross Domestic Product at market prices is the total market value of all the production that has taken place within the national boundaries. As this value is calculated at constant (i.e. 1980) prices the series is virtually a volume index of UK domestic production. It can be seen from the index that the volume of production in 1979 was above that of the 1980 base year. Overall output again fell to 1981, but recovered from 1981 to 1984.

Such a fall in total output has adverse implications for the economy as whole. Clearly, much of the change in the other series we have looked at was indeed the consequence of what can be called a recession.

(b) Through arbitrage, and allowing for risk and liquidity, interest rates tend to move in line with each other. It thus appears from the data on the yield of treasury bills that interest rates were unusually high at the beginning of the period. This would be consistent with a credit squeeze designed to limit the growth of monetary aggregates and reduce inflation. Indeed, this was the basis of the 'monetarist experiment' attempted by Mrs Thatcher's government when first elected.

A credit squeeze would tend to reduce aggregate demand. It has been found, however, that consumer demand for credit is rather inelastic with respect to interest rates alone. But the effects on industry tend to be greater. Many firms require credit to bridge the gap from production to sales, high interest charges thus cause cash flow problems. Smaller firms may be forced into bankruptcy, particularly if their debtors delay payment in order to take advantage of the high interest rates. Larger firms will tend to reduce their loans by curtailing short term investment and meeting demand by running down stocks thus allowing production cut backs. These effects seem manifest in the figures for stocks and manufacturing investment.

High interest rates will also tend to cause an inflow of 'hot money' in the external assets and liabilities category of the balance of payments. Such capital inflows will raise the demand for sterling and thus the sterling exchange rate against other currencies. It appears from the index for 'extraction of mineral oil and gas' that this rise in the exchange rate was exacerbated by a rise in the production of North Sea oil. As the UK decreased its imports of oil and increased its exports the consequent demand for sterling would again exert upward pressure on the sterling exchange rate. This would tend to reduce the competitiveness of UK exports (This effect is often known as the 'Dutch disease'). The data shows that the sterling exchange rate did rise at the beginning of the period. As manufacturing is particularly dependent on exporting, this (together with the direct effects of high interest rates we have looked at) could account for the dramatic fall in manufacturing output and employment.

(c) Expectations are a major determinant of investment, stock building and labour hoarding. If industrialists were convinced that a major recession was about to occur, perhaps because of the strength of the Government's commitment to reduce inflation, this could exacerbate any downturn in activity. The CBI regularly conducts surveys of business confidence and it would be useful to know to what extent the recession was led by and then deepened by a downturn in expectations.

In a such an open economy as the UK's, the overall level of activity is greatly affected by the volume of world trade. If the government of many of the UK's trading partners were simultaneously attempting to reduce inflation this could have resulted in a downturn in world trade. Indicators of the volume of this trade would thus be useful in order to assess its impact apart from any influence of domestic policy.

Keynesian economists also believe that the fiscal stance of the government is an important determinant of aggregate demand and hence the level of economic activity. It would thus be useful to have data on the levels of taxation and government expenditure. But one must be careful in interpreting such data as taxation will fall and public expenditure rise in a recession without any change in fiscal stance. This effect is known as 'fiscal drag'. It would therefore also be relevant to look at the composition of public expenditure, for example, welfare payments versus public investment. If welfare payments rise sharply, this is the result of the recession rather than a deliberate attempt to avoid it.

Also useful would be data on inflation so as to calculate real interest rates. Earlier data on manufacturing employment would allow one to see to what extent the decline is part of a long-term structural change. Data on demographic trends, the size of the labour force and the duration of unemployment by age and sex might enable one to assess to what extent the rise in unemployment reflected people entering the labour force rather than those already in it losing jobs and failing to find new employment.

Question 3
(a) The term 'public ownership' is usually used to describe industries which are owned and controlled by the state. The radical Labour Government of 1945–50 initiated an extensive programme of nationalisation.

The economic arguments in the manifesto statement are as follows. By creating a monopoly which combines previous production within one state enterprise economies of scale will be achieved, i.e. unit cost will be reduced. **201**

The state can inject finance into the industry to ensure that most modern technology is used. State ownership will ensure that reduced unit costs are passed onto the consumer, part of this reduction in costs will result from avoiding the wasteful duplication of having separate distribution networks, transport routes and advertising. In a competitive market, research and development will be secret and there is the discouraging consideration that it might be copied, these problems are avoided in state enterprise. Indeed, if there are continual economies of scale, setting price equal to marginal cost will result in a financial loss, thus, unaided, private enterprise could not achieve this prescription for allocative efficiency.

'Privatisation' is the term used to refer to the sale of public enterprises to the private sector. The term is also used to describe deregulation and the contracting-out of public sector activities.

The pro-privatisation statement is far less specific proclaiming that the advantages are 'self evident'. Nevertheless, the 'liberation of managers' probably refers to the reduction of political interference in the running of the industry and allowing management to act without constantly having to justify its actions to ministers. For example, in order to reduce the PSBR nationalised industries have been subject to limits imposed on their borrowing, equally they have been forced by governments to contain prices rises to reduce inflation or, more recently, increase prices to raise revenues. The claim that productive efficiency will be increased is most tenable if privatisation results in more competition; competition in product markets can make firms cut their costs in an effort to match the prices of rivals or to lower prices to attract customers from rivals. In the absence of rivals there could still be the threat of takeover or shareholders voting directors out of office if profits are poor. In addition there might be less reliance on the state to bail the industry out in times of difficulty.

(b) Comparisons of public and private sector enterprises are fraught with difficulties. For example, few goods are provided by both sectors; nationalised industries have both commercial and social responsibilities hence performance criteria can differ, for example, high profits can reflect exploitation of monopoly power and neglect of unprofitable essential services rather than cost efficiency; imposed differences in access to finance between the two sectors can affect comparisons of performance; the success of a privatised industry can depend on the terms of its privatisation and will be affected by influences which are not necessarily linked to privatisation itself.

The most comprehensive comparison of performance between public and private enterprises was conducted by Pryke in 1982. He looked at three industries where there was both public and private provision, i.e. airlines, the sale of gas and electricity appliances, and ferries and hovercraft. In each case it seemed that the public enterprise compared badly with its private sector counterpart. But Pryke's survey has been criticised: for example; Pryke tended to compare the public sector with only the 'best' of the private sector; the difference in scale between the public airline and the private was so vast it is not clear comparison was meaningful; in the case of gas and electrical appliances the nationalised industries also maintained their showrooms as advice centres and bill payment points. It is also the case that no clear conclusions seem to emerge from the other studies that have been carried out in this area of economics.

In terms of incentives it is perhaps necessary to divide the Government's privatisation programme into two stages. The early privatisations involved industries in which there was clearly competition from rivals in the product market. Although such privatisations have continued, the latter stage has seen the privatisation of vast public monopolies such as British Telecom and British Gas. Indeed, to appease the incumbent management and ease the path to privatisation, proposals to allow competition have been severly limited in scope. It is also unlikely that management will believe that governments would fail to come to the aid of industries providing essential public utilities. The sheer size of these monopolies also makes takeover extremely unlikely. Thus it is not clear whether complacency is reduced by such privatisations.

Most of the recent research (for example from Yarrow and also Button) on the effects of privatisation suggests that regulatory policy and competition in the market is far more important than the form of ownership itself. Indeed, as public ownership has been common where competition is unlikely, this could account for results which suggest comparatively poorer performance. It might even be the case that a privately owned firm which, to compensate for a lack of competition, is subjected to regulation such as the 'RPI–X%' price regulation formula or by control of profits might respond with excessive marketing and over capitalisation and hence perform worse than would a publicly owned firm.

Answers to multiple-choice questions

1	E	11	B
2	B	12	B
3	A	13	B
4	D	14	A
5	A	15	C
6	E	16	B
7	E	17	C
8	D	18	C
9	C	19	A
10	E	20	E

Appendix

Addresses of Examination Boards

Joint Matriculation Board, Devas Street, Manchester M15 6EU

Northern Ireland Schools Examinations Council, Beechill House, 42 Beechill Road, Belfast BT 8 4RS

Oxford and Cambridge Schools Examinations Board, 10 Trumpington Street, Cambridge and Elsfield Way, Oxford 0X2 8EP

Oxford Delegacy of Local Examinations, Ewert Place, Summertown, Oxford 0X2 7BZ

Scottish Examinations Board, Ironmills Road, Dalkeith, Midlothian EH22 1BR

Southern Universities' Joint Board for School Examinations, Cotham Road, Bristol BS6 8DD

The Associated Examining Board, Stag Hill House, Guildford, Surrey GU2 5XJ

University of Cambridge Local Examinations Syndicate, Syndicate Buildings, 1 Hills Road, Cambridge CB1 2EU

University of London Schools Examinations Board, Steward House, 32 Russell Square, London WC1B 5DN

Welsh Joint Education Committee, 245 Western Avenue, Cardiff CF5 2YX